Valley Forge

Making and Remaking a National Symbol

Lorett Treese

Valley Forge

Making and Remaking
a National Symbol

A Keystone Book

The Pennsylvania State University Press
University Park, Pennsylvania

Library of Congress Cataloging-in-Publication Data

Treese, Lorett, 1952–
    Valley Forge : making and remaking a national symbol / Lorett
Treese.
        p.   cm.
    "A keystone book."
    Includes bibliographical references (p.   ) and index.
    ISBN 0-271-01402-4 (cloth). — ISBN 0-271-01403-2 (pbk.)
    1. Historic sites—Pennsylvania—Valley Forge—Conservation and
restoration—History.   2. Washington, George, 1732–1799—
Headquarters—Pennsylvania—Valley Forge.   3. Valley Forge (Pa.)—
History.   4. Parks—Pennsylvania—Valley Forge—History.   5. Valley
Forge National Historical Park (Pa.)   I. Title.
E234.T74   1995
974.8' 13—dc20   94–29460
                                                                CIP

Published by The Pennsylvania State University Press, University Park, PA 16802-1003

It is the policy of The Pennsylvania State University Press to use acid-free paper for the
first printing of all clothbound books. Publications on uncoated stock satisfy the minimum
requirements of American National Standard for Information Sciences—Permanence of
Paper for Printed Library Materials, ANSI Z39.48–1984.

For MAT
and for my mother,
who celebrates her birthday on June 19th

Contents

List of Illustrations   ix

Preface   xi

1. The First Hundred Years at Valley Forge   1

2. The Centennial and Memorial Association of Valley Forge   17

3. A Rocky Beginning for the Valley Forge Park Commission   37

4. The Park Commission Triumphs   53

5. The Churches at Valley Forge   81

6. Historical Accuracy vs. Good Taste: Valley Forge in the 1920s and 1930s   105

7. The "Complete Restoration" of Valley Forge   129

8. New Uses for an Old Story   155

9. The Siege of Valley Forge   171

10. A Struggle for Growth and Professionalism at the Washington Memorial   187

11. New Interpretations at Valley Forge   199

Epilogue: Valley Forge—Past, Present, Future   215

Notes   223

Bibliography   255

Index   263

List of Illustrations

1. Washington's Headquarters at Valley Forge, c. 1861
2. Valley Forge Centennial illustration from *Harper's Weekly*
3. Old mill and tenant houses in Valley Forge
4. Plan of Valley Forge Park, c. 1902
5. Valley Forge's first monument
6. Washington's Headquarters, c. 1910
7. The second historic structure acquired by the park
8. Map of Valley Forge Park, 1908
9. Dedication ceremony for monument, 1911
10. Valley Forge sheep
11. Early preservation effort at Redoubt #3
12. National Memorial Arch
13. Two early photographs of Varnum's Quarters
14. Two drawings of Dr. Burk's chapel plans
15. Washington Memorial Chapel during construction
16. Worker excavating forge
17. Valley Forge's replica of Houdon's statue of George Washington
18. Dr. Burk's grave
19. One of the first replica huts at Valley Forge
20. Map of Valley Forge, 1941
21. Replica hut built in 1935
22. Replica hut designed by George Edwin Brumbaugh
23. Row of Brumbaugh's huts
24. Advertisement for Washington Inn
25. The bake ovens that never were
26. Postcard depicting the Mansion House
27. Valley Forge in the spring during the 1940s
28. Grave marker dating from the 1930s
29. Statue of General Von Steuben

Preface

"Are you finally going to tell the truth about Valley Forge?" he asked me. In researching this book, I had the opportunity to meet many people belonging to a number of organizations associated with this renowned historic site, most of them deeply committed to the place and concerned about what went on there. One dedicated gentleman was quite curious about what I was writing, and very serious when he posed that loaded question.

His question told me that the gentleman was well aware of a current lack of consensus about exactly what had happened at Valley Forge. His manner also told me that it was important to him that his particular view be promulgated as the correct one. Like most Americans, he perceived history as a search for a single, discoverable truth to be staunchly defended once it had been found.

Professional historians view history differently. They are well aware that the books and papers they produce contain not "the truth" but their own interpretation of a past that can never be completely recaptured, and that they cannot escape the biases and prevalent attitudes of their own time in judging the people and events of the past. In his book *The Past Is a Foreign Country*, David Lowenthal writes: "The past as we know it is partly a product of the present; we continually reshape memory, rewrite history, refashion relics."[1] He adds that even those who define themselves as revisionists do not so much set the record straight as add one more version to an existing body of interpretations.[2] In his book on creative interpretations of the American Revolution titled *A Season of Youth: The American Revolution in Historical Imagination*, Michael Kammen writes, "Even our most essential traditions have been subject to some startling shifts."[3]

Valley Forge really has several histories. There is the history of the Continental Army's winter encampment of 1777–1778, but there is also a history of how that particular story has been told—something the professionals call its historiography. And because the immense popularity of the Valley Forge story led to the preservation of a large physical site, there is in addition a history of what has been done at Valley Forge to pay tribute to this event, to illustrate it and evoke it, and to make its meaning clear to visitors. Interpretations of the Valley Forge story have changed over the years, and so has the Valley Forge landscape.

In the early nineteenth century, Americans tended to be indifferent to their history, although they increasingly glorified the survivors of the Revolutionary War as this generation began dying off. Americans were also surprisingly indifferent to the physical remains of history and allowed many historic structures to be unsentimentally demolished. Mount Vernon had nearly been sold to commercial developers when a group of women intervened; their efforts were an example to those who later came together to preserve something of the campground at Valley Forge.

"Remaking the past to embody their own wished-for virtues was a major Victorian enterprise," Lowenthal writes.[4] As American society became increasingly industrialized and urban-based, and as more and more foreigners arrived on American soil, Americans looked nostalgically back to the Colonial and Revolutionary periods, longing for the traditions and values that were thought to have prevailed before society's changes began to threaten the future. Ancestral societies that only older-stock Americans were eligible to join were established. Old buildings were restored and battlefields preserved. In America's Romantic Era, the tale of a dismal military winter camp at Valley Forge began taking on legendary qualities. Valley Forge became the place where virtue had triumphed through sacrifice and perseverance. Other historic sites associated with George Washington were spoken of as "shrines," making Valley Forge seem even more sacred because so much human suffering, it was thought, had been so willingly dedicated to so worthy a cause. The hallowed ground seemed to cry out for physical preservation and glorification.

Between the end of the nineteenth century and World War I, American nationalism found physical expression in the erection of monuments designed to inspire respect for the virtues they celebrated. Valley Forge got its own share of monuments—some excellent works of art, others less significant, but all now artifacts in their own right.

During the first third of the twentieth century, there was a gradual shift from the tendency to memorialize the past toward attempts to physically recreate it. Many historic sites tried to match the remarkable popular appeal of the re-created colonial capital at Williamsburg, and Valley Forge was no different. However, in a recent article in *New York Review*, Ada Louise Huxtable expresses the modern view of sites like Williamsburg, saying:

> The blend of new and old, real and fake, original and copy, in even the best of these restorations defies analysis; it is dedicated to a wholly artificial construction that is supposed to convey a true (that is, tangible) experience of American art and history. But if these "re-creations" teach something to those who might otherwise remain innocent of history, they also devalue what they teach; the intrinsic values of the real place are transformed and falsified.[5]

In an article titled "Visiting the Past: History Museums in the United States," Michael Wallace writes that after World War II "the populist openings of the thirties were checked and reversed, and the meaning of 'historic' narrowed once again, as the bourgeoisie set out to uproot 'un-Americanism' and celebrate, with renewed complacency, 'the American Way of Life.'"[6] During the Cold War period, communism seemed to threaten the very existence of America. It was hoped that the nation's history and its historic sites could influence Americans to uphold American values and be prepared to defend them. Groups that had long been involved with Valley Forge, as well as one significant newcomer, made attempts to use the ambience of the place to promote Americanism.

The Civil Rights Movement brought a new appreciation for diversity and prompted a new generation of historians to discover the history of women, blacks, and ethnic minorities. Vietnam and Watergate brought to American society an iconoclasm that may have inspired the reevaluation of long-accepted historical accounts, while new scientific instruments made it possible to gain new insight from existing sites, documents, and artifacts. In the last twenty-five years, professionals have come up with new interpretations of the history of Valley Forge and the remains at its physical site.

Today, more than four million people a year visit the park and view its landscape, but what do they really see when they look at buildings like Washington's Headquarters, monuments like the National Memorial Arch or re-created structures like the log huts that were once supposed to give the place a Williamsburg air? In an article titled "Harnessing the Romance of the Past: Preservation, Tourism, and History," Patricia Mooney-Melvin writes:

> Every site, no matter how faithfully preserved, represents a collection of pasts. In addition to the accumulation of its own history, a

site is a combination of where it currently is and what it is "supposed" to represent. People, politics, level of research, the absence or presence of preservation funding, and management approaches to particular sites all influence what the visitor sees.[7]

A Valley Forge visitor sees both the remains of more than a century of commemoration and much intellectual contention over the appropriate way to experience the Valley Forge story. Structures in the landscape at Valley Forge reveal more about the tastes and attitudes of succeeding generations than they do about Washington's army.

No, I am not trying to tell "the truth" about the winter encampment at Valley Forge. My story begins just after Washington's army marched out. This book is about Valley Forge in its role as a historic site of national importance: a place where people go to learn about or pay tribute to one incident in American history. This book examines the words, the structures, and the objects that have been used to tell the Valley Forge story at this physical place. In a larger sense, it is about how the Valley Forge experience has been promoted, packaged, and often exploited, and it examines what has perhaps been the longer, harder, and less well known ordeal of Valley Forge.

I owe sincere thanks to a number of people at the National Park Service who helped me research the archival material at Valley Forge National Historical Park. Chief among them are Joan Marshall-Dutcher, Joseph Lee Boyle, and Phyllis Ewing. I also thank Betty Browning, Dona McDermott, and Fran McDevitt for their assistance, as well as Bob Dodson, E. Scott Kalbach, Barbara Fox, Tom McGimsey, and Superintendent Warren D. (Denny) Beach, who all provided information through interviews.

I owe a great deal to the Valley Forge Historical Society, and particularly to its president Meade Jones for her cooperation and support and permission to research the society's files and minutes. In addition, I thank Betty McHenry and the office staff at the Valley Forge Historical Society for their patient assistance.

I am grateful to the current rector at the Washington Memorial Chapel, the Rev. Dr. Richard Stinson, and to the former rector as well, the Rev. Sheldon M. Smith. I extend my thanks to the parish office staff and especially to carillonneur/historian Frank DellaPenna.

I also thank Robert Miller, Betty Miller, Charles Hepburn, and Hal Badger at the Freedoms Foundation, as well as Mrs. Aloysius S. Banmiller of the Valley Forge DAR.

Finally, I want to thank the helpful staff members of the following institutions: the Historical Society of Pennsylvania, the University of Pennsylvania Archives, the Pennsylvania State Archives, the Chester County Historical Society, the Historical Society of Montgomery County, the *Norristown Times Herald* Microfilm Library, the Mid-Atlantic Regional Office of the National Park Service, Falvey Memorial Library at Villanova University, the Winterthur Library, and the Winterthur Archives. My thanks also go to my editor at Penn State Press, Peter J. Potter; to my manuscript editor, Peggy Hoover; and to the scholars who reviewed my manuscript, Wayne Bodle, and Dwight Pitcaithley of the National Park Service.

Two works were particularly helpful to me in developing my bibliography. These are Harlan D. Unrau's internally distributed *Administrative History of Valley Forge National Historical Park* and Barbara McDonald Powell's "The Most Celebrated Encampment: Valley Forge in American Culture, 1777–1983" (Ph.D. dissertation, Cornell University, 1983).

I reserve my warmest gratitude for my husband, Matthew A. Treese, for his help with my research, but mainly for the affectionate encouragement that sustained me through this project. Without Mat this book would not have been written.

1

The First Hundred Years
at Valley Forge

In the summer of 1828, John Fanning Watson took his horse and gig over the Schuylkill River at a place called the Swedes' Ford and set off to visit Valley Forge, where little more than fifty years earlier George Washington's army had spent the winter of 1777–1778. Watson was then working in a bank in Germantown, but he was also a dedicated antiquarian in the process of preparing his multivolume *Annals of Philadelphia*, the collection of anecdotes and oral history for which he is today remembered. Like more and more Americans in the 1820s, he had enough time and disposable income to become a tourist, seeking adventure and amusement in parts unknown. Planning a story for a Germantown newspaper, he neatly recorded his impressions in a small notebook, creating one of the earliest tourist accounts of Valley Forge. He wrote admiringly of "Hill & Dale & wood & meadow & cultivated field" and the general beauty of the rich eastern Pennsylvania countryside. [1]

Upon reaching his historic destination, Watson searched for physical remains of the presence of the Continental Army. The hills of Valley Forge he found "all in a wild wooden state."[2] Near Valley Creek, which flows between two steep hills called Mount Joy and Mount Misery, he discovered modern factories, but in one wooded area near the road he did locate what he described as a "relic," the ruin of what had obviously been a defensive redoubt.[3] He also visited the small house where Washington had established his headquarters and where he was certain that the compassionate general had anxiously "felt for the sufferings of his ill clad followers."[4]

What Watson failed to find was evidence of attempts to preserve or glorify the physical Valley Forge. From the time of the Revolution until Watson's own day, Americans had taken surprisingly little interest in their own history, possibly because the Revolution that created the nation was perceived as a deliberate break with the past. History had not been stressed in the schools of the early republic and even Watson's *Annals*, so fascinating to historians today, received little attention from his contemporaries. Nor had Americans been preserving their historic places; Ben Franklin's house had been destroyed in 1812, and George Washington's presidential mansion in Philadelphia would meet a similar fate in 1832.[5]

The historic incident of the winter encampment at Valley Forge would be rediscovered in the Romantic Era of the mid-nineteenth century when the dreary tale of thousands of soldiers suffering and surviving the winter in a military encampment would be transformed into an inspiring legend in which virtue had triumphed after sacrifices had been made. The Valley Forge story would capture the popular imagination, bringing many more tourists to Valley Forge and eventually creating a need to preserve the remains of the encampment. Watson's travel account gives an early glimpse of the way in which nineteenth-century Americans would come to think about Valley Forge.

"What emotions press upon the *reflecting mind!*" Watson wrote. "On those hills, were miserably hutted the *forlorn hope* of the country in its day of most gloomy peril."[6] He continued, "Poor sufferers! their clothing was scanty—, their blankets rags, & their feet always without stockings and almost shoeless!"[7] In Watson's imagination, patriots standing guard duty on cold winter nights wistfully conjured up hearth and home and patriotically contemplated the wrongs that their beloved country had endured.[8]

Watson also commented on the obvious prosperity of the area in his own day, and had he arrived the summer before Washington he might have made the same observation. In 1777, Valley Forge had been checkered with small, enclosed fields. About two-thirds of the area's land had been under cultivation for general farming. Farmers also raised horses, cattle, swine, and sheep. Oak, chestnut, and hickory trees growing on the steeper hills were a source of fuel and charcoal.[9] Swiftly flowing Valley Creek had provided power for local industry. A thriving industrial community had grown up where the creek flowed into the Schuylkill River. The wealthy Potts family had long been operating the forges from which the area took its name. There had also been sawmills, charcoal houses, a gristmill, a blacksmith, a cooper, and a company store. Dams channeled water into millraces that turned the waterwheels for some of these business operations.[10]

In August 1777, British commander Sir William Howe landed his formidable army at the head of the Chesapeake Bay and made for Philadelphia. Howe defeated Washington at a battle at the Brandywine River, and his forces met a contingent of Americans in a skirmish at Paoli. The two armies met again at Germantown, where fog and confusion robbed the Americans of victory. In mid-December, Washington decided to settle his men at Valley Forge for the winter. The terrain was defensible, the location would prevent Howe from raiding much of Pennsylvania's agricultural heartland, and, Washington hoped, the rich farms in the valley would help supply the soldiers during the winter.

No battles were fought at Valley Forge, but the presence of Washington's army devastated the countryside. Soldiers dug up the landscape to build entrenchments and redoubts. The farmers' fences and woodlots were sacrificed to provide shelters for the men. The residents' livestock and stores of grain were commandeered. One account implied that the soldiers also made off with a great deal of movable property, while the locals themselves were nearly reduced to want by the time the troops moved on.[11]

For a while, the American military continued using the old campgrounds at Valley Forge. They served as a hospital camp, an ordnance depot, and a place for detention of prisoners of war.[12] Some six months after Washington's army left, Captain Thomas Anbury, a British prisoner, was marched through Valley Forge under guard. He was quartered in one of the old soldiers' huts, where he recorded his surprise to observe that Washington's defenses had been so weak. Conversation with local loyalists made him aware of the sufferings of area residents, among whom the loyalists still could not understand why Howe had not attacked Valley Forge the previous winter.[13]

Even before the war was officially over, Valley Forge farmers were working to restore the area to its bucolic, antebellum state. There was no spring planting in 1778, but farmers returned their land to cultivation as quickly as possible. They pulled down the soldiers' huts for fuel and fencing material. By 1779, tax records showed that their livestock holdings had nearly reached pre-encampment levels.[14] In September 1781, American Lieutenant Enos Reeves lost his way en route to Philadelphia and found himself at Valley Forge. He wrote:

> We . . . came thro' our old Encampment, or rather the first huts of the whole army. Some of officers' huts are inhabited, but the greater part are decayed, some are split up into rails, and a number of fine fields are to be seen on the level ground that was cleared, but in places where they have let the shoots grow, it is already like a half grown young wood.[15]

Industry also rapidly returned to Valley Forge. While the war continued, the American government established a musket factory there. A British raiding party destroyed the old forges, but Isaac and David Potts together with their relative William Dewees soon built a new forge and dam and began operations at a rolling and slitting mill. In the early 1800s, America's market economy grew, providing many opportunities for industrialists. The production of wrought iron at Valley Forge continued only until about 1816, but John Rogers constructed new facilities for the manufacture of domestic hardware. About the same time, Valley Forge acquired a saw factory, and the production of boiler plates began in the valley. By 1818, the Valley Forge also had a crucible steel furnace, built by the Rogers family. To serve the thriving community, Isaiah Thropp opened Valley Forge's first public store in 1822.[16]

At Valley Forge, the second quarter of the nineteenth century began with some economic uncertainty, but the area soon saw new life. Valley factories were converted for textile production, an industry in which efficient factory system methods were emerging. Charles Rogers ran one large mill, and just west of the village Isaiah Thropp began operating a second mill.[17] To the east of Valley Forge, in 1824, farmer Alexander Kennedy opened a lime quarry and built kilns to burn lime. His two sons expanded the business, and a prosperous village, known first as Kennedy's Hollow and later as Port Kennedy, grew up near Valley Forge. This town also became known for the remarkable caverns discovered during quarry operations.[18] By the 1830s, the valley's many successful businesses had attracted the transportation industry, bringing canal and later rail service to Valley Forge so that its products could more easily reach the cities.[19] In 1837, one resident wrote a relative: "The place is growing fast and may in a few years be something of a town."[20]

The industrial revolution brought quiet Valley Forge the same questions and conflicts the rest of the world was grappling with. Would industrialism create a new social order? What would be the relationship between worker and capitalist? A Scot named Robert Owen was advocating communal industrial communities in which members owned property jointly, shared all labor, and divided the rewards. Owen is most famous for the utopian community he established at New Harmony, Indiana. His principles inspired the foundation of a similar community at Valley Forge.

In 1826, a number of Philadelphia and Wilmington families founded the "Friendly Association for Mutual Interests." Their key benefactor was William Maclure, president of Philadelphia's Academy of Natural Sciences and a devout disciple of Robert Owen. The association purchased buildings at Valley Forge and engaged James Jones of Chester County to supervise the colony. Jones established himself and his own family in the small house that had been Washington's Headquarters during the winter encampment.[21] Association members wrote for themselves a constitution expressing their commitment to pursue useful employment and share in the profits of their venture. Members promised to remain "MORAL, SOBER, and INDUSTRIOUS." Domestic chores would be shared; orphans would be provided for; food, clothing, and furniture would be distributed to all members who were in need. The Friendly Association ambitiously planned a permanent village with commercial buildings and dwellings of equal accommodation for all.[22]

The Friendly Association lasted less than a year. In general, Americans proved to be too individualistic for Owen's brand of utopian socialism. Maclure turned critical and came to doubt that the community at Valley Forge really understood Robert Owen's principles.[23] It has also been speculated that the community members suffered persecution because they reportedly did not believe in God.[24] Many members withdrew, but James Jones remained and purchased Washington's Headquarters. Apparently the Friendly Association was quickly forgotten, for during his visit in 1828 Watson never mentioned the very recent presence of this Owenite community.

On a hill in the woods near the Schuylkill River, Watson did notice the remains of rustic tables and benches where, he had heard, a great many people had recently feasted together.[25] Apparently Watson just missed the Harvest Home Meeting of Chester and Montgomery counties that had been held July 26, 1828, the first recorded mass meeting at Valley Forge. Had Watson been present on that clear, warm day, he might have seen 4,000 people assembled there. Although they called their gathering a Harvest Home, it was officially an Independence Day celebration held late in July for the convenience of farmers whose chores had kept them too busy for a holiday earlier in the month. At noon, the Declaration of Independence had been read; later there was music and oratory.[26]

Part of the day had been devoted to feasting and toasting. In a shady wood, the revelers had been seated at thirteen tables, each 164 feet long and each laden with beef, ham, potatoes, and bread. The formal and informal toasts showed that the gathering was also a political rally. Glasses were raised to the current president, John Quincy Adams, and his many virtues; to Adams's administration; to the union of the states; to Henry Clay, the champion of his country's rights; to the people; and to the government of Pennsylvania. Survivors of the American Revolution were increasingly cherished as death claimed more and more of them, and several had been invited for this special occasion. Peter S. Duponceau, a Frenchman who had been a captain at Valley Forge and an aide to General Von Steuben, rose to declare himself a friend to the incumbent president, preferring Adams to his political rival Andrew Jackson, in part simply because the name "Adams" had nostalgic connections with Revolutionary days.[27]

In 1844, Valley Forge saw another large political rally when Daniel Webster arrived to make a campaign speech for presidential candidate Henry Clay. By this time, many more Americans were voting and taking an interest in politics. Webster's reputation as a great orator ensured that the village would be thronged with eager people clutching banners, wreaths, and patriotic emblems. After Webster's train arrived at the little Valley Forge railway station, he politely surveyed the village's points of interest, including Washington's Headquarters.[28]

The printed program commemorating the 1828 Harvest Home did not dwell much on the story of what had happened at Valley Forge. Only briefly did it mention "the ground rendered sacred by the sufferings of the American Army under Washington" and the soldiers who had wintered there "amid snow and ice, and scarcity, and the apprehension of attack from a vastly superior British force."[29] The growing popularity of the Valley Forge story can be inferred from the fact that Webster capitalized much more on it and even attempted to link his candidate with the heroes of Valley Forge through the fact that both Clay and Washington had called themselves Whigs. "Ladies and Gentlemen," Webster began,

> there is a mighty power in local association. All acknowledge it, and all feel it! . . . There are in this vast multitude who, like myself, never before stood on the spot where the Whig army of the

Revolution, under the immediate command of their immortal leader, went through the privations, the sufferings, and the distress, of the winter of 1777 and 1778. . . . It is impossible to recall the associations of such a place without deep and solemn reflection. And when we, as Whigs, professing the principles of that great Whig leader and that Whig army, come here to advocate and avow those principles to one another, and professing to exercise the political rights transmitted to us by them, for the security of that liberty which they fought to establish, let us bring ourselves to feel in harmony with the scenes of the past. [30]

A record dating from the same year gives evidence of a grassroots desire on the part of local residents to gain national recognition and fame for Valley Forge and to preserve something of the physical place. In 1844, Isaac A. Pennypacker, a doctor in nearby Phoenixville and the grandson of a Revolutionary War veteran, addressed John Fanning Watson inquiring what could be done to preserve and promote Valley Forge. "When I think of the Epoch of that gloomy winter and know the importance of that period in the contest for Liberty, I cannot but feel that Valley Forge has been most shamefully neglected," he wrote. [31]

The fame of Valley Forge would spread in 1850 thanks to a series of letters written by Henry Woodman for the *Doylestown Intelligencer* and later published as a book. Woodman was a Quaker who had spent his early years at Valley Forge. During the winter that Washington's army had camped in the valley, Woodman's mother had been a nineteen-year-old farm girl and his father had been a soldier serving with the North Carolina troops. Woodman wrote that his mother's family's house had been occupied by both General George Weedon and General Baron Johan DeKalb. After the war was over, Woodman's father had revisited Valley Forge on his way back home, hoping to find food and lodging there. He had fallen sick and after his recovery had stayed on as a laborer, marrying the local Sarah Stephens some five years later. [32]

Henry Woodman told of an incident that he claimed occurred in 1796. It seems that his father had been plowing a field at Valley Forge when an elderly gentleman dressed in black had arrived on horseback. Dismounting, the gentleman greeted the elder Woodman cordially and began asking a great many questions about local agriculture. The farmer apologized for being ill prepared to give good answers, saying that he was not a Valley Forge native and had not been brought up to farming, although he had camped at Valley Forge during the Revolutionary War. "This gave a new turn to the conversation," Woodman wrote. The stranger identified himself as George Washington and expressed his delight to find an old soldier engaged in the peaceful and useful occupation of farming.[33] It is entirely possible that Woodman's father did speak to Washington, although Woodman might have had the date wrong. Washington's diaries mention a fishing trip to Valley Forge in 1787 during a hiatus in the Constitutional Convention. The diaries also contain information on farming practices in the valley recorded by Washington, apparently acquired from interviewing local farmers.[34]

Woodman's letters provide a picture of Valley Forge during Woodman's own lifetime. As a child he had gathered wild grapes and chestnuts in the area then still known as "The Camp." He had seen the foundations of soldiers' huts, and had come across the ruins of an old hut chimney. He had discovered decaying bones exposed by soil erosion. He had pointed out Washington's Headquarters to travelers.[35] Woodman added:

> It was a very common thing, since my recollection, to find on the grounds some memento of that period. I have often in company with my elder brothers and other boys, sometimes with grown persons, generally strangers, who, when in the neighborhood, had a curiosity to visit the place, and sometimes alone have I spent hours in traversing the ground in search of these relics of the Revolution not that they were of any great value, but [to] possess them as curiosities [was] to remind us of that period.[36]

Woodman also described the Valley Forge of mid-century. Valley Forge was then a village of forty houses and a railway station. Its cotton mills had made the area increasingly prosperous. The Rogers family and the Thropp family had become the local captains of industry. Charles H. Rogers had built a 40-foot observatory on a hilltop and equipped it with a telescope.[37] From the observatory, Woodman reported, one could see

> a very beautiful and diversified prospect of the most lovely and interesting scenery in its native grandeur, highly cultivated farms, splendid mansions and commodious farmhouses, neat cottages and handsome villages, the navigable river, the railroad thronged with cars, beautiful streams, hills and dales, "fountains and fresh shades" in abundance, till observation is satisfied in passing.[38]

In Woodman's last letter, he mentioned having received "flattering accounts
. . . of [his letters'] reception, not only in this my adopted county [Bucks
County], but in other parts of the country, and in the halls of our National
legislature," confirming his opinion "that the subject is one of deep interest,
and worthy of being rescued from oblivion."[39]

Valley Forge got more national recognition as the professional historians
and biographers of the Romantic Era rediscovered the Valley Forge experience. In his 1860 biography of George Washington, Benson J. Lossing
wrote:

> For in all the world's history, we have no record of purer devotion,
> holier sincerity, or more pious self-sacrifice, than was there exhib-
> ited in the camp of Washington. The courage of the battlefield
> dwindles almost into insignificance when compared with that sub-
> lime heroism displayed by the American soldiery at Valley Forge, in
> the midst of frost and snow, disease and destitution.[40]

Though the observatory blew down in 1861, Valley Forge attracted
increasing numbers of visitors from the greater Philadelphia area. In the
early 1870s it accommodated many sightseers and picnickers when Charles
H. Rogers leased the old campgrounds to the Philadelphia and Reading
Railroad Company.[41] In 1873, a local paper mentioned that the Valley Forge
postmaster had leased his fine gardens for summer amusement. Visitors
would find that "the Village has a good brass and quadrille band, capable of
giving good music for dances or military marches."[42] That August the same
paper noted: "The largest party that visited the favorite picnic grounds at
Valley Forge this year, was that of the Bethel Colored Church, of Philadelphia, which arrived on last Wednesday. Upwards of 1,200 [railway] tickets,
we are informed, were sold for this excursion."[43]

The Centennial Celebration and World's Fair held in 1876 is said to have
touched off the Colonial Revival Movement. The fair did feature historical
exhibits, but they generally served to glorify the present day by comparison.
In the words of cultural historian Karal Ann Marling, "Its old fashioned
artifacts gave visible proof of just how wondrous the modern present really
was."[44] The nostalgic fascination with the domestic life of the Colonial and
Revolutionary eras that characterizes the Colonial Revival Movement can
really be traced to modern trends toward industrialization, commercialization, and urbanization that disturbed many Americans and fostered their
interest in the history, settings, and objects of the past. Spurred on by

authors like Alice Morse Earle, people began collecting antiques to furnish new houses built in revived colonial architectural styles. Historic houses open to visitors, often furnished with the relics of former inhabitants or donated curiosities, began to multiply. Preservationist groups with names like The Association for the Preservation of Virginia Antiquities and the Society for the Preservation of New England Antiquities were formed.

As another by-product of the Colonial Revival Movement, hundreds of historical associations were founded and more than fifty patriotic societies were formed. Many upper- and middle-class Americans who were troubled by the increasing number of immigrants newly arrived from southern and eastern Europe joined societies in which membership depended on whether one could trace an ancestor back to the American Revolution or the Colonial period. These organizations duly erected monuments and grave markers to old soldiers, and incidentally conferred a kind of pedigree on their living members. Some of these organizations included the Daughters of the American Revolution, the National Society of the Colonial Dames of America, the Sons of the American Revolution, and the Society of the Cincinnati. [45]

As America's fascination with the past took hold, Delaware Valley residents anticipated that people from all over the nation would want to take day trips to Valley Forge while visiting the world's fair in Philadelphia. In 1873, a local paper had advised: "Valley Forge, which is second to no place in America as to Revolutionary fame, should be made a grand objective point in the Centennial Celebration in 1876." [46] With the same idea in mind, Theodore W. Bean, a lawyer from Norristown, Pennsylvania, published a book called *Washington at Valley Forge One Hundred Years Ago; or, The Foot-Prints of the Revolution*. His preface identified the volume as a guidebook for Centennial tourists and claimed that the book contained "all that the pilgrim to this spot will require to renew in his heart the debt of gratitude which we owe to the illustrious men who made these hills as notable as their lives have become memorable in the common history of our country." [47]

Bean encouraged visitors to look for existing traces of the winter encampment, such as the still-visible remains of entrenchments, but he also painted a contemporary picture of Valley Forge. By Bean's day, Valley Forge was served by three railroad lines: the Northern Pennsylvania, the Reading, and the Pennsylvania Central. Bean listed the names of important property owners, such as Isaac W. Smith, who owned a woolen factory, and his sister Sarah Shaw. He mentioned Charles H. Rogers, who owned two hundred acres there, and Stanley L. Ogden, the "landlord of the Valley Forge

Mansion Hotel located a short distance up the hill from Washington's headquarters." He spoke of Hannah Ogden, a descendant of the Jones family and the current resident at Washington's Headquarters. According to Bean, Mrs. Ogden "keeps the premises in good condition, everything being precisely as when occupied by the General-in-Chief."[48]

Ironically, while Valley Forge was becoming an increasingly popular tourist destination, very little real historical research on the encampment of 1777–1778 was being done. Watson, Woodman, and Bean all had little to say about exactly what happened that winter. Some people were still extremely misinformed. As late as 1873, one individual passing through Valley Forge by rail had been told by a fellow traveler: "Yes, this is Walley Forge. Yonder is the hills on which was fought the biggest battle of our forefathers, and that's Washington's headquarters right over there, where the General stayed and boss'd the job."[49] As if to make up for a lack of hard data, many legends and traditions arose during the course of the nineteenth century. They grew and changed and were enlarged on as they were eagerly handed down.

The powerful visual image of bloody footprints became almost a logo for the winter encampment. Washington's letters to Congress and the reports of other officers had frequently protested that certain regiments were ill clothed. In one letter, Washington mentioned a lack of shoes so severe that the men's "marches might be tracked by the blood from their feet."[50] In a biography of George Washington, Washington's adopted son, George Washington Parke Custis, related that during the army's march to their winter campgrounds in December 1777 Washington had been observed eyeing something on the ground. He stopped and asked an officer, "How comes it, sir, that I have tracked the march of your troops by the bloodstains of their feet upon the frozen ground?"[51] In his speech at Valley Forge, Daniel Webster mentioned that the bloody footprint story had been told at Washington's own dinner table.[52] John Fanning Watson, who based his writing on oral tradition, mentioned bloody footprints in another context. He wrote that he had heard from Valley Forge veteran Charles Macknet that "when on duty, shoes were *borrowed* of one another—on occasion of alarm, when all had to be abroad, then many feet had to touch the frosty ground & some footsteps were mark'd with blood—!"[53] Woodman mentioned bloody footprints three times, claiming that his information came from eyewitnesses who "had seen the snow and ground over which the soldiers had to pass in performing the duties of the camp, marked with the blood that flowed from their feet.[54] Bean repeated the Custis vignette in a history of Montgomery

County published in 1884 and suggested it even in the subtitle of his 1876 guidebook, *Foot-Prints of the Revolution*.

Other Valley Forge traditions involved the hero George Washington who had long been venerated as a symbol of national identity and stability, and one tradition in particular illustrated his compassion and care for his troops. Writing sideways in the margin of his travel notebook, Watson recorded that Washington had reportedly once traded places with a cold and hungry sentinel, allowing the young soldier to get a hot meal.[55] A periodical called *The Casket* expanded on this story in April 1830 and added appropriate dialogue:

> A young man not quite twenty, from the western part of Massachusetts, was on guard before the General's door, marching back and forth in the snow, on a tremendous cold morning. Washington came out and accosted him, "My friend, how long have you been on guard here?" "Nearly two hours, sir." "Have you breakfasted?" "No, sir." "Give me your gun and go breakfast at my table." He did so, and General Washington marched the rounds until he returned.[56]

More than sixty years later, the *Ladies' Home Journal* carried essentially the same tale.[57]

An equally persistent legend tells how a Quaker silently observed Washington as he knelt in the snow in a bower of trees to pray for the deliverance of his troops and his country. This tale was first published in the 1808 edition of a biography of Washington by the colorful itinerant preacher and traveling book salesman, Mason L. (Parson) Weems. Weems never revealed his source, but he identified Washington's observer as "a certain good old FRIEND of the respectable family and name of Potts." The sight had supposedly so impressed Potts that he confided to his wife Sarah his belief that Washington was a man of God and that the nation was saved. This charming story had certain inconsistencies, such as the fact that Washington had never been overtly religious. In addition, between 1774 and 1782 Isaac Potts, who owned Washington's Headquarters during the time of the encampment, had been living in Pottsgrove, not Valley Forge. And even if Potts had visited the winter encampment, his wife at the time had been named Martha, not Sarah.

Nevertheless, the prayer-in-the-snow story captured the endorsement of the respected Virginia historian Bishop Meade in 1857. From the mid-1800s, various artists attempted to illustrate it, creating visual images that ended up in churches and schools. In her book *George Washington Slept Here*, Karal Ann Marling describes the story as an "icon" in the collective conscience of Americans,[58] and that being the case, most nineteenth-century accounts of Valley Forge included the prayer story. Watson mentioned it only briefly, but Woodman claimed that he had heard it from residents before he "saw the account published."[59] In biographies of Washington both published in 1860, George Washington Parke Custis and Benson Lossing each quoted the prayer story in footnotes using almost the same words. In these versions, more detail appears. The Quaker Isaac Potts is strolling along the creek when he hears a solemn voice. He notices the general's horse tethered to a sapling and finds Washington on his knees, "his cheeks suffused with tears." In this version, Potts confides to his wife that if God would listen to any human, Washington would be the one, and therefore America was assured of her independence.[60] Bean picked up this version in *Foot-Prints*, down to Washington's tear-stained cheeks.[61]

By the last quarter of the nineteenth century, the prayer story was apparently coming under its first attacks. In 1874, in a family history of the Pottses, Mrs. (Isabella) Thomas Potts James offered some documentation for the tradition, saying she had copied her version of the prayer legend from material written by Ruth Anna Potts, Isaac Potts's daughter, who had died in 1811.[62] A 1901 magazine article also mentioned this document, while an account written in 1904 contended that the prayer story was "no mythical tale."[63] As if to give physical weight to the legend, an 1875 newspaper story told how a Reading resident had been given a cane carved from the wood of the tree under which Washington had prayed.[64]

Seemingly contradicting the exemplary character of Washington is another peculiar story with roots in the nineteenth century, about a secret escape route maintained for Washington in case the camp was surprised by the British. Woodman briefly speaks of "secret doors" at Washington's Headquarters for the speedy escape of the commander-in-chief.[65] Another account written in the late 1880s or 1890s tells of a secret tunnel. By that time, Washington's Headquarters was open to the public and a modern addition had been made to the building in an attempt to re-create a log dining room that had been erected during the encampment. When visitors entered this log structure, this writer says, "lights are brought and the guide pilots the way down a dark, damp stairway into a dismal subterranean chamber some thirty odd feet below the surface, and tells us of the local tradition which asserts that from it a secret passage led to the Schuylkill river and offered a means of escape in an emergency."[66] A newspaper travel account written in 1904 contended that the escape tunnel had been built not by the courageous Washington but by the Potts family to be used in case of Indian attack.[67]

It is currently believed that the secret tunnel legend was inspired by a root cellar dug while the nineteenth-century Jones family occupied Washington's Headquarters. In a letter to a nephew written in 1890, Nathan Jones speaks of having helped to dig a "milk cave" back in the 1840s but denies the existence of a secret tunnel at that time.[68] However, the secret tunnel story has delighted so many tourists over the years that even today visitors are disappointed to learn there is no evidence that any escape route existed in Washington's time.

There is also no evidence to support the claim of the DeHaven family that their ancestor Jacob DeHaven lent George Washington $450,000 in cash and supplies while the army was encamped at Valley Forge. This tradition first appeared in print in a history of the DeHaven family penned by Howard DeHaven Ross.[69] Periodically, the descendants of Jacob DeHaven make attempts to get the "loan" repaid with interest. Various individuals took up this cause in the 1850s, 1870s, and 1890s. The issue came up again around 1910, 1920, and 1960. As recently as 1990, the *New York Times* reported on the status of a class action suit filed in U.S. Claims Court by a DeHaven descendant from Stafford, Texas. By then the DeHavens calculated the amount owed their family at more than one hundred billion dollars, but they reported they were willing to accept a "reasonable payment"—and maybe a monument at Valley Forge.[70]

This remarkably persistent tradition has been thoroughly debunked by Judith A. Meier, of the Montgomery County Historical Society, whose genealogical research revealed that there were no DeHavens living in the immediate area until after 1790 and that Jacob DeHaven had never been rich enough to make such a fabulous loan. Still, past experience shows that a DeHaven claim is certain to arise about once every generation.

In the century or so since Washington left Valley Forge, the place had become transformed. Watson, the lone visitor of the 1820s, had been replaced by scores of tourists drawn by the accounts of antiquarians, professional historians, and local boosters. Although few people could recite many facts about the winter encampment of 1777–1778, there was a consensus that something important had happened at Valley Forge, where endurance, perseverance, and faith had paved the road from the bleakest despair to moral victory. As the Baptist minister Henry L. Wayland preached in 1878, Valley Forge clearly demonstrated that the providence of God ruled over the fates of people and nations. Valley Forge showed that "we must pay the price of every blessing by toil and suffering."[71]

It was a lesson that had enormous appeal for Victorian Americans. The next question was whether some physical remains of the place where this lesson could be learned should be exalted, honored, and preserved for future generations of Americans.

2

The Centennial and Memorial Association of Valley Forge

One December evening in 1877, several public-spirited gentlemen with a keen interest in history arrived at the home of Mr. Isaac W. Smith in the village of Valley Forge. All upper-middle-class professionals from the surrounding area, their purpose was to plan a celebration to mark the centennial of the winter encampment at Valley Forge. This celebration, they decided, would not take place on the One Hundredth Anniversary of that gloomy December day when Washington's army had marched into the valley, but would instead commemorate the warm, sunny June day when the troops had marched out. The gentlemen resolved that on the following June 19 there would be parades, music, and oratory on a grand scale at Valley Forge. They appointed officers and formed committees to organize this salute, which they hoped would attract thousands. Finally, they gave themselves a name: the Valley Forge Centennial Association. [1]

Once the Christmas holidays were over, the Centennial Association sent out invitations. Among those invited were President Rutherford B. Hayes and the First Lady, the President's entire cabinet, the Vice President, the

Speaker of the House, the Chief Justice and the entire Supreme Court, the members of important congressional committees, the state senate and house of representatives, plus the state supreme court. Since the celebration was supposed to have a military flavor, they also invited the General and Lieutenant General of the U.S. Army, various officers of the Navy, the Boston Ancient and Honorable Artillery Company, the New York Seventh Regiment, the Fifth Maryland Regiment, the Chicago Zouaves, the Norfolk Blues, and the Charlestown Blues. This was going to be no small-town affair.[2]

Little more than a month later, a committee from the Valley Forge Centennial Association was en route to Harrisburg to ask the state to grant them money. The cash they wanted would not be required for the June extravaganza; the gentlemen expected to raise considerable money through the sale of concession privileges and the collection of rebates from the railroad companies that would bring the crowds to Valley Forge. A local newspaper revealed that the Valley Forge Centennial Association sought state funding for another reason: "The money is wanted less for current expenses than to purchase Washington's old headquarters."[3]

The Centennial Association had already decided that the Valley Forge experience deserved not just an elaborate celebration but a lasting memorial. According to Henry J. Stager, a Norristown printer who would later write and publish a limited-edition history of this organization,

> It was suggested that no more fitting memorial could be designed than Washington's Headquarters, which had already stood the storms of more than one hundred years, and was filled with precious memories of the great Chieftain whose home it had been during the most trying memorable days of the Revolutionary struggle.[4]

The organization was no doubt influenced by what had already transpired at other historic sites. In 1850, the governor of New York persuaded the state legislature to purchase the structure that had been George Washington's headquarters at Newburgh, New York, making it America's first historic house museum.[5] And although the governor of Virginia was not successful in getting that state's legislature to appropriate funds to save Mount Vernon from becoming a hotel, Ann Pamela Cunningham, who described herself as a "Southern matron," founded the Mount Vernon Ladies' Association in 1852, and by 1859 her organization owned this tourist attraction.[6] More recently, the old Ford Mansion that had been Washington's headquarters in

Morristown, New Jersey, had been saved in 1873 by a group of gentlemen calling themselves the "Washington Association."[7]

The immense popularity of George Washington as a historic figure throughout the nineteenth century was no doubt responsible for these successful preservation efforts. In the two antebellum projects, it was hoped that the reverence for Washington inspired by the houses would have a unifying effect on America. Ann Pamela Cunningham's use of language also illustrated the nation's reverence toward this founding father when she spoke of Mount Vernon as a sacred place, a "shrine of pure patriotism," that would be visited by many "pilgrims."[8] The same sort of language was increasingly applied to other historic sites throughout the rest of the 1800s and into the twentieth century.

Washington's Headquarters was not as architecturally impressive as these other sites associated with Washington. It was a small two-story, three-bay,

Fig. 1.   The earliest known photograph of Washington's Headquarters at Valley Forge, c. 1861. The building was privately owned at the time and used as a residence. (Courtesy, Valley Forge National Historical Park)

gable-roofed stone Georgian structure with a floor plan similar to that of a townhouse, asymmetrical with only two small rooms per floor and a stair hall running the length of the building. Its small kitchen wing might have postdated the Revolution. Originally, it might have been built as a summer residence for the relatively wealthy eighteenth-century Potts family, who had owned considerable property and commanded the industrial operations in the valley. In the nineteenth century, Washington's Headquarters was believed to have been built around 1760, but current thinking suggests it may have been built as late as 1773.[9] It belonged to Hannah Ogden, daughter of James Jones, the former supervisor of Valley Forge's failed Owenite community.

On Washington's Birthday 1878, the Valley Forge Centennial Association reorganized to meet their objective of purchasing Washington's Headquarters. They changed their name to the Valley Forge Centennial and Memorial Association, resolving to appoint a lady regent to head a committee of patriotic women who would raise the funds to purchase their memorial.[10] In the wake of the abolition movement, Americans had grown more accustomed to seeing women in leadership roles. Ann Pamela Cunningham had relied on a network of middle- and upper-class socially prominent women and spoke of them as the "vestals" of American heritage at Mount Vernon.[11] By the end of the nineteenth century, thanks to her example, women were considered appropriate custodians of the historic places where America's heritage was preserved and its patriotism was fostered.[12]

For their first female regent, the Centennial and Memorial Association of Valley Forge selected Anna Morris Holstein. Born in Muncy, Pennsylvania, in 1824 and married to William Hayman Holstein in 1848, she had served as an army nurse during the Civil War.[13] Most important, however, was her applicable recent fundraising experience. Ann Pamela Cunningham had initially sought funds only in the South, but eventually broadened her operations to include thirty state chapters each under the direction of a lady vice-regent who coordinated that state's correspondence and fundraising activities.[14] Anna Morris Holstein had been part of the Mount Vernon Ladies' Association and had raised money in Montgomery County. It was hoped that she would be able to duplicate the success of Ann Pamela Cunningham and use her contacts to raise funds both nationally and locally for Valley Forge's worthy cause.[15]

Mrs. Holstein and her committeewomen soon came to terms with Mrs. Ogden. Because the modest house was so full of "precious memories," Hannah Ogden wanted a pricey $6,000 for it. It was proposed that the

Centennial and Memorial Association pay Mrs. Ogden $500 on May 1, $1,000 on August 1, $1,500 on October 1, and secure a mortgage for the other $3,000.[16] A gentleman of the Centennial and Memorial Association advanced the initial $500.[17]

At the end of May and the beginning of June 1878, the Centennial and Memorial Association issued more invitations to their upcoming celebration. Local papers printed the notice: "The Valley Forge Centennial [and Memorial] Association extends a cordial invitation to all people to join in celebrating the one hundredth anniversary of the occupation of Valley Forge by the Continental Army under beloved Washington, on the 19th of June next." Those attending would observe "an imposing spectacle never again in our time to be witnessed at Valley Forge."[18] Five members of the Centennial and Memorial Association visited Washington, D.C., to personally urge President Hayes to attend. When they were graciously received by the President himself, they read a brief address on the history of Valley Forge. The President listened politely and declared that he felt great affection for the voters of Pennsylvania, but he declined the invitation, pleading the prior engagement of a wedding in Princeton on June 20.[19]

Although the President and the other high-profile invitees would not be coming, the local community was expected to turn out in great numbers, and the Centennial and Memorial Association swung into action to accommodate them. Early in June they took bids from those who would operate concession stands.[20] The ladies of the organization also hoped to profit by selling food, so they advertised for donations of ham, tongue, fruit, coffee, and tea to be sold at their lunch pavilions,[21] and they arranged for students at the Chester Springs Orphan School to wait tables for them.[22]

The early morning hours of June 19 saw much activity at Valley Forge. Neighboring towns had been requested to ring all public bells at 5:00 A.M.[23] This joyous noise was accompanied by the salute of thirteen cannon at sunrise.[24] According to the day's proceedings, printed one year later, by 7:00 A.M. the roads to Valley Forge were "thronged by the yeomanry of the surrounding country," who swarmed around the small headquarters building. Special trains began arriving around 8:30 A.M., steadily disgorging passengers, who increased the already growing crowd.[25]

The day's spectacles soon began. The governor of Pennsylvania and his staff were formally received. Together with other government officials, the governor reviewed a huge parade of military and civil marching societies. Moving majestically through the fields of Mr. I. Heston Todd of Valley Forge, thousands of men in uniform performed military drills.[26] The breathtaking display was immortalized in a drawing in New York's prestigious *Harper's Weekly*.

The day's oratory was held in an enormous tent shipped in from Massachusetts. One theme evident in all the speeches was the contrast between the despair and suffering of encampment days and the gladness of this day of celebration. All speeches touched on the moral lesson of Valley Forge: that willing sacrifice can lead to triumph. Pennsylvania's governor spoke of a Valley Forge "hallowed by hunger and cold, disease and destitution."[27] Centennial and Memorial Association member Theodore W. Bean mentioned "the shoeless soldiers, the frozen ground, the cheerless hills, [and] the lowering leaden sky that arched them over with gloom."[28]

A lengthy poem composed by Mary E. Thropp Cone—who had grown up near Valley Forge and married Andrew Cone, owner and publisher of the *Oil City Times* and, in 1878, ambassador to Brazil—enlivened the program. Though neither the Honorable Mr. Cone nor his poet wife was able to attend the ceremony, the leading citizens of West Chester had asked Mrs.

Fig. 2.   Valley Forge Centennial, 1878. In this *Harper's Weekly* illustration, thousands march in formation during the celebration hosted by the Centennial and Memorial Association.

Cone to lend her talent to the occasion. She wrote the poem in Brazil, and in it she described her own memories of the scenes of home and her gratitude to the heroes of the past who had made America great.[29]

Everyone was patiently waiting for the address of Henry Armitt Brown, thought to be one of the most brilliant orators of the day. When he finally spoke, Brown reviewed the history of Valley Forge at great length, using storyteller language and vivid images to thoroughly captivate the audience. He set the stage by describing the soldiers' arrival in December 1777: "The wind is cold and piercing on old Gulf road, and the snow-flakes have begun to fall. Who is this who toils up yonder hill, his footsteps stained with blood?"[30] Using historians' accounts and the words of actual soldiers, he continued with tales of a bleak winter, frozen roads, men's limbs blackened with gangrene, and the horror of camp amputations. Brown too made the contrast between Valley Forge in the eighteenth and nineteenth centuries:

> The heroic dead who have suffered here are beyond our reach. No human eulogy can make their glory greater, no failure to do them justice can make it less. . . . Their trials here secured the happiness of a continent; their labors have borne fruit in the free institutions of a powerful nation; their examples give hope to every race and clime; their names live on the lips of a grateful people; their memory is cherished in their children's hearts, and shall endure forever.[31]

A few days after the celebration Mrs. Holstein wrote: "That was indeed a grand oration of Armitt Brown. It thrills one to *read* it; what must it have been to have *heard* it, amid such surroundings?"[32]

Mrs. Holstein missed the inspiring speech because she was busy all day in the headquarters area with her lady assistants. Provisions had been donated by the wagonload, and the ladies were presiding at makeshift tables protected by tents, dishing up lunches by the hundreds. Their efforts raised $410 toward the purchase of Washington's Headquarters. For a while during the day, no soldiers were posted at the headquarters and the ladies were left alone to fend off souvenir hunters intent on breaking off pieces of the stone building to keep as personal mementos.[33]

The success of this first mass gathering held solely to commemorate the Valley Forge experience appeared to demonstrate that there was a tremendous interest in Valley Forge. As a result, the Centennial and Memorial Association adopted a charter formalizing their plans to purchase Washington's Headquarters, open it to the public, and create a memorial park. On July 5, 1878, the Centennial and Memorial Association was officially chartered to purchase, improve, and preserve the lands at Valley Forge General Washington used, together with the structures on them.[34] The association adopted bylaws similar to those of the Mount Vernon Ladies' Association and Mrs. Holstein became an official leader, her mission to form a nationwide network of vice regents who would raise money for their organization throughout the United States. Anyone could join the Centennial and Memorial Association. A contribution of just $1.00 bought a membership, a vote, and a stock certificate suitable for framing.[35] Eventually President James A. Garfield's wife, Lucretia, and his daughter and mother each bought a share of stock.[36]

Initial fundraising efforts were successful. By the spring of 1879, the association had collected $3,000 toward the purchase of Washington's Headquarters and had secured a mortgage for the remaining amount. On May 1, the association paid Mrs. Ogden's price and the deed to headquarters was transferred to William Holstein, who conveyed it to the association. The Centennial and Memorial Association had acquired its lasting memorial, plus about one-and-a-half acres of land.[37]

A few weeks later, a local newspaper headlined an article "THE CENTENNIAL IS TO BE RIVALLED ON JUNE 19 — PREPARATIONS TO DEDICATE THE WASHINGTON HEADQUARTERS." The article described plans already in motion for more oratory, another lunch, and a state championship rifle match on that day.[38] Other accounts of the planning effort followed. One sweltering day in early June, with the thermometer registering an unseasonable 100° in the shade, Centennial and Memorial Association members were forced to hold a planning session outdoors on the Valley Forge picnic grounds. Eventually, an engraved invitation circular embellished with a picture of Washington's Headquarters was issued.[39]

Reporters were on the scene on Dedication Day at Valley Forge. One was able to telegraph his story of that morning's events to West Chester, where it made the evening edition of the *Daily Local News.* He spoke of a clear, crisp morning and estimated that 10,000 people had arrived by 10:00 A.M, with more pouring in each minute.

> At the time I write, the grounds present a beautiful appearance. The sloping hills and low-lying valleys that border the river, . . . the dark strips of woodland dotting the landscape here and there,

form one of the loveliest and most entrancing views in all of Chester County.

He named the dignitaries who had already arrived, and described the parade that had proceeded from the railroad depot to the village picnic grounds located near an old mansion that had been remodeled and turned into a fine hotel called the Washington Inn. [40]

Descriptions of the day's most interesting event would not reach the newspapers until the following day. Washington's Headquarters would be formally dedicated with the laying of a new cornerstone by the Freemasons, an international secret fraternity officially called the Free and Accepted Masons, to which George Washington himself had belonged. This peculiar colorful ceremony began when officials of the Masonic Order arrived by train and were led to a platform arranged with their arcane paraphernalia. The Right Worshipful Grand Master, Michael Nesbit, solemnly mounted with his entourage and called for silence. The Masons' Grand Chaplain pronounced the invocation, asking that the "Supreme Architect of the Universe" bless the nation, the state, and the Centennial and Memorial Association. At the direction of the Grand Master, objects were placed inside the hollow cornerstone, making it a sort of time capsule. These objects included a Bible; several gold, silver, and bronze medals; a copy of Henry Armitt Brown's oration of the previous year; a number of local newspapers; and several books on the American Revolution. Masonic officers then carefully tested the cornerstone with plumb, level, and square and pronounced it tried and true. Finally, the Grand Master spread cement on the cornerstone and used his gavel to ceremonially tap it into place. The stone was anointed with corn, wine, and oil, to bring peace and prosperity to the community. [41]

Once this exotic dedication was over, the crowds repaired to the rifle range that had been set up east of the village, stretching 500 yards across Gulph Road and running parallel to the road that ran through the village toward Port Kennedy. All afternoon, people eagerly watched the targets through field glasses. It was not until 7:30 P.M that the Pennsylvania Team from Philadelphia was declared the winner and accepted a gold medal from a Centennial and Memorial Association member. All the shooting frightened some horses, resulting in several demolished wagons and one injury. [42] A day later, the *Daily Local News* reported on the seamier side of the celebration. The crowd, officially estimated at between 6,000 and 10,000, had attracted pickpockets. Two men lost pocket watches, one lost a pocketbook, and a third had all his money stolen while watching the dedication ceremony. "A lady from Philadelphia," the story concluded, "was about getting on the 5:30 train when some one snatched her gold watch. She followed the thief, but he made his escape, and in the meantime she missed the train."[43]

The Centennial and Memorial Association had a deed and a new cornerstone at the Headquarters, but they needed cash to pay off their mortgage and get clear title to the building. Mrs. Holstein and her associates tried to raise the money by hosting balls, concerts, lectures, and musicales wherever enough interest could be generated. At Pottsville, Pennsylvania, patriotic ladies erected colorful tents and attired their pretty daughters as gypsies— hastily trained to tell fortunes for a modest fee. The Pottsville ladies adorned their gypsy camp with waterfalls, springs, and wells gushing lemonade. They hauled in a church choir, a band, and an orchestra. The event even featured an archery competition among a dozen Pottsville belles, plus a trotting race.[44] Local newspapers encouraged schools to raise money for Valley Forge,[45] and the Norristown Philharmonic Society planned a series of concerts to help out.[46]

Such creative efforts did not bring in sufficient money, however, and in 1882 the association still owed $3,000 on the Headquarters, and members reported having trouble meeting interest payments and making needed repairs to the building. One newspaper lamented:

> The amount is so trifling that Philadelphia alone could raise it in a few hours. And yet the utmost apathy prevails in reference to it. . . . Had the gifted Henry Armitt Brown lived much more would now have been accomplished for Valley Forge. His eloquent words touched all hearts, and revealed what a heritage of sacred memories of Valley Forge belonged to the nation.[47]

Unfortunately, the wealthy of Philadelphia were also being asked to contribute to the preservation of Independence Hall and Fairmount Park, and appeals to Harrisburg were getting no response. The Centennial and Memorial Association feared it would face foreclosure.

The association finally received the financial help it needed from an organization called the "Patriotic Order Sons of America" (POS of A), which had been organized in 1847 and whose members still call it "our nation's oldest Patriotic Society of Native Americans." In August 1885, a delegation of ladies from the Centennial and Memorial Association delivered an appeal for help while local POS of A members were convening in Norristown.

Henry J. Stager, president of Pennsylvania's POS of A organization, was honored to adopt their cause and agreed to solicit money from other POS of A contingents, known as camps, throughout the state.[48]

Stager encountered but managed to overcome the same apathy the Centennial and Memorial Association had experienced. In one promotional pamphlet, he suggested that each camp hold some sort of celebration on Washington's Birthday 1886 and donate the proceeds.[49] When sufficient cash failed to materialize, Stager followed up with a letter. Only 35 camps had responded, he admonished—where were Pennsylvania's other 146? "Was there ever a stronger appeal for financial aid to show the practical patriotism of our Order than this, and could we permit another to step in our place and relieve us of the labor and high honor of success in this noble work?" he demanded.[50] Stager sent a third appeal in July 1886, reporting that one-third of the Pennsylvania camps had so far contributed $2,200. Couldn't the other two-thirds come up with the rest of the cash?[51]

While Stager hounded his membership throughout 1886, POS of A brought the parades and brass bands back to Valley Forge. On Decoration Day (Memorial Day) that May, several camps converged there. Washington's Headquarters was gaily festooned with flags, streamers, and bunting. Spectators once again arrived by train, carriage, and wagon to listen to speeches and inspect the grounds at Valley Forge.[52]

In November 1886, POS of A representatives met with the Centennial and Memorial Association to report that they had raised $3,370.98, enough to pay all the debts at the Headquarters and to prompt a change in the structure of the Centennial and Memorial Association.[53] In Stager's third appeal to his camps, he had written:

> The object is, simply to clear off the indebtedness of the $3,000 mortgage now upon Washington's Headquarters at Valley Forge. In doing so, we will not only receive a mortgage for the full amount named, but also three thousand shares of stock in the Centennial [and Memorial] Association, which will give us a full majority vote in its future direction and care.[54]

When POS of A turned over its proceeds, it received 3,600 shares of stock issued to Henry J. Stager as trustee. Anna Morris Holstein remained nominal head of the association, with the title of regent, while Stager became vice regent, with the power to vote all the POS of A shares. POS of A members also assumed thirteen places on an eighteen-member board of directors.[55]

Local newspapers applauded this restructuring. The *Daily Local News* editorialized about the plans of this reorganized body to make Valley Forge a "national possession," saying, "The Patriotic Sons of America are working exactly in this line, and their disinterested efforts deserve to be commended with success."[56]

POS of A would also help the Centennial and Memorial Association obtain an even more significant amount of money. In January 1887, a POS of A member visited Harrisburg to solicit the governor's support for a state grant of $5,000. By lucky coincidence, Pennsylvania's governor had been a general in the Civil War and Anna Morris Holstein had been the nurse attending him after he lost a leg. In April 1887, the Pennsylvania state legislature appropriated $5,000 for "the improvement, extension and preservation of the lands and buildings occupied by General George Washington, as his headquarters at Valley Forge, during the winter of 1777 and 1778."[57]

The $5,000 would be used to make Washington's Headquarters look like it had when Washington was there. As the *Daily Local News* put it, "The whole building will be made to resemble the structure of ye olden time as near as possible."[58] Its kitchen addition was altered to expose a breezeway with an arched opening between the main building and kitchen. This attractive architectural feature had been hidden by stucco when the breezeway was enclosed during the building's occupation by the Jones family. A log structure meant to re-create a log dining room built during the encampment and mentioned in a letter Martha Washington sent Mercy Otis Warren in March 1778 was annexed to the kitchen wing.[59] Walls were replastered, and modern window frames were replaced with period reproductions. Old wood from interior repairs to some of the floors and woodwork was carefully saved and delivered to a Norristown planing mill, where it was sawed up to be made into canes, collar buttons, and other marketable souvenir items.[60]

In 1891, Anna Morris Holstein prepared a pamphlet on Washington's Headquarters that was available for sale to visitors with paper or muslin cover for 10 or 25 cents. In the pamphlet, Mrs. Holstein was enthusiastic about how much the Headquarters now resembled the building George Washington had known:

> [It] appears to-day almost precisely as it did when Washington was domiciled within it. The doors, with bolts and locks, are the very same his hands have moved; the floors . . . are those over which the great chieftain has walked in many weary hours; the window

glass and sash are unchanged since the days when his anxious eyes looked through them at the soldiers' huts upon the hills.[61]

While the window glass and most of the floorboards might have been original, it is now thought that the hardware Mrs. Holstein was so proud of were nineteenth-century replacements for earlier, smaller bolts and locks.[62]

Despite the desire for authenticity, the Centennial and Memorial Association made a number of changes to the grounds around headquarters that would have been decidedly out of place in Washington's day. The grounds were landscaped with shrubbery, flowers, and walks that would have seemed very foreign in an eighteenth-century industrial community or military camp. The Centennial and Memorial Association also added shade trees, asking each of the thirteen original colonies to donate a tree representative of that state.[63] While visiting Mount Vernon in the late 1880s, one POS of A member acquired an elm sapling for the grounds, certified by Mount Vernon's gardener to have descended from a tree planted by Washington's own hands.[64] For many years, the Washington elm stood proudly on the right as visitors faced the entrance of headquarters. Mrs. Holstein wrote about her plans to place a canon on either side of the door and to set up pyramids of cannonballs as lawn ornaments. She also mentioned a flagpole from which a donated flag some 30 feet long regularly flew.[65] In 1899, the association received another donation—a model of a schoolhouse built as a float for a POS of A parade. The Centennial and Memorial Association dutifully placed it behind headquarters, where it remained until 1905.[66]

A caretaker's cottage was constructed in one corner of Centennial and Memorial Association property. This tiny building contained only four rooms and a kitchen. Two different visitors would later condemn its architectural style as too "Eastlake" (a modern version of Gothic) to be in keeping with "ye olden" flavor of headquarters.[67] However, it would enable the caretaker to move out of cramped quarters in the kitchen annex and attic of the old building. Drawing a salary of $360 per year plus free rent at the cottage, the Centennial and Memorial Association caretaker was the only member of the organization ever paid for his work.[68]

Long before the POS of A became involved with Valley Forge, the Centennial and Memorial Association had wanted to furnish Washington's Headquarters with antiques. In 1887, Mrs. Holstein reiterated this desire, writing: "The intention is to furnish the main building with furniture of the Revolutionary period. As it is not at all probable, we can now collect anything belonging to Genl Washington. We will have to get it, where we can."[69] She was hoping for donations, and in 1888 a local paper publicly requested suitable heirlooms: "If deposited at Washington's headquarters at Valley Forge, they would be well cared for, prized, seen and admired by hundreds. While being kept by individuals, they are only seen by members of a family occasionally."[70] Over the years, Mrs. Holstein personally solicited contributions from her contacts, including Frederick D. Stone, at the Historical Society of Pennsylvania. In 1892 she reminded Stone that she would be glad to have a clock he had mentioned and would appreciate the society's help with pictures and photographs.[71]

On December 17, 1894, nine local women assembled in Norristown to organize a Valley Forge DAR chapter, and Anna Morris Holstein became its first regent.[72] In 1900, the Centennial and Memorial Association granted this chapter permission to furnish Washington's bedroom at headquarters. It held a concert and raised $103.45, which formed the nucleus of a fund on which they could draw.[73] In their minutes, they noted, "it was the general sentiment of the members present to use *only genuine old furniture* if possible."[74] In the early months of 1901, the ladies visited antiques dealers and managed to get a bureau, chairs, and a washstand;[75] they had some trouble locating a suitable bedstead, and once one was found it was discovered that the bedposts were too high for the low ceilings at the Headquarters, so the piece was altered accordingly.[76] A separate carpet committee attempted to provide a rag rug made of scraps collected and prepared by each member of the chapter. They tried to have their carpet woven on the Martha Washington loom at Mount Vernon, but in the end they provided a carpet woven locally.[77]

Other DAR chapters followed the example set by Valley Forge. In 1902, the Chester County DAR asked to furnish another room on the second floor of headquarters. There were some dissenting votes on the board at the Centennial and Memorial Association, but permission was finally granted.[78] The Chester County ladies came up with a bedstead, two bureaus, a looking glass, and another one of those rag rugs then considered so essential to colonial interior decor.[79] In 1903, the Merion DAR asked to furnish an attic room that had a round window and was believed to have been George Washington's observatory. The minutes of the Centennial and Memorial Association read: "There was some objection to further occupancy of the Building, and a spirited discussion ensued, but the privilege was granted by a vote of eight in favor to five opposed."[80] The Merion daughters used a less formal arrangement of objects in an attempt to make the room look inhabited. In their literature they proclaimed their success, writing that they had "seen numerous visitors turn away hastily, fearing that they had intruded upon a private room."[81] After all three rooms were open to visitors, one tourist commented on the wealth of relics on view at headquarters, noting that the building had three furnished rooms, two done to evoke Mount Vernon and one in a country style.[82]

In the 1880s and 1890s, while the Centennial and Memorial Association acquired and restored Washington's Headquarters, the industrial community at Valley Forge was going through difficult times. Economic decline began in 1881 when Isaac Smith relocated his woolen mill in nearby Bridgeport. Later a paper mill folded, and in 1890 the Thropp mill complex burned down. Valley Forge's population dropped from an all-time high of 500 to about 125.[83] Houses were abandoned, and area residents were beginning to describe the village as an eyesore, contrasting sharply with the natural beauty of the valley. Port Kennedy's lime business failed, and the Kennedy family went bankrupt. An ironworks in the same town failed in 1893, and by 1900 Port Kennedy was also nearly abandoned.[84] Local problems were exacerbated between 1893 and 1897 as the nation experienced the worst economic downturn since its foundation.

Visitors from outside the immediate area commented on the valley's sad state. In 1895, the *Philadelphia Press* ran an article on Valley Forge entitled "A Deserted Village." Its writer spoke of crumbling mill buildings idle for more than a dozen years, with gaping holes in their windows and vines growing up their neglected walls. He observed rows of decaying tenements still sparsely occupied by a few black families.[85] Clifton Johnson, writing for *Women's Companion* in 1902, made the same observation, noting: "A melancholy air of industrial ruin hangs over the Valley."[86] He discovered that the few remaining residents found only occasional work at a local quarry, a brick works, and a stone-crushing operation. As a mid-winter visitor, Johnson had surprised the village hotel owner and had listened to the cook complain about how impossible it was to keep help at that time of year in such a deserted place.[87]

The same articles mentioned that Valley Forge came alive in the summer. It seems that the village was being transformed into a seasonal resort. Soon after POS of A allied itself with the Centennial and Memorial Association, thousands made it a tradition to take part in an annual celebration on June 19, which was becoming known as Evacuation Day. On Evacuation Day in 1887, there was music, marching, and oratory from 10:00 A.M until dusk.[88] By June 1890, as many as 10,000 people came. Valley Forge had become an

Fig. 3.   Old mill and tenant houses in Valley Forge. After the Revolution, Valley Forge resumed its role as an industrial community. This photograph most likely dates from the late nineteenth century, when Valley Forge suffered economic decline. (Courtesy, Valley Forge National Historical Park)

attraction not only for patriots and POS of A campers, but also for people out to make a quick buck. The *Daily Local News* wrote of

> the stands of sharpers which lined the roadway from the railroad station in the valley to the pavilion away up on the hillside, where the principal exercises of the day were held. "Sweat cloths," wheels of fortune, and all the paraphernalia of open air gambling was conspicuously arrayed and the swindlers in charge drove a thriving trade until driven out . . . by special officers.[89]

Extra effort went into planning for the exercises for Evacuation Day in 1903, which was the 125th anniversary of the day Washington marched his men out of Valley Forge.[90]

Many summer visitors passed the time by hunting for genuine relics of the American Revolution. The plows of Valley Forge farmers had long been unearthing grapeshot, cannonballs, and other objects apparently left behind by the soldiers in 1778. After the nation's Centennial in 1876, the Colonial Revival Movement made such objects seem more important and valuable, and by the end of the nineteenth century major finds were being announced in the newspapers. In 1888, it was reported that the caretaker at headquarters had found an antique hatchet.[91] In 1890, some Valley Forge workers unearthed a twelve-pound cannonball, a broken bayonet, a sword, and an old case knife. Some of these items were placed on exhibit at Washington's Headquarters.[92] In 1900, a visitor from Marshallton, Pennsylvania, bought a belt buckle plowed up by a Valley Forge farmer and said to have been worn by one of Washington's personal bodyguards.[93]

Summer tourists were also keenly interested in the grimmer aspects of Valley Forge. It has been said that the nineteenth century was preoccupied with death—demonstrated by the cemeteries that became sculpture gardens, and etiquette books devoting entire chapters to mourning customs and fashions. All the accounts of men starving and suffering at Valley Forge implied that many had died there, and nineteenth-century visitors roaming the hills and fields were fascinated to contemplate the prospect of thousands of unmarked graves beneath their strolling feet.

To satisfy the morbid curiosity of visitors to Valley Forge, several individuals made the first attempts to locate burial grounds holding the dead from the encampment period. Local residents believed that many graves had been dug on the north side of the campground, just south of the road connecting the village of Valley Forge with Port Kennedy (now Route 23). Landowner William Stephens remembered how he and his father had heard from old Uncle Abijah about a spot near a sassafras tree just a few hundred yards from their own house (now known as Varnum's Quarters), where tradition had it that perhaps 600 men were buried. Stephens's curiosity prompted him to start digging a trench. "After a little time," he wrote, "I came to the bottom of a grave which showed a layer of black mold. This mold was about three feet from the surface and about a foot or more deep." The fact that he discovered no buttons or buckles indicated to Stephens that the dead had been buried naked at Valley Forge.[94] A little to the east, visitors could see a headstone carved with the initials "J.W.," and a newspaper story quoted an area resident who contended that a person could walk from this grave to the Todd Mansion (now known as Huntington's Quarters) several hundred yards away by stepping from grave to grave.[95] In 1902, it was reported that workers constructing a cement walkway in this area had unearthed five graves with well-preserved skeletons.[96]

Valley Forge's other acknowledged burial ground was on the south side of the encampment just inside what had been the outer line defenses against possible attack. In 1896, scattered graves with rough headstones could be found in the woods atop a small knoll where General Anthony Wayne's men had camped (now known as Wayne's Woods).[97] Today, Outer Line Drive winds downhill around Wayne's Woods, twisting north and then abruptly south in a wide arc connecting it with Baptist Road. The road encloses an area commonly hailed a century ago as a camp burial ground. A Mr. Latch of Devon, Pennsylvania described how this sloping ground had revealed itself as a burial place in a dramatic way: "Unable to dig graves sufficiently long, the living buried the dead with 'crouched knees.' Spring showers and summer rains washing the earth away, left protruding knees as ghastly monuments."[98]

The interest in graves naturally led to the first of what would be many Valley Forge ghost stories. The *Philadelphia Press* writer covering his visit in 1895 wrote:

> It is said that the spirits of the dead Revolutionary soldiers flit along the hillsides on stormy nights and visit the shadowy spots where they once gathered around the camp fire and that ghostly campfires have been seen flickering among the trees on starless nights and the faint echo of a challenge and countersign from the lips of spirit sentinels.

He spoke of other ghosts in the dilapidated village tenements. One dwelling had been the home of a man shot trying to rob the railroad station agent. It seemed that no village family would live in the place, not even rent-free.[99]

If other places associated with George Washington could be spoken of like sacred shrines, then surely the tales of ghosts and the supposed graves of Revolutionary War soldiers made the whole encampment area sacred ground, prompting the Centennial and Memorial Association to try and expand their operations and purchase more land. In 1890 they bought an adjoining acre-and-a-half from Nathan Jones for $1,200. This tract included a spring behind the Headquarters from which Washington was said to have obtained his drinking water.[100] In 1891, Mrs. Holstein received a letter from Robert Crawford, who owned another adjoining lot, including what was thought to be Washington's old barn. Crawford offered his property for $4,000, and Holstein hoped to find some patriot with enough money to buy it and hold it for the cash-poor Centennial and Memorial Association.[101] As 1892 wore on and the property found no buyer, Mrs. Holstein became increasingly worried. She confided to Frederick D. Stone at the Historical Society of Pennsylvania how important it was that her organization "thus control a property which might become troublesome and annoying to us." She continued: "I think I mentioned to you, a year ago, that the Romish Church would like to have it. But Captain Crawford would prefer that it should again form part of the Hd. Qur. tract."[102] In 1894, the Centennial and Memorial Association was finally able to buy the property for $3,000. [103]

Considerably further out of the reach of the association was the 190-acre Carter Tract, which included much ground on which Continental soldiers had camped, the supposed site of the old forge in the valley, and the oak under which Washington was said to have prayed. Carter had had a bid from a brewing company in 1890, but he hoped to find a buyer who would preserve this hallowed ground rather than set up business there. [104]

For the kind of growth and expansion it wanted, the Centennial and Memorial Association needed more cash. After receiving the grant of $5,000 from the state, they had optimistically sought $25,000 from the federal government between 1888 and 1890. Theodore W. Bean drew up a bill to this effect, and a Centennial and Memorial Association committee visited Washington. Bean found a Mr. Yardley to introduce the bill in the House and sought the assistance of Pennsylvania's Senator Cameron. [105] The proposition languished and was finally dropped under opposition from President Grover Cleveland, who was afraid every other historical association in America would seek an equal amount. [106] Having failed with the federal government, the Centennial and Memorial Association again looked to the state of Pennsylvania. In 1892, they planned to ask for $10,000. In 1893, a bill passed awarding them $5,000, but Governor Robert E. Pattison vetoed it. In May 1897, the Centennial and Memorial Association's legislative committee reported that efforts to obtain state money were being temporarily abandoned "as the time was not considered opportune."[107]

Without government appropriations, the Centennial and Memorial Association collected operating funds by charging a 10-cent admission fee at Washington's Headquarters and selling pictures, prints, and mementos. In 1893, they offered a silver souvenir spoon engraved with a picture of Washington's Headquarters on the bowl, designed by association member Rebecca McInnes. [108] The association had spent some time disputing whether the handle should represent a musket or a continental soldier. [109] In 1895, the association also marketed a china plate with a picture of the Headquarters building. [110]

By that time, it was unlikely that the Centennial and Memorial Association would ever see government money again. This local organization had followed current trends in historic preservation by acquiring a house associated with George Washington and giving it a period look with antique furniture. Its members had involved local chapters of the national organizations of the POS of A and the DAR. They had organized public ceremonies and opened a historic site to the public, bringing thousands to Valley Forge and giving a dying industrial community new life as a summer resort and historic shrine. Their efforts received enough public attention to lay the groundwork for creation of Pennsylvania's first state park, established at Valley Forge in 1893. The new park was empowered to acquire, or "condemn," the land on which redoubts, entrenchments, or campsites had existed, to preserve these sites, and to make the area accessible and meaningful to the public by building roads and erecting markers.

The Centennial and Memorial Association must have realized that the park would also draw off additional funding they might have received from the state. Nevertheless, the association welcomed creation of the park and expected to work hand in hand with this new Valley Forge organization. After all, Anna Morris Holstein and Francis M. Brooke, the latter chosen to head the first state park commission, were cousins. It must therefore have come as a shock on Evacuation Day, June 1905, when the Centennial and Memorial Association treasurer reported that a committee from the park had come to tell them that the park commission was about to take their beloved Washington's Headquarters away.[111]

3

A Rocky Beginning for the Valley Forge Park Commission

While the Centennial and Memorial Association struggled to acquire and maintain its historic house, it focused enough attention on Valley Forge for other groups and individuals to engage in a kind of debate about exactly what constituted a fitting tribute to the winter encampment of 1777–1778. What should be preserved of this holy ground? And what should be added to the landscape?

Having lost her wealthy ambassador husband to death, Mary E. Thropp Cone, who had written a poem for Evacuation Day 1878, returned to her native Pennsylvania. In June 1882, while the Centennial and Memorial Association was desperately trying to raise funds for Washington's Headquarters, she wrote a lengthy letter to the *Phoenixville Messenger*, its prose no less poetic than her verse:

> Back again to Valley Forge after having visited Holyrood and Westminster, Versailles and the Vatican, the Forum and the Coliseum; after having threaded the silent streets of Pompeii and sailed

up the lonely Amazon, and I have seen no spot in the Old World or the New, so dear, so delightful or so interesting to me as Valley Forge, with its sacred memories, its hallowed associations. . . .

Is there any other spot between the Atlantic and the Pacific of which Americans have greater reason to be proud than the encampment ground of Valley Forge? Surely the virtues here displayed deserve to be remembered with as much gratitude and admiration as the brilliant but less difficult achievements of Bennington, Monmouth and Yorktown. True, we have had parades, encampments, and celebrations here; but these, however imposing, are ephemeral, never, except at the Centennial, satisfying public expectation, and hence, perhaps, the apathy of the people so much complained of, so disgraceful. [1]

Editor and publisher John O. K. Robarts took up where Mrs. Cone left off. One week later, he wrote:

It is true the Headquarters are in a good state of preservation, and the interior mainly as Washington and his Martha left it, but still that does not come up to the full measure of what it wanted. Those walls do not tell the names of the Generals, the regiments, the States represented there in that season of peril, now so well known. And as the years go by, the records of all this will become fainter and fainter still. What is needed then, is a substantial granite shaft, plain, but imposing, upon which may be chiselled the story as outlined above, so that people of this age and of the ages to come, may there read what now they will have to go to printed and perishing pages to learn. [2]

In the second half of the nineteenth century, monuments were springing up at many historic sites, a trend that peaked between 1870 and World War I, a time of intense nationalism in the United States. On historic battlefields, monuments marked troop positions and enabled visitors to mentally recreate the honor and glory of great battles. They acknowledged the memorable deeds of heros and warriors and ennobled the sacrifice of life, allowing contemporary people to demonstrate their allegiance to the ideals of the past. [3] As Mrs. Cone had noted, other historic sites associated with the Revolution already had imposing and enduring granite shafts, but Valley Forge had none.

Thanks to agitation by Mrs. Cone and Robarts, Valley Forge soon had a new organization. On December 18, 1882, Mary E. Thropp Cone organized a meeting at the public hall in the village of Valley Forge to celebrate the 105th anniversary of the winter encampment and to see that Valley Forge would soon get the monument it deserved. Robarts reported that those she gathered together resolved that "Valley Forge should have a monument to perpetuate the memories of the Continental heroes who suffered here" and added: "It is to be earnestly hoped that a Soldiers' monument upon the heights of Valley Forge will be the result of the meeting brought about by that sterling lady, Mrs. Mary E. Thropp Cone."[4]

By the following spring, Mrs. Cone's organization had a charter and a name: The Valley Forge Memorial Association. Naturally, Mrs. Cone was elected president. She proposed to raise $5,000 by private subscription and reported that her group had already collected about $500.[5] They must have been greatly encouraged when, within a year, Congress considered a bill encouraging the erection of monuments on Revolutionary battlegrounds. This proposed bill would enable the U.S. Treasury to match dollar for dollar the funds raised by any historical association that could collect $5,000 to this end.

Although the Valley Forge Memorial Association failed to achieve its purpose and soon disbanded, Mrs. Cone's efforts may have had other effects on Valley Forge. Her fundraising coincided with the period during which the Centennial and Memorial Association had the greatest difficulty collecting money and despaired that their mortgage might be foreclosed on. It is possible that the Valley Forge Memorial Association actually drew money away from headquarters. A Valley Forge guidebook published in 1906 hinted at another effect, suggesting that when the Valley Forge Memorial Association failed to raise the money it needed for a monument from the federal government, they turned to the state of Pennsylvania, abandoned the monument idea, and joined in agitation for a large public-land reservation at Valley Forge.[6]

By the end of the nineteenth century, other voices besides those of Centennial and Memorial Association members were calling for the actual site of the winter encampment at Valley Forge to be preserved as some sort of park. One of the earliest came from Theodore W. Bean, author of *Foot-Prints of the Revolution* and member of the Centennial and Memorial Association, who proposed that his own organization purchase the campground, the funds again being supplied by POS of A.[7] When the 190-acre Carter Tract was offered for sale, a *Daily Local News* editorial asked: "What shall be done with historic Valley Forge? The beautiful tract of land which recalls memories of patriotic devotion seldom, if ever, equalled in the history of America, has long been private property, and of recent years has almost gone begging for some one to buy it." The newspaper suggested two alternatives: "That the Society of the Daughters of the Revolution, of which Mrs. Benjamin Harrison is President, shall acquire the property, and the second, that it shall be reserved, either by the state of Pennsylvania or the Federal Government, as a park."[8]

The park movement found a successful champion in Francis M. Brooke, a descendant of General Anthony Wayne. In the 1890s, Brooke was a state legislator and committee chairman. He had attended the Centennial celebration in 1878 and was among the thousands who had been inspired by the moving words of Henry Armitt Brown. In 1892, he began lobbying Harrisburg for legislation to establish a state park at Valley Forge, which resulted in a bill signed by Governor Robert E. Pattison in 1893 creating the Valley Forge Park Commission. The state legislature also appropriated $25,000 to enable the park commission to buy roughly 250 acres of the land on which Washington's army had camped and where the earthworks the army built in 1777–1778 were still visible. After Brooke's death in 1898, the minutes of the park commission offered this tribute: "To his patriotic interest in the preservation of the memorials of the Revolutionary struggle this Commission owes its origin."[9]

The Valley Forge Park Commission was a ten-man committee whose members were directly appointed by the governor for five-year terms with no compensation. The first park commission consisted of prominent Philadelphia businessmen as well as officers of historical and patriotic associations, such as the Historical Society of Pennsylvania and the Society of the Cincinnati. It met for the first time on June 17, 1893, at the Historical Society of Pennsylvania and elected Francis Brooke as their president. Though they were important and knowledgeable men in their own fields and organizations, they realized they had but surface knowledge of Valley Forge, so they resolved to visit the campground together with members of another patriotic organization called the Pennsylvania Sons of the Revolution.[10]

The statute creating the Valley Forge Park Commission said that the state itself was appropriating land at Valley Forge. The original task of the park commission was to establish the boundaries of this park by determining exactly where Washington had positioned his men and built his defensive earthworks. Its ongoing task was to preserve this land forever as nearly as possible in its "original condition as a military camp." Land where Washington's soldiers had camped automatically belonged to the state of Pennsylvania.[11] Although its former owners would be compensated, they had no choice but to sell. The commission was also empowered to maintain the park as a public place and to make its historically important sites accessible to visitors. The 1893 statute specifically excluded land already owned by the Centennial and Memorial Association.

Francis Brooke wrote Frederick Stone, a fellow park commissioner and officer of the Historical Society of Pennsylvania, that their first task would be to draw a map of the Revolutionary campground "according to the best obtainable information."[12] To do this, they also needed to know exactly what had happened at Valley Forge, but they quickly discovered that little real documentary research had ever been done. Their task would necessarily begin with the collection of information. Brooke sent a letter to every major library and historical society in the nation, requesting that all known maps and information be referred to the park commission.[13] The *Pennsylvania Magazine of History and Biography*, published by the Historical Society of Pennsylvania, advised its readers that the Valley Forge Park Commission was "aware that there are many unpublished original documents relating to the camp, and [was] desirous of obtaining the deposit of orderly-books, diaries, letters, and maps, for preservation and for the further elucidation of its history."[14]

When the park commissioners began their work, the earliest known research on maps of Valley Forge was that Jared Sparks did for his biography of George Washington. In 1833, Sparks had drawn a map based on the personal recollections of a Valley Forge resident. The Sparks map had come into the possession of Cornell University. In the 1890s, several exciting map discoveries came to the attention of the Valley Forge Park Commission. Samuel W. Pennypacker—son of Isaac A. Pennypacker, who had made one of the earliest calls for the preservation of Valley Forge in his letter to John Fanning Watson in 1844—was traveling in Europe. In Amsterdam, Pennypacker was able to purchase an original set of drafts and plans drawn by a French engineer during the Revolutionary period, among which, he was delighted to discover, was a contemporary map of Valley Forge. He told of his discovery in an address to POS of A members delivered in 1898 when he presented the precious map to their organization.[15] The map is now in the collections of the Historical Society of Pennsylvania.

Valley Forge's most famous map was apparently discovered at about this time by Lawrence McCormick. This map had been hidden in a nearby old residence called the John Havard House. The handwriting on it was similar to that of Washington's chief engineer, French Brigadier General Louis Duportail, who had lived in the Valley Forge area from 1795 to 1801. This map, which is known as the "Duportail map," also ended up in the collections of the Historical Society of Pennsylvania. Though hailed as a monumental discovery, a copy of the Duportail map was already among Jared Sparks's materials, so apparently its existence was known during the lifetime of this scholar. [16]

In 1893, the Valley Forge Park Commission hired an engineer named L. M. Haupt to conduct a topographical survey of 460 acres "more or less" in the roughly triangular tract of land between the Schuylkill River, Valley Creek, and Washington Lane (now Baptist Road Trace). [17] Based on their ongoing documentary research and this topographical study, the commission began to lay out the boundaries of the 200-odd-acre park and to identify the current private owners of this land. The Valley Forge Park Commission then attempted to obtain the land they wanted at the lowest possible cost and least possible inconvenience to its present owners.

As recently as 1891, the *Daily Local News* had speculated: "Land in this vicinity is not regarded as high in price, and the owners of the Valley Forge property are said to be anxious to sell." This newspaper account, written two years before the park commission had been created, estimated the value of land at Valley Forge at about $10 an acre. [18] The park commission optimistically sent letters to current owners asking them to name their price. [19] To the dismay of its members, the park commission discovered that the perceived value of land at Valley Forge had increased sharply in the brief time since their organization had been established. Local landowners got little sympathy from the area press. The *Daily Local News* quoted the *Media Record* in castigating owners who "fondly hug the delusion that [the State] will pay fabulous prices for what is little more than scrub land at best. . . . To now attempt to extort fabulous prices for this ground savors strongly of a spirit and purpose that is grossly mercenary, if not actually mean." [20]

Rather than haggle with owners, the park commission worked to establish independent county "juries of view" to examine the land in question and determine its value. In February 1894, the Montgomery County jurors met at the Washington Inn at Valley Forge and went as far as they could up the overgrown hillsides by carriage, "and thence on foot, through the mud, brush and rain," carefully examining the actual ground for themselves. [21] The juries also met with witnesses called by landowners and the park commission both.

The owners and their partisan witnesses made some interesting claims.

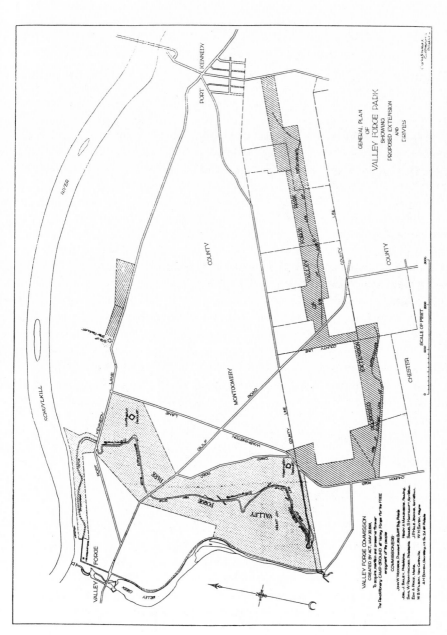

Fig. 4. Plan for the first expansion of Valley Forge Park, c. 1902. Created in 1893, the Valley Forge Park Commission based the first official boundaries of their 200-acre park on a topographical survey and documentary research. (Courtesy, Valley Forge National Historical Park)

George McMenamin, son of landowner B. F. McMenamin, testified that just eighteen acres of Valley Forge farmland had produced some 1,800 bushels of corn in a single season. A newspaper sarcastically reported: "Such a remarkable yield had never before been heard of by the jurors or the Park Commissioners' counsel, and they were inclined to believe that George was mistaken. The witness, however, adhered to his statement during a rigid cross-examination."[22] Other owners testified that their holdings had potential as possible quarries or that valuable deposits of potters' clay lay just beneath the surface. The prices claimed by private owners and their witnesses were fully 50 percent higher than those claimed by witnesses for the park commission.

The owners continued to be blasted by the press for their lack of patriotism and apparent intent to fleece the taxpayers of Pennsylvania. The *Daily Local News* quoted the *Phoenixville Messenger*: "It is strange that when people who appear to be surcharged with patriotism have a chance to put money in their pockets they forget the bonny Red, White and Blue, and become grabbers of the most heroic stamp."[23] A few weeks later, the same paper quoted the *Lancaster New Era*: "It [the original appropriation for the park] looked like a fat goose to these land owners, and they resolved it would not be their fault if that goose was not well plucked."[24]

By October 1894, all the testimony was in and the jurors made their reasonably impartial valuations. Land in Montgomery County would be sold for an average of $135.01 an acre, and land in Chester County would be sold for an average of $169.12 an acre.[25] This was more than the park commission had originally expected to pay, but it was also less than half of what some owners had expected to receive. The *Daily Local News* concluded: "The people of the State will be glad to learn that it is possible to carry out a patriotic project in spite of the attempts of a few to make money out of it."[26]

After the controversy over the acquisition of land, the park commission entered a dormant period, precipitated by an almost total lack of funds and no doubt made worse by the depression beginning in 1893. During the second half of 1894, there were few commission meetings because, according to the president's report, there was little business to discuss.[27] Early in 1895, the president reported that the cash awards being made for land were consuming the park's entire appropriation. The commission was so low on operating funds that their watchman had not been paid since December.[28] Francis Brooke's trip to Harrisburg to solicit money resulted in an appropriation of $10,000, but this went toward existing debt, leaving the park commission with no cash to make improvements to the land it had purchased. [29] The park commission report printed at the end of 1896 stated that the park had only $136.72 on hand. The complaint was raised that "no items of personal expenses of any Commissioner incident to the work have been paid from the state funds, though in some instances these items have not been inconsiderable." And the watchman was still waiting for back wages. [30]

In 1897, Brooke prepared a report addressed "To the Senators and Representatives of the State of Pennsylvania" asking for $60,000. He bitterly compared the amount of attention Valley Forge was getting with the money dedicated to the preservation of historic sites associated with the Civil War and wrote:

> The National Government has properly spent many millions of dollars on the battle fields of the Rebellion [the Civil War] and this work is not yet done. Our own State Legislature has appropriated over a half million of dollars to Gettysburg alone, besides what it has spent elsewhere for like purposes. Yet the battles of the Rebellion bravely fought to a successful issue, were only fought to preserve the Union, established through the unexampled suffering of the soldiers at Valley Forge. [31]

Despite Brooke's efforts, the park commission saw no new funds in 1897 or the following three years.

In 1899, Park Commissioner Holstein DeHaven wrote a form letter addressed to "Dear Senator" describing the commission's sad state at that point. "At present I consider that the Valley Forge Commission does not exist," the writer complained, "there being only two members and no officers to carry on the work." By this time Francis Brooke had passed away and another member had resigned. The names of two other potential members had been withdrawn before the state senate had confirmed their appointments. And because there was absolutely no money, those remaining unhappy members of this inactive commission had no means to do their job. The writer concluded: "I think it is a disgrace and a shame to have the present state of affairs existing." [32]

The official report of the Valley Forge Park Commission printed at the end of 1900 noted that the commission had been faced with an empty treasury plus bills amounting to $3,500. By this time, the commissioners had also assessed their future needs in caring for the land they had acquired some six years earlier, and estimated their current requirements at $73,200. [33] The following calendar year, the press finally took up the cry that the state legislature had ignored Valley Forge for far too long. The *Daily Local News* editorialized:

> We spend annually thousands of the State funds for needless projects, and extravagant measures. Our taxpayers can keep up political officials in grand style, but a paltry five thousand dollar appropriation is marked off the list, that there may be enough money to go around for less patriotic purposes. [34]

This statement appeared in the same editorial announcing the dedication of an impressive monument at Valley Forge. In 1901, Valley Forge finally got its stone shaft, a marker some 50 feet high and 10 feet square at the base, embellished with a bronze tablet displaying an artist's conception of the Revolutionary encampment. It seemed very much like what the National Memorial Association had envisioned about two decades earlier. For years this monument held the distinction of being the most impressive manmade structure at Valley Forge. It was ironic that in 1901 the new monument was not located within the boundaries of the park, nor did it owe its existence to the impoverished park commission or the stingy Pennsylvania state legislature.

Technically the new monument was not really the first monument raised at Valley Forge. That honor belonged to a humble red sandstone marker erected on the left bank of the Schuylkill at the site of a bridge that had been built by Major General John Sullivan. In 1777–1778, this bridge had allowed food supplies to reach the camp from the north. When Washington's army evacuated Valley Forge, they had marched over the same bridge, but the historic structure had been washed away shortly after that. No one knew exactly when or how the sandstone marker got there, but in his 1850 articles on Valley Forge, Henry Woodman mentioned it standing on the opposite shore identifying the location of "Sullivan's Bridge, 1778."[35]

Perhaps inspired by this first marker, in 1840, canal boat workers from the Schuylkill Navigation Company and the Union Canal Works decided to further glorify the former location of Sullivan's Bridge by placing a second marker on the Valley Forge side of the river. At that time, travelers and boatmen could still see the heaps of stone that had been the pilings for Sullivan's Bridge.[36] It may have been during one of the year's idle periods that the boatmen formed a union and began taking subscriptions, eventually raising enough money for a stone that would stand six feet high. Their marker lasted until 1850, when it was washed away. Around that time it was

Fig. 5. Valley Forge's first monument, dedicated in 1901 by the Daughters of the Revolution of 1776. Popularly called the Waterman Monument, it was erected near a headstone at one of the supposed burial grounds and dedicated to all soldiers who died and were buried at Valley Forge.

replaced by a local resident, a Dr. William Wetherill. By the end of the century, however, this monument too had been damaged by floods caused by ice breaking up on the river in the springtime, and in no way did it compare with the new stone shaft farther south.[37]

Valley Forge's latest monument had been inspired by a small headstone lying in the fields of a Valley Forge farmer named I. Heston Todd, who had long been avoiding it with his plow out of respect for the dead. The headstone was nothing elaborate, but it was the only marked grave at Valley Forge and bore the initials "JW" and the date "1778." As visitors began tramping through the fields and woods at Valley Forge, it became obvious that relic hunters were chipping away at the headstone. The Sons of the American Revolution asked and obtained permission from Todd to protect the relic with a wire cage.

It was known that troops from Rhode Island had made camp not far from the headstone, and a letter in the collections of the Rhode Island Historical Society indicated that "JW" was John Waterman, a civilian quartermaster and assistant commissary in General Varnum's brigade. In the late-nineteenth-century atmosphere of ancestor worship, those who could trace their families back to the Revolutionary or colonial era frequently held large, national reunions. Professor Daniel Howard of West Chester used the 1894 Waterman family reunion as an occasion to let Waterman's descendants know about the existence of the headstone.[38]

In 1895, Howard received word from the Rhode Island Sons of the American Revolution that the Rhode Island legislature had appropriated $2,000 to erect a monument on Waterman's grave and had established a commission for this purpose.[39] That fall, Francis Brooke got a message from Pennsylvania's Governor Daniel Hastings notifying him that the governor of Rhode Island was coming to Valley Forge to inspect the grave and make further plans for the monument. Brooke was instructed to show the proper amount of respect.[40]

Rhode Island's Governor Lippert made it clear that he wanted to cooperate with the Valley Forge Park Commission, but the Waterman grave was not located on ground that had been purchased by the park. I. Heston Todd, who owned the gravesite, had once been a park commissioner, but Governor Hastings had since removed him. Todd was very much at odds with the park commission and was not inclined to cooperate with Governor Hastings. He wanted to see Rhode Island erect a monument to Waterman, but he also wanted to ensure that neither the state of Pennsylvania nor the park commission got any credit for it. He offered to deed a plot of land directly to Rhode Island in return for assurance that its title would never revert to Pennsylvania. He also wanted a piece of the Rhode Island appropriation, although he later denied that he had demanded any kind of payment. If the state of Pennsylvania interfered with his plans, Todd threatened, he would dig up John Waterman and leave the park commission with a worthless plot of land.[41]

The park commission countered this threat by trying to lure Rhode Island's appropriation to another site. Declaring that it was unable to deal with the unreasonable demands of Todd, Rhode Island's monument commission had decided to spend an additional $8,000 to erect a bigger and better monument in memory of all Rhode Island soldiers who had served at Valley Forge. The park commission suggested that they put their monument near the site of an old earthwork then called the Star Redoubt (now Redoubt #1), which had commanded the site of Sullivan's Bridge. It was assumed that the site had been defended by Rhode Island men, because their brigade had been encamped immediately east of it while the headquarters of Rhode Island's General James Mitchell Varnum had been located nearby. By 1897, Governor Lippert endorsed this recommendation and the Rhode Island legislature made it law.[42]

The site of the old Star Redoubt was on land privately owned by William M. Stephens, whose family had lived in the Valley Forge area for many generations before the Revolution. When the park commission tried to condemn the little more than one acre that Rhode Island's monument would require, Stephens strongly objected to losing a tiny plot from the very center of his farm. He also pointed out that the park commission had no money to finish paying for the land it had already condemned. At the end of 1897, Francis Brooke got a letter from Stephens's lawyer informing him that Stephens planned to contest this condemnation and that no amicable agreement was possible.[43] In 1897, an impartial jury of view put a dollar value on the contested plot, but Stephens tried to get the appointments revoked and the verdict set aside. Finally, Stephens sued the state of Pennsylvania, an action that was sure to incur considerable delay before Rhode Island could start building anything on his land.[44] Indeed, the Stephens case was not called for trial until 1902,[45] at which time a jury awarded Stephens $2,100. The Valley Forge Park Commission report for that year requested the funds it needed to make this payment.[46]

By 1904, a Rhode Island monument near the site of the Star Redoubt was still under consideration, but by then the park commission was against it.[47] Notes on negotiations with Rhode Island continued to appear in park commission minutes in 1908 and 1910.[48] Then the 1912 park commission report mentioned that Rhode Island had dropped the entire plan to erect a monument at Valley Forge. By that time, several other states had attractive monuments in place, and the report declared: "Rhode Island may be the last to act as she was the last to act in the adoption of the National Constitution, but for such a state of affairs the commission feels that she is alone responsible."[49]

In much of the meantime, John Waterman's simple headstone remained neglected, having attracted no other attention than the placement of its wire cage. A 1901 magazine article described its forlorn appearance, mentioning that the cage had not been set over it "for the purpose of keeping John Waterman in, as some irreverent visitor has remarked, but for keeping vandals out. It is rather difficult to understand how relic hunters who came before the cage ever managed to leave as much as they did of this lonely monument."[50] As lonely as Waterman's headstone may have been, the Waterman grave itself was located on a slope where it seemed that the faint outlines of many other unmarked graves could still be made out, equally forlorn and deserving of some sort of recognition.[51]

In 1897, members of an organization called the National Society, Daughters of the Revolution of 1776 began negotiating with I. Heston Todd, taking up where the state of Rhode Island had left in efforts to glorify the spot with a monument. To them, Todd conveyed the land he had wanted to give to Rhode Island, and the organization established a fund and began receiving donations.[52] Before his death in office, President McKinley had supported the daughters in their patriotic efforts. The daughters unveiled their shaft in October 1901, and had President McKinley lived he would probably have attended. As it was, Pennsylvania's governor was there to witness the dedication.[53]

From the very day it was dedicated, this monument has confused many a visitor. Even today, it is popularly but incorrectly called the "Waterman Monument," and few are certain exactly what it is dedicated to. It was never intended as a monument solely to John Waterman. It was erected on the site of one of Valley Forge's supposed burial grounds and was dedicated to all those who died at Valley Forge. Its inscription reads: "To the memory of the soldiers of Washington's army who sleep in Valley Forge." Yet even the park commission indicated confusion in their 1902 report when they described it as a memorial to "the endurance of the Revolutionary Patriots who during this severe winter, underwent the hardships incident to the severe cold, and withstood the ravages of disease which almost wiped the army out of existence."[54] On the contrary, the area's first impressive monument was dedicated to those at Valley Forge who did *not* endure, withstand, or survive. The obelisk was not intended to replace Waterman's headstone, which continued to stand nearby until 1939, when park commissioners were alarmed to discover it missing. Upon learning that the daughters had removed it and planned to donate it to a museum, park commissioners convinced the organization's officers to transfer its ownership to themselves so that it could be placed in the park museum. It is now the property of the National Park Service at Valley Forge, and its former location has become uncertain.[55]

The fanfare over the striking new monument overshadowed the private placement that same year of another grave marker at Valley Forge. Local resident R. Francis Wood had unearthed some bones on his farm and had written park superintendent A. H. Bowen for permission to inter them on park property. He wrote: "They are the remains of a soldier of the Revolutionary Army, who was shot on the farm by the then owner," presumably for stealing and with the authorization of a continental officer.[56] Permission was granted, and Wood buried the soldier near the redoubt then called Fort Huntington (now Redoubt #4), putting up a simple stone, which actually became the first monument *in* the new park. Today, park rangers refer to it as the "chicken thief monument."

At the turn of the century, the park at Valley Forge was essentially without impressive markers and interesting structures like Washington's Headquarters. What did it have? The park commission had purchased a strip of land along the river that connected to a pentagon-shape area bordered today by Route 23, North Gulph Road, and Baptist Road Trace. This adjoined a triangular area situated between Valley Creek and the line separating Chester and Montgomery counties. On park land were the two major lines of earthwork entrenchments that once formed the inner lines of defense against potential attack at Valley Forge. There were also two redoubts that the park had named Fort Washington (now Redoubt #3) and Fort Huntington (now Redoubt #4). The park essentially consisted of mounds and depressions in the earth indicating where something had once been. The park was a wild place, so overgrown that even park personnel had not fully explored it. In 1897, park guard Ellis Hampton wrote Francis Brooke: "As I was walking over the hills I discovered, what seemed to be, a line of entrenchments. They lie in the tract of Mahon Ambler on the Southeast side of the hill, 300 feet east of the long line of entrenchments."[57]

The need for better care of Valley Forge was heightened by turn-of-the-century improvements in transportation that were bringing more and more visitors to the area. In the 1890s, Valley Forge got a second railroad station on the south side of the tracks that was soon surpassed by a new stone building constructed in the early 1900s. Valley Forge narrowly missed getting trolley service when the Phoenixville and Bridgeport Electric Railway Company tried to lay tracks through the park. This project apparently languished because the park commission said it did not have the power to grant right-of-way. The matter was referred to the state attorney general and was promptly strangled by red tape.[58]

At the turn of the century, visitors arrived at Valley Forge to pay tribute to traditional American ideals in a changing society. In a popular novel published in 1906, *Lady Baltimore*, author Owen Wister has two characters discuss exactly what was wrong with contemporary Americans. "They've lost their sense of patriotism," one character asserts. People were only interested in making money, and these upstarts had a notorious lack of respect for their betters, the people of formerly powerful and prominent families. Yes, there were "those who have to sell their old family pictures [and] those who have to buy their old family pictures." Not only that, but the South had its "Negroes" to contend with, while the North had its "low immigrant groups."[59] What would become of America?

America needed places like Valley Forge. The park commission needed an infusion of money if it was to shape the land it had acquired there and enhance appreciation of the Valley Forge experience.

4

The Park Commission Triumphs

The Valley Forge Park Commission found a powerful friend in Governor Samuel W. Pennypacker. In his inaugural speech, Pennypacker boldly stated:

> No people are ever really great who are neglectful of their shrines and have no pride in their achievements. . . . The good example set by Philadelphia in its care of Independence Hall and Congress Hall should be followed by the State. The fields of Fort Necessity, where Washington first became known; of Bushy Run, where Bouquet won his important victory, and the camp ground of Valley Forge should be tenderly cared for and preserved. [1]

Samuel W. Pennypacker had been born in nearby Phoenixville in 1843. Instead of attending Yale, he had chosen to fight in the Civil War. He had studied law with a Philadelphia attorney, becoming a lawyer himself and later a judge. Though largely self-educated, he was known as the "Sage of Schwenksville" and considered something of an expert on the history of the

Pennsylvania Dutch. Pennypacker had been the one who had guided Henry Armitt Brown around Valley Forge in preparation for his famous speech in 1878. As governor, Pennypacker made frequent trips to Valley Forge. In 1904, a Philadelphia newspaper reported on one excursion at which "the governor was the life as well as the leader of the party. His enthusiasm over the preservation of the sacred camp was more obvious than that of any other of those present."[2]

It was Governor Pennypacker who finally got the park commission the cash it needed to put Valley Forge on a firm financial footing and make vast improvements at the park. In 1905, he signed a bill appropriating money for the purchase of additional land at Valley Forge, the building of roads, the erection of an observation tower, and the placement of markers to indicate the campsites of the Continental Army's various brigades. In 1906, the *Daily Local News* observed: "Within the last two years the Valley Forge Park Commission has done much to beautify the old campgrounds, and its work is not one-half completed. The commission was created in 1893, but the work of improving Valley Forge did not begin until about two years ago."[3] In 1908, after Pennypacker had been replaced by another governor, the same paper noted that of the total $261,000 the state had so far spent on Valley Forge, $219,000 had been appropriated during Pennypacker's four-year term.[4]

The revitalization of the park commission made possible by Governor Pennypacker also raised the question of whether this organization should be the sole custodian of the physical Valley Forge and the primary arbiter of what happened at the place. The governor certainly helped the park commissioners put an end to a threat that had loomed large enough at the turn of the century to threaten their very existence.

During the final quarter of the nineteenth century, preservation became a legitimate function of the federal government. Federally funded monuments on the battlefields of the Civil War and the American Revolution had been the first step in this direction. In the 1890s, Congress went further and created several national military parks, including Gettysburg, which became a national military park in 1895. By the end of the nineteenth century, those with hallowed ground worth preserving were clamoring for more federal dollars.

As early as 1883, voices had been raised in favor of making Valley Forge a national park. Senator David Vorhees of Indiana visited Valley Forge. Immediately upon his return to Washington, he introduced a resolution authorizing the Committee on Military Affairs to look into making Valley

Forge a national park.[5] His efforts were perhaps premature, and nothing came of them.

The timing was better in December 1900, when no less than seventeen historic and patriotic organizations met at Independence Hall in Philadelphia to pursue the idea of a national park at Valley Forge. The *Philadelphia Press* gave itself credit for prompting this meeting.[6] The Daughters of the American Revolution had also made a resolution some three years earlier to work toward a national reservation at Valley Forge,[7] and the DAR was among the organizations represented at Independence Hall. They were joined by the Colonial Dames, the Society of the War of 1812, the Society of Colonial Wars, the Brotherhood of the Union, the Patriotic Order Sons of America, various Chester and Montgomery county historical societies, and the Centennial and Memorial Association of Valley Forge.[8]

Their chief complaint was that Valley Forge had been neglected. True, the park commission had acquired land, but this was only a fraction of the soil on which Washington's troops had spent the winter of 1777–1778. Without other state appropriations, which did not seem to be forthcoming at the time, the park could acquire no more land, nor could it do anything with the property it already owned. Because private owners had once protected the graves, the earthworks, and the other historic spots on their own property, Valley Forge seemed worse off under the park commission than it had been before its creation.

The December 19 meeting at Independence Hall continued that evening, featuring patriotic speeches that were frequently interrupted by bursts of enthusiastic applause. Dr. George Edward Reed, president of Dickinson College, voiced the earliest recorded suggestion that the Valley Forge story might be useful to help Americanize new immigrants. By the 1890s, it was estimated that fully 15 percent of the nation's population was foreign-born, causing other Americans to become increasingly concerned about whether the newcomers could learn American values and be absorbed into American society. Reed said, "One of the necessities of our time is to keep the spirit of patriotism alive in the hearts of all our people, a specially important duty in a country like ours, which has grown so rapidly and whose population is composed of so many different nationalities."[9] U.S. Senator Boies Penrose received much applause for his promise, "I am here to pledge my earnest effort toward the accomplishment of this project until the field shall have been formally set apart by Congress as a memorial of the heroism of the Continental Army."[10]

Efforts to create a national park at Valley Forge were unsuccessful in 1901, but enthusiasm did not seem to lag. Senator Penrose found the House Committee on Military Affairs unwilling to report any more bills for national parks that session, but his movement found a champion in President McKinley, who went on record in favor of federal acquisition of Valley Forge.[11] The movement's leaders, who started calling themselves the National Park Association, sent out form letters to raise money acknowledging their initial setback but promising to present the issue in Congress again.[12] By the end of the year, Senator Penrose joined forces with Congressman Irving P. Wanger, who hailed from nearby Norristown, and the two men jointly sought an appropriation of $200,000 for the purchase of Valley Forge.[13]

Late in January 1902, the National Park Association decided to send a massive delegation to Washington. An assassin's bullet had robbed them of their friend in the White House, but they planned to present a memorial to his successor, President Theodore Roosevelt. Leaders of the movement lunched with the President.[14] The following day, members of the National Park Association explained their patriotic purpose to the Senate Committee on Military Affairs. From ten o'clock in the morning until late in the afternoon, the committee rooms were packed, and it was reported that not one voice was raised against the proposition.[15]

The Valley Forge Park Commissioners, who opposed the movement, stayed home. The general feeling among these gentlemen was that Pennsylvania should finish what it had begun. All the park commission needed was money. Samuel W. Pennypacker became the commission's spokesman during his campaign for governor:

> I think it would be a great mistake to take the Valley Forge campground out of the hands of the State of Pennsylvania. . . . The State is abundantly able to take care of Valley Forge, and it will preserve in a most fitting manner the Revolutionary Camp.[16]

As governor, Pennypacker successfully squelched the movement with a letter to Senator Penrose. The park commission was doing well, he proclaimed, it needed cooperation and money, not redirection from groups like the DAR. "We want to do everything we can to help [the park commission] and to prevent the interference which comes from persons outside the State and certain well-meaning but ill-advised women within it." Pennypacker enlisted Penrose's aid: "Should the matter come up in Congress, I rely upon you to help me. Should a bill be presented, you can probably kill it easily by having added to it that the Government also take Bunker Hill from Massachusetts and Stony Point from New York."[17]

The movement for a national park at Valley Forge was never launched again during Pennypacker's lifetime. In 1916, the *Phoenixville Daily Republican* created a contest soliciting letters both for and against a national park at Valley Forge. The letter of a Fred A. Tencate stated:

> In conversation with the ex-Governor [Pennypacker] within the past year he advised me not to try to ever have Valley Forge Park transferred from the State to the Nation, and whilst I realized that he did so purely out of State pride, I could not coincide with his views and since his lamented death, I have again begun the agitation.[18]

This later movement too went nowhere. In his history of the Centennial and Memorial Association, Henry J. Stager reported that Anna Morris Holstein and Theodore W. Bean had both "repeatedly urged" that Valley Forge be made a national park.[19] If this encouraged the park commission to view the Centennial and Memorial Association as a threat, it may have helped hasten the demise of this organization.

When the park commission was first established in 1893, there seemed to be no reason why it could not cooperate with the Centennial and Memorial Association. Within a week of the park commission's first meeting, the commissioners received a cordial message from the Centennial and Memorial Association offering them the use of Washington's Headquarters for their meetings. The park commission acknowledged the offer but continued to meet in Philadelphia, perhaps simply because it was geographically more convenient for most of the members.[20] While the agitation for a national park continued, the *Norristown Times Herald* urged cooperation between the three entities that would potentially exist at Valley Forge. "The three proprietors need not clash," it advised. "Each would have its own sphere of action and all would be working for a common purpose."[21] Even the national publication *Harper's Weekly* hoped that "under the control of the government the various interests would be unified for the good of the entire campground."[22]

Though the Centennial and Memorial Association reported that the takeover of Washington's Headquarters had been an unpleasant surprise, there were early indications of trouble. Stager's history reported that as early as June 19, 1894, it was known that the park was contemplating annexing the Headquarters to its property. "This the Board of Directors prepared to dispute," the association minutes read. [23] In a pamphlet, *A Brief Review of Valley Forge and Its Environments*, Stager flatly stated: "The Headquarters are not for sale." He suggested that the park commission acquire the structures that had been quarters of Washington's generals and protect the earthworks they already owned. [24] In 1900, the Centennial and Memorial Association's minutes noted that state officials, particularly those at the state capitol, were not giving proper credit to their organization or to the work of the POS of A. [25]

With Pennypacker in office as governor, money in the park treasury, and the national park movement successfully diverted, perhaps it seemed that the time was right for a decisive attack on the Centennial and Memorial Association. The park commissioners' official justification for seeking to eliminate this organization appeared in the commission report published at the end of 1904. The report admitted that Washington's Headquarters was in admirable condition and that the building's attractive furnishings and surroundings made it a mecca for tourists and picnickers. However, entrance to the building cost each visitor 10 cents.

> Should this be? [the park commission asked] Is it not rather humiliating to require the payment of a small sum of a visitor when we realize that all of the Headquarters of Washington throughout the country, which are preserved and open, are free to the visitors? [26]

Another reason was perhaps suggested by a 1900 guidebook to Valley Forge, which commented: "Washington's Headquarters is the chief object of interest beyond the line of fortifications." [27] The park commission owned a lot of overgrown heaps of earth; the Centennial and Memorial Association had a valuable tourist attraction. The underlying question was whether that attraction properly belonged in private hands or in public hands.

Hearing the call of the park commission, the Pennsylvania legislature took action at their next session, amending the act that had created the park by striking the phrase that had always protected the Centennial and Memorial Association's property. Association members heard about this at their annual meeting on Evacuation Day in 1905. They received a visit from a delegation from the park commission who quoted the amended act and proposed the immediate takeover of the building. According to Stager's history, the park sought "a friendly agreement with the Association as to the price to be paid." Recorded in the association's minutes for that day were the words "The Association did not consider it had been fairly treated by the State." [28]

The association tried to thwart this hostile takeover by naming a price so high that the park would not be able to pay it. They resolved on a seemingly unreachable $25,000,[29] and might have gone even higher as they managed to find real-estate experts who valued their property between $35,000 and $50,000.[30] As they had during the land confiscation of ten years before, the press seemed to take the part of the park commission. A query to Philadelphia's *Public Ledger* asked what was a fair price for Washington's Headquarters? The answer came that the state should set the price. This was not a case where private individuals wanted to tear it down or divert the property to another use. If the state was ready to assume the care of the building, the Centennial and Memorial Association should step aside and let them do so.[31]

When the state proposed to arrive at a price through the assessment of an independent jury of view, the Centennial and Memorial Association sought an injunction restraining the park commission. The Montgomery County Court of Common Pleas denied their injunction, and they decided not to appeal to the U.S. Supreme Court, fearing that the state would in the meantime enact some other legislation that would render any expensive and time-consuming efforts ultimately futile.[32]

When the jury of view awarded the association $18,000, its members decided to accept the offer rather than appeal. Their conditions were that the state would allow them an additional $200 for their personal property at the Headquarters and permit them to place a plaque in the building attesting to their role in acquiring and restoring the structure.[33]

At their annual meeting the following year, members of the Centennial and Memorial Association discussed the prospect of dissolving their organization. The park commission had denied them permission to meet at Washington's Headquarters, so they gathered at the nearby Washington Inn, where they could probably see their beloved building from the windows. Their treasurer acknowledged receipt of $18,000.00 which would leave them with $16,486.27 in cash after their legal expenses were paid. They resolved to defer the question of dissolution for one year while members considered how to distribute these funds.[34]

It was actually 1910 before the Centennial and Memorial Association petitioned a local court for legal dissolution because in 1907 a new question arose concerning their money. Meeting again at the Washington Inn that June, the association received a proposal from the park commission that they give funds back to the park. The association scornfully acknowledged receipt of this letter, sending back word that "the [Centennial and] Memorial Association knows of no warrant in law to pay over the money and respectfully declines to do it." Association members scratched their heads over how the park commissioners figured that the sum they had paid for Washington's Headquarters should now be handed back.[35]

In 1912, the park commission won this odd debate. The matter was resolved by an independent auditor appointed to hear all concerned parties and decide on the legal issues. The auditor's report summarizing the conclusions at law was included in Stager's history of the Centennial and Memorial Association. It was decided that the association had been organized to act as a charity, and its funds were held in trust for public use. Because it had never been operated for the profit of its members, its funds could not be distributed among those members, nor could they be returned to the individuals who had purchased its decorative stock certificates. Association funds legally belonged to whoever would carry out the original mission of the organization.[36] It seemed absurd and incredible, but the very body that had confiscated Washington's Headquarters was the only organization then in a position to carry out the objective of preserving this building. The park commission essentially got Washington's Headquarters for free.

The auditor's conclusions ended with glowing words implying that there had actually been a spirit of cooperation between the Centennial and Memorial Association and the park commission and that the association had been meekly willing to give its property to the park. "The luster of this proud achievement [the preservation of Washington's Headquarters] should not be dimmed by even a suggestion that the donors would undo it; and no such suggestion has come from any of them."[37] Despite these words, the association appealed the decision, but it was upheld by the Common Pleas Court of Montgomery County and the Supreme Court of Pennsylvania.

That the association's relationship with the park had long ceased to be amicable is witnessed by the controversy that persisted for four years over the small sum of $200 that the park had promised the association for their personal property at headquarters. This property included the souvenirs the association had been selling there. The park commission had originally agreed to pay the association a total of $18,200, but then the commissioners decided they had allowed too much for personal property when they discovered that some objects had already been marked "sold." In 1906, the park commission offered a check for $113.84 but failed to pay this amount until April 1910, by which time they were deeply involved in campaigning for the rest of the association's money.[38]

Nor was the park commission especially cooperative in allowing the association to place their plaque in Washington's Headquarters. At the end of 1905, the park declared that such a plaque must carry no individual names and must not be placed on the walls of the Headquarters lest it "desecrate" that building. [39] By 1907, an association committee was lobbying the Pennsylvania legislature for their support on the plaque issue, and later they made it known that they would not even consider formally dissolving their organization until the park agreed to the plaque. In 1908, they were told that they would be allowed to place their plaque at the headquarters providing the park commission approved its wording. [40] The plaque, with the simple words "This tablet commemorates the patriotic service rendered by the Centennial and Memorial Association of Valley Forge aided by the Patriotic Order of the Sons of America in acquiring, restoring and preserving these headquarters, 1878–1906," was finally mounted in the entry hall at the Headquarters in 1909. [41] The park superintendent reported that there was "no ceremony attached to the erection of this tablet."[42]

Fig. 6. Washington's Headquarters, c. 1910, after the state park commission had evicted the Centennial and Memorial Association. Note the cannon, which could be found throughout the grounds of Valley Forge in the nineteenth century whether they were from the Revolution or not. (Courtesy, Valley Forge National Historical Park)

The park made some changes at Washington's Headquarters. They did away with the 10-cent admission fee but allowed the caretaker they installed there to sell souvenirs and collect a 10 percent commission.[43] A stone wall soon replaced the old picket fence that had long surrounded the building. In the decade after they got their hands on the Centennial and Memorial Association's money, they repainted and refurbished the house and began a refurnishing project. The park commission concluded that none of the original furnishings from the encampment period could be traced and decided to furnish the building in the general style of the late eighteenth century.[44] Furniture was purchased from John Wanamaker, owner of a large Philadelphia department store, and Alfred Lewis Ward. The project was supervised by Ward's and Wanamaker's decorators.[45] A park commissioner demanded that the furniture supplied by the Chester County DAR be removed, and in 1914 the organization complied.[46] Furnishings supplied by other DAR chapters remained in place at that time. When the refurnishing project was done, the building was protected from the winter's cold and damp by a new heating system that brought warm air through pipes from another source, greatly lessening the danger of fire in the historic building.[47] In 1917, a magazine article commented: "The details of the restoration are throughout so complete that in every room the past seems very real."[48]

During Governor Pennypacker's administration, the park was also able to acquire new land. In 1904, the park commission purchased land along what would have been the camp's outer line defenses, where many brigades had camped. In 1906, the park acquired several contiguous parcels where other soldiers had camped, and a few other tracts to straighten out the boundaries.[49]

This expansion brought a second structure within the park's boundaries in 1906: a parcel with a dilapidated old building that had rotting rafters and floors. At the time, the building was thought to have been a schoolhouse built between about 1790 and 1830.[50] One aging area resident remembered attending school there around 1824 or 1825.[51] The structure had more recently been used as a stable and henhouse.[52] Another former area resident said that her elderly sister remembered it as "a very old building occupied by Negroes, when she was a little girl."[53] When Governor Pennypacker arrived to inspect the schoolhouse, a local newspaper reported, "a casual examination by the Governor of the state at once convinced him that the structure was of a much earlier date. He soon found the date 1783 cut by a schoolboy, with his initials."[54]

Having decided that this additional structure was historic enough to remain standing, the park commission began restoring it—and found what they considered to be evidence of an even earlier date. Old stones dug out of the foundation showed carved names of two more schoolboys and the years "1714" and "1716."[55] The park commission report printed at the end of 1908 stated: "From records obtained by a member of the Commission it is ascertained that [the schoolhouse] was built in 1705 by Letitia Penn Aubrey, a daughter of William Penn."[56] Because the park commission did not identify these records, and they have never been rediscovered, and because the carved "1714" and "1716" were never discovered in later work on the building, the quality of this evidence cannot be judged.

The park commission concluded that the school must have functioned as a hospital during the winter encampment, but they restored it as a school. Restored field hospitals were popular in military parks, but in roughly the same time period a log hut was being built and fitted out as a hospital at Valley Forge.[57] The "Letitia Penn Schoolhouse" ended up with a master's

Fig. 7.   The second historic structure acquired by the park. Pennsylvania Governor Samuel W. Pennypacker, a Valley Forge booster, was convinced it was an eighteenth-century school. Park officials determined that it had functioned as a hospital during the winter encampment, but today it is believed to have been built after 1790. (Courtesy, Valley Forge National Historical Park)

desk, student benches, a blackboard, and inkwells. One visitor commented that it had been "restored with a faithfulness to detail which even includes the dunce's cap."[58] The park commission discussed allowing the widow of the park's first caretaker at the Headquarters to set up a little business there selling souvenirs.[59]

Current research indicates that the park's enthusiasm for this building was a bit misplaced. It is now once again believed to date from between 1790 and 1810, or perhaps later.[60] It certainly did not owe its existence to Letitia Penn Aubrey. Although it was situated on land that William Penn had reserved as a manor for his daughter, a grant that was confirmed to her in 1701, it is doubtful that she and her husband did anything with this land besides attempt to sell it for cash.

The money appropriated for Valley Forge during Samuel W. Pennypacker's administration finally enabled the park to construct roads. Back in 1896, the park commission had complained that visitors were damaging the grounds by wearing their own paths among the historic earthworks, because of the lack of roads, and that "with the best of motives they work an irreparable injury."[61] By 1904, the park commission reported that they had completed a road along the entrenchments on Mount Joy, enabling visitors to view and appreciate them without climbing all over them.[62] A newspaper article described the path, now called "Inner Line Drive," that wound uphill from the Valley Forge train station affording beautiful views of the Schuylkill far below.[63] In 1906, the park completed a winding boulevard, now called "Outer Line Drive," connecting Port Kennedy via the outer line defenses to Fort Washington and Inner Line Drive.[64] By 1908, park guards were reporting problems with automobiles hurtling through the park at speeds far in excess of the posted limit of 10 miles an hour.[65]

The new roads seemed to encourage park officials to view a second trolley venture with more enthusiasm. All commissioners seemed happy with a project proposed by the new Phoenixville, Valley Forge & Strafford Electric Railway Company, which was raising $65,000 to connect these three towns by trolley.[66] In 1909, the company was busy buying rights-of-way before beginning work on tracks that would stretch along the outer line, crossing Gulph Road, Baptist Road, and Inner Line Drive and continuing along Valley Creek to Washington's Headquarters. Valley Forge never did get trolley service, however. By 1921, the park commission was afraid the trolley would prevent restoration of the creek area to its eighteenth-century appearance. The trolley company refused to move the tracks from the east side of Valley Creek, so the park superintendent was instructed to remove them.[67]

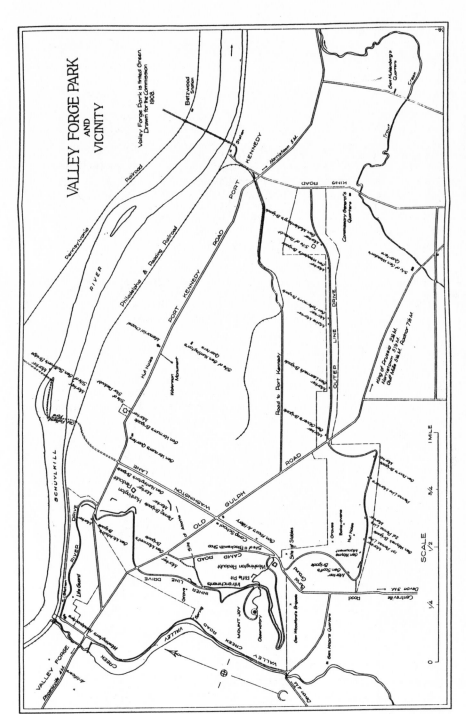

Fig. 8. This 1908 map of Valley Forge Park is from the 1910 park commission report. (Courtesy, Valley Forge National Historical Park)

In 1909, Valley Forge was graced with a new observation tower on the summit of Mount Joy. At the turn of the century, such towers were springing up at many amusement parks and scenic spots. The park commission had observed: "All battlefields and historical parks have one or more—all but Valley Forge."[68] Money that had been appropriated for the park during Pennypacker's administration finally enabled the park to commission Variety Iron Works to build a tower typical of those engendered by the turn-of-the-century tourist boom. It had a concrete foundation and a corrugated iron roof. It was 75 feet high and 25 feet square at the base. Visitors who climbed to the top found plaques directing their attention to various points of interest visible from that elevation. The tower was demolished in 1988.[69]

By the time the tower appeared, there was actually something to see in the fields of Valley Forge. The era of monuments had begun with a vengeance, and Valley Forge seemed eager to catch up with Gettysburg, where so many monuments had already been set up that the battlefield looked like a Victorian cemetery. Between 1906 and 1908, the park paid for a series of simple markers to identify the locations of the camps of each colonial brigade in the Continental Army. In 1909, the Montgomery County Historical Society contributed a new granite boulder on the site of the old, damaged marker commemorating Sullivan's Bridge.[70]

The park had long been hoping that each of the thirteen original colonies would erect monuments to the troops from their respective states, but the first state to do so had not really been one of the thirteen original colonies. Research by a visitor named Nathan Gould determined that soldiers who hailed from what was Maine had served with the Massachusetts companies at Valley Forge.[71] In 1906, the park commission informed Maine's legislature that the park would welcome their proposed marker.[72] A Maine commission purchased an appropriate boulder, which was unveiled on October 17, 1907, with the governor of Maine attending the ceremonies.[73]

Because the Maine marker was relatively small and simple, its unveiling preceded the huge monument that Pennsylvania was constructing. In 1905, Governor Pennypacker had signed an appropriation for $30,000 for an enormous statue of General Anthony Wayne, which he and the park commission hoped would raise the competitive ire of other states and bring more monuments to Valley Forge.[74] The governor also involved himself with the state commission that was inspecting designs for the proposed monument. The commission unanimously decided on a design by Henry K. Bush-Brown and signed a contract with this sculptor after visiting his studio in Newburgh, New York. Bush-Brown's plaster model was cast in bronze in

Philadelphia and, according to members of the monument commission, "pronounced to be one of the world's best Equestrian statues by those who through experience and education in Equestrian statues are competent judges."[75]

This monument was dedicated around Evacuation Day in 1908. Some 3,000 people came in carriages and autos, including Former Governor Pennypacker. After the hulking statue was officially unveiled by Bush-Brown's daughter, Pennypacker delivered a lengthy speech on the life of Anthony Wayne. The monument, he suggested, was appropriately placed. "By no chance, therefore," he intoned, "does it happen that his statue is set upon the center of the outer line at Valley Forge. It is where he [General Wayne] stood in the cold and the drear of that gloomy and memorable Winter."[76] Governor Pennypacker always remained proud of the Wayne statue. In 1909 he wrote a friend, "I am much pleased that you like the appearance of the camp ground at Valley Forge and the Monument of General Wayne."[77]

The summer following the dedication of the Wayne statue saw the beginning of the Pennsylvania Columns. Henry Bush-Brown was again chosen as the artist, but by this time Samuel Pennypacker was no longer in office and the completion of the columns was delayed for several years for lack of funds. In 1909, Park Superintendent A. H. Bowen wrote another park commissioner that Bush-Brown said he was working on "eagles" to mount atop the columns.[78] This was a problem because there was no money to pay for these embellishments until 1910, when the commission urged an appropriation to pay both for the eagles and for the bas-reliefs depicting Pennsylvania officers needed to complete the project.[79]

Once the columns were finally completed, Park Superintendent S. S. Hartranft complained that Bush-Brown had left the site before the second eagle had been fastened to its column. Moreover, the work had not been done according to specs. Instead of being attached to the column with a long metal rod, the eagle had been attached with short bolts and was leaning noticeably.[80] Though this problem was reportedly rectified, one eagle remains slightly crooked to this day. Hartranft also mentioned that one of the park foremen had expressed the opinion that the columns' foundations were inadequate. He noted that he had heard it rumored that Bush-Brown had been given this commission because he had lost money on General Wayne. What was the real story with these monuments? Hartranft wondered. The superintendent concluded: "The sudden appearance of these mushroom columns in the park without the due knowledge of all of the Commission seemed some like a dream."[81]

While the Pennsylvania columns waited for their eagles, the ladies at the Valley Forge chapter of the Daughters of the American Revolution erected a second monument to the unknown dead at Valley Forge. Their monument was located at the other site where, according to tradition, many Revolutionary soldiers were buried: the slope near the outer line defenses on the south side of the park. At the dedication of their monument in 1911, a clergyman in his invocation mentioned the many heroes who lay buried in the area reached by the sound of his voice. In unveiling the monument, the regent of this chapter dedicated it to "Those dead heroes who perished so long ago for American liberty—not in the glory of battle with drums beating and banners flying, but from disease and privation, in the desolation of a winter camp."[82]

Between 1911 and 1914, three states followed the example of Pennsylvania in commemorating the service of their Continental soldiers, though none of

Fig. 9.   The 1911 dedication ceremony for monument commissioned by the Valley Forge DAR. The location was then thought to be an unmarked burial ground for Revolutionary soldiers. (Courtesy, Valley Forge National Historical Park)

their monuments was quite as lavish as General Wayne on his horse. The Massachusetts monument unveiled in 1911 was a sort of curved stone bench pierced by a shaft. It seemed to invite the visitor to pause and admire the view. The simple Delaware marker unveiled in 1914 was cut from Brandy-wine granite. The same year, the Commonwealth of Pennsylvania unveiled yet another monument—this one honoring Major General John Armstrong, who had commanded the Pennsylvania militia. The Camden Elks Lodge initiated the drive for a New Jersey monument. New Jersey's governor, Woodrow Wilson, adopted the project and appointed a commission. By the time the monument was unveiled in 1913, Wilson had been elected President of the United States and could not attend the ceremonies. Spectators were not deprived of a White House aura, however, since Wilson sent his daughter Eleanor to represent him. The president of Wilson's monument commission explained: "With remarkable foresight, the President provided himself with several charming daughters in order to avoid disappointment on occasions similar to this."[83] Miss Wilson apparently captivated the press, and words appeared in print complimenting her "unassuming girlish manners and her ever-present bright smile," not to mention her pretty white shirtwaist and skirt and her blue hat trimmed with roses. Miss Wilson dutifully pulled the cord to reveal the statue of a soldier mounted on a column. She was presented with a huge bouquet of American Beauty roses.[84]

As the monuments sprang up, the Valley Forge park commission worked to do something about the landscape. Ever since the park's formation, employees had been clearing a dense undergrowth of wild grapes and other brambles from park land, their work proceeding as steadily as possible given the weather and the park's chronic lack of funds. In 1906, during Pennypacker's administration, park commissioners were finally able to come up with a plan for what they called the "natural adornment" of the park.[85] They began by moving the picnic area away from Washington's Headquarters and closer to the nearby redoubt they called Fort Huntington. This was a long walk from the train station, but those who couldn't make it could go to the private picnic grounds near the Washington Inn.[86]

A number of dogwood trees discovered at the base of Mount Joy inspired the park commission to create a defined dogwood grove there. As springtime visitors sauntered or drove along Inner Line Drive, they found themselves surrounded by white and pink dogwoods. The Chestnut Tree Blight around 1911 forever changed the composition of the forest by killing all mature American chestnut trees, but the ensuing removal of dead and damaged trees may also have inspired the creation of "vistas," or lines of sight, created by the deliberate removal of trees so that visitors could gaze from one historic attraction to another. By 1917, the park commission minutes referred to their various vistas by name, calling them "Knox's Point Vista," "The Creek Vista," and "The Tower Vistas."[87] After the park acquired land on either side of Valley Creek, this gorge was also landscaped with hemlock and oak. The oaks grew from five bushels of acorns gathered from the grounds of nearby historic Saint David's Church. They were planted in random patterns by an industrious corps of boy volunteers.[88] Then in 1919 the park superintendent reported: "We have purchased a flock of sheep with the idea of running them on the Park for the purpose of keeping the grass down and also for ornamental purposes."[89] The park now required a shepherd, and the commission advertised for a "married, sober, industrious, thoroughly experienced shepherd, . . . Scotchman preferred."[90]

The major redoubts of the park were reconstructed in the early years of the twentieth century. In 1906, the redoubt the park had named Fort Washington got some attention and was furnished with an observation platform so visitors could examine it without standing on it. More work was planned in 1912. A park committee described this effort as "a very simple and inexpensive undertaking, requiring the use of ordinary intelligence without any special demand upon the imagination."[91] The simple undertaking consisted of clearing Fort Washington of trees and obstructions, reinforcing what mounds of earth were visible, and installing some cannon and flagpoles. Colonel George A. Zinn of the Army corps of engineers was consulted regarding installation of the field guns.[92] Once Fort Washington was presentable, it attracted so many visitors that their carriages and automobiles clogged the road at this point, creating traffic problems and prompting the park to consider widening the road.[93]

When the park finally acquired the land where the so-called Star Redoubt had been, they found the reconstruction much more problematic. This structure had been essentially plowed under, and its exact shape could not be determined by the indistinct mound still visible. Park commissioners decided that the redoubt had been built in a star shape by examining the symbol that represented it on the Duportail map. It was reconstructed on its traditional site based on what had been learned from work done at Fort Washington.[94]

In 1917, the forts restoration committee reported that some money was still left for the restoration of Fort Huntington. Work was purposely delayed because Pennsylvania's then governor, Martin Brumbaugh, another Valley

Fig. 10. In 1919, the park superintendent wrote, "We have purchased a flock of sheep with the idea of running them on the park for the purpose of keeping the grass down and also for ornamental purposes." The commission also advertised for a "married, sober, industrious, thoroughly experienced shepherd, . . . Scotchman preferred." (Courtesy, Valley Forge National Historical Park)

Forge enthusiast, wanted to visit and inspect the fort, but the governor found he had no time to spare due to the exigencies of World War I.[95]

The shadow of war was already looming over Valley Forge at the dedication of the Von Steuben statue in 1915, a time when anti-German sentiment was already sweeping Europe. This statue, designed by the German sculptor J. Otto Schweizer, who had been born in Zurich, had been raised by the German-American Alliance. The dedication at its original location on Outer Line Drive between the Wayne statue and the Valley Forge DAR monument was attended by German-American residents of Philadelphia and the surrounding area. Although the ceremonies featured German music and songs, the theme was German-American loyalty to the United States. The president of the German-American Alliance declared:

Fig. 11.   Early preservation effort at earthwork once known as Fort Washington, now Redoubt #3. A fence was erected to keep tourists outside. (Courtesy, Valley Forge National Historical Park)

"One of the duties of the National German-American Alliance is to mark historical sites with monuments which instill patriotism into the hearts of the American people." Other speakers declared that German-Americans were and always had been loyal to their adopted country.[96] The statue was eventually surrounded by linden trees grown from German seedlings of the same variety as those on the avenue in Berlin known as Unter den Linden.

America was already at war by the time its national monument, the National Memorial Arch, was dedicated in 1917. The arch finally brought Valley Forge what the Valley Forge Memorial Association had really wanted—a gift from the entire nation to the historic campground. After the efforts of the Valley Forge Memorial Association had dwindled to a stop, the park commission had speculated about visiting Washington in 1894 to ask for a national monument on Mount Joy. The park commission envisioned "a colossal bronze figure of a private soldier on guard and looking down on the Old Gulf Road. He should be young in years, whose wan face, ragged uniform and worn out shoes would typify the hunger and cold so heroically borne in that historic camp."[97] What the park eventually got was something quite different.

In 1908, Congressman Irving P. Wanger of Norristown introduced a bill in Congress to appropriate $50,000 for two federally funded arches at Valley Forge. These were to be christened the Washington and Von Steuben arches, and they were to be located at the two major entrances to the park. This expensive proposition occasioned some debate in Congress when other politicians questioned whether money should be spent on monuments at a time when the United States was forced to issue bonds to run the government. Democrats were generally against the expenditure, but Republicans argued that America was not yet so poor that she could not afford to be patriotic.[98]

A Senate committee amended the bill by changing the two arches to a single arch honoring Washington, and so the national monument would be truly worthy of the nation's gratitude to the army at Valley Forge, they doubled the appropriation. The bill was approved in 1910, and Congress resolved that the secretary of war would oversee the project, approving plans and specs and authorizing the location of the arch.

The arch was designed by Paul Philippe Cret, a professor at the University of Pennsylvania. Cret was born in Lyons, France, in 1876 and had studied at the Ecole des Beaux Arts there and in Paris. He would remain affiliated with the University of Pennsylvania until his retirement in 1937 after a long and influential career as one of America's most respected architects. Cret is known today for his public buildings in the Beaux Arts style, which drew inspiration from the Renaissance and the work of classical antiquity. In the Philadelphia area, Cret's work includes the Federal Reserve Bank building, the Barnes Foundation museum, the Rodin Museum (with Jacques Greber), the Ben Franklin Bridge, the Henry Avenue Bridge, and the University Avenue Bridge, among others.

Cret's final design for the arch drew its inspiration from the Arch of Titus in Rome. It had many directly derived ornamental details, such as its coffered ceiling and the winged female figures on its spandrels. In ancient Rome, triumphal arches had been constructed to honor victorious generals, so the idea of an arch honoring George Washington seemed appropriate even though the concept was anachronistic. The arch drew some early fire from the *Philadelphia Record*, where an editorial observed that Roman arches had always been part of the urban setting of Rome—a triumphal arch seemed ridiculous in a lonely rural landscape.[99]

A second controversy arose when Congressman Wanger questioned the arch's location. The park planned to build the arch along the boulevard they had constructed along the outer line defenses. Wanger wanted it on Gulph

Road where the Continental soldiers had left their bloody footprints as they marched into the area.[100] In 1911, Wanger wrote a bitter letter to the park superintendent, saying:

> If it were not for the entire lack of consideration given by the Valley Forge Park Comm. to my views touching the site and design of the memorial arch I might almost persuade myself that the comm. realized that I had something to do with the enactment authorizing the arch and appropriating the money for its erection.[101]

At the urging of the secretary of war, the commission met with Wanger and heard him out, but did not change the proposed location of the arch.[102]

In 1914, when the arch was nearing completion, it was discovered that no money had been set aside for dedication ceremonies. The park commission hastily asked the War Department for funds, but officials there merely replied that the surplus of the original appropriation could be applied for the dedication.[103] When the park commission found that it had no money left, the secretary of war was asked to sponsor a bill appropriating $5,000 for suitable dedication ceremonies. By then, the United States had a new secretary of war, who responded that he had not initiated the building of the arch and did not plan to become involved.[104] This put the arch in limbo. Until a dedication officially transferred it to the care of the park commission, it did not belong to the park. And until the arch belonged to the park, no state money could be spent on its repair and maintenance. An article in the *Philadelphia Public Ledger* speculated whether the arch would long remain in this state, the forces of nature gradually transforming it from a classical arch to a classical ruin.[105]

The arch was finally dedicated on June 19, 1917. A special train of Pullman cars brought an impressive number of U.S. Congressmen to Valley Forge, where they crowded onto and around a grandstand draped with bunting and American flags.[106] Professor Paul Cret could not attend because he was already on his way to France, where he served in the French army as an interpreter attached to the First Division of the American army. Pennsylvania's governor, Martin Brumbaugh, who for personal religious reasons did not sanction war, had a difficult time delivering a suitably patriotic speech that did not compromise his principles. Victory in Europe depended on the economic and emotional support of America. During World War I, antiwar sentiments could literally prove dangerous to the individual who uttered them. Brumbaugh spoke about "the spirit of Valley Forge," which he said

Fig. 12. National Memorial Arch. The park's largest monument was designed by architect Paul Philippe Cret and dedicated in 1917. Scaffolding suggests that the figures in the photograph may be workmen. (Courtesy, Valley Forge National Historical Park)

was "with the Allies in the western line": "It is breathing hope in Russia. It has asserted itself in Greece. It is brooding over China and has already quickened Japan and animates the peoples of the islands of the Sea." His message was that the spirit of Valley Forge and its lesson of triumph through endurance would continue in those troubled times to bring hope to humankind. [107]

Valley Forge was criticized during World War I by those who wondered whether the park commission was doing enough for the war effort. Some believed that America needed more than a spiritual lesson from Valley Forge. The importance of sending food to the allies was being emphasized throughout America. Park Commissioner W. H. Sayen wrote Governor Brumbaugh in an attempt to justify the wartime role of the park. Sayen declared that 30 acres of park land were cultivated with food crops, which was as much as the reduced staff at the park could cope with. Sayen complained: "A great many of these people who are attacking the state for not cultivating its public parks, own privately large golf links from one hundred to two hundred acres and on which they propose to enjoy themselves and destroy the pleasure grounds for 80,000 children." [108]

Generally speaking, the park commission got on well with Governor Brumbaugh, who proved to be the park's second great friend in Harrisburg. In 1916, the park commission report complimented the governor, saying, "With the present State administration there happily came a Governor who knew Valley Forge, and the Commonwealth is to be congratulated upon the work he made possible by suitable appropriations." [109] During Brumbaugh's term, the park was finally able to resume the growth it had witnessed during Samuel W. Pennypacker's administration. The park commission nearly doubled the size of the park by buying hundreds of acres along Valley Creek plus large tracts contiguous to what it already owned, and it constructed the Camp Road linking Forts Washington and Huntington.

In 1918, the park acquired property that included the house that had been General James Mitchell Varnum's headquarters during the winter of 1777–1778. The house was a three-bay, two-story stone structure with a hall-and-parlor interior plan typical of the Delaware Valley during the beginning of the eighteenth century. Probably built sometime between 1711 and 1735, it became the oldest building in the park. Up until 1898, it had been the residence of the Stephens family, but in the early twentieth century it was falling into ruin. The commission considered it an important acquisition but recognized that its restoration would be expensive. Commis-

Fig. 13. Two early photographs of Varnum's Quarters, purchased by the park in 1918. *Upper*: before DAR renovation of 1920s; what may be the original roofline is faintly visible. *Lower*: after renovation but before drastic restoration of 1934, which lowered the roof. (Courtesy, Valley Forge National Historical Park)

sioners were able to get the Philadelphia Chapter of the DAR to renovate and preserve the house and install a caretaker there.[110]

Several other acquisitions reveal an unconscious pattern in the development of the park during the first quarter-century of its existence. Since the time of the encampment, the valley had been an industrial setting. By 1920, the park commission had driven away most of the remaining industries from the villages of Port Kennedy and Valley Forge. Port Kennedy's Ehret Magnesia Company was among the businesses that fell victim to the park. As the park expanded during Brumbaugh's administration, it acquired land with dwellings where some of this company's employees were living. During World War I, Ehret was manufacturing a product the navy needed for the war effort, so the park commission allowed Ehret's employees to continue occupying their homes. After the war was over, the park commission heard rumors that Ehret would spend some $100,000 on new workers' dwellings plus other improvements on its land adjoining the park.

The park commission planned to acquire this property eventually and did not want to spend an additional $100,000 for it. The Ehret Magnesia Company was asked for information but refused to cooperate. The commission retaliated by immediately designating the tract in question as a future portion of the park, meaning that the company would not be able to recover the costs of any improvements made from that time onward.[111] This stymied the company's plans to enlarge their own operations during a time when many of America's businesses were rapidly expanding. The park commission saw nothing wrong with this state of affairs and flatly declared:

> The contention of the Ehret Magnesia Company that it is being harassed in the operation of its work by the Valley Forge Park Commission is not tenable. It is true that the Commission has taken steps, necessary to protect public interest, which were objected to by the company, but the Commission feels that the interests of the public are paramount to the interest of the Company.[112]

At the western end of the campground, another business came into conflict with the park commission. The commission condemned land on the southwest side of today's intersection of Routes 23 and 252. Thomas and Anna Cutler owned the land, but they had leased a mill there to one Ebenezer Lund, who operated a business called the Valley Forge Worsted Mills. The park commission planned to allow Lund to operate until his lease ran out, after which they wanted to tear the old mill down. Lund complained of being "tied hand and foot by your commission," unable to make needed repairs at the factory because he would not be able to recover the cost of these improvements from the state.[113] The park commission offered no help, so Lund went to court and was awarded $31,500 for damages sustained in the confiscation of his leasehold. He informed the park that he would be clearing out as soon as he could move his machinery.[114] In an undated memo on Valley Forge Worsted Mills stationery, Lund expressed his anger. The park, he charged, had ruined Valley Forge for business. An entrepreneur could not even offer secure employment. "Labor will only stay long enough to get learnt and until they can get another position." When all the valley's businesses were gone, he guessed, the last of its residents would move too, since people could not "eat their houses."[115] Valley Forge would become a dead place. Indeed, the closing of Lund's operation indeed marked the end of viable industry at Valley Forge.

The park commissioners would have liked to improve Valley Forge even more by curtailing what they deemed other objectionable commercial operations on property belonging to the Washington Inn. The inn kept hogs penned up not 300 feet from the headquarters building. The park superintendent wrote: "The odor from this piggery is very objectionable and we believe unwholesome to those who are obliged to be on the ground continuously."[116] The Washington Inn also had a cesspool that overflowed. Happily feeding around the grounds were chickens, which became the main course at the hotel's popular chicken-and-waffle dinners.[117] It would, however, be many years until the park commission could acquire the property of the Washington Inn and make that too blend in with the scenery being created at Valley Forge.

In the first two decades of the twentieth century, as they acquired the bulk of the land on which Washington's soldiers had camped, the park commissioners did their best to preserve and maintain all structures deemed to be of colonial or Revolutionary origin—the structures that would have existed when the Continental army was here. Surrounding those structures, the commissioners fostered the creation of an attractively landscaped memorial park that had markers indicating what was no longer visible to the tourist. Other markers, such as the Wayne statue and the National Memorial Arch, were meant to inspire awe and instill pride in the visitor.

A revitalized park commission had managed to fend off the threat of a national park and sweep away the competitive Centennial and Memorial Association. It received little criticism for this, or for the fact that it was killing the businesses that fed two communities. What criticism the park did receive centered on how it was going about its program, not about the park commission's overall plan. Local resident E. B. Cassatt complained about the park guard who would not let him and his wife ride horseback over certain park trails. [118] He criticized the park's landscaping, observing that their vistas were three times as broad as they needed to be and were inappropriate because they had certainly not been there during the winter of 1777–1778. In addition, Cassatt charged, the Wayne statue had been "disfigured" when park employees cut down the woods that had crowned the little knoll on which it stood. [119]

In the same period, there was a parallel controversy about who would interpret the message of Valley Forge. For years, park administrators had had to contend with Bernard McMenamin, better known as "Barney the Guide," who picked up odd dollars by escorting visitors who wanted to see Valley Forge's points of interest. [120] One visitor wrote a park superintendent about another unofficial guide who liked to plant himself at the top of the observation tower and solicit contributions after reciting a spiel on Valley Forge: "The principal thing noteworthy in the young man's talk was his bad grammer [sic]." [121] But the park commission would discover it had much more serious competition in the Rev. Dr. W. Herbert Burk, a clergyman from Norristown who had acquired property well east of what was then the park and who had some very definite ideas about what visitors to Valley Forge needed to know.

5

The Churches at Valley Forge

It was Washington's Birthday 1903 and the Rev. Dr. W. Herbert Burk, rector of All Saints' Church in Norristown, Pennsylvania, was delivering his sermon. His subject was of course George Washington, whom he identified as a dedicated churchman—a vestryman and warden in his own Truro parish. The rector argued that Washington's greatness was the product of his religious nature, something the rector described as a rare quality in "that dark age of Deism which welcomed the cheap infidelity of 'Tom' Paine" and the "selfish maxims of Poor Richard."[1]

In Burk's mind was a vision, the inspiring image of a solitary and steadfast Washington kneeling in the snow at Valley Forge and placing his trust in God during one of his life's darkest hours. The rector urged his congregation:

> Would that there we might rear the wayside chapel, fit memorial of the Church's most honored son, to be the Nation's Bethel for all days to come, where the American patriot might kneel in quest of

that courage and that strength to make all honorable his citizenship here below, and prove his claim to that above![2]

The chapel that did eventually rise at Valley Forge would give Burk the lifetime job of defending Washington's religious nature against those who questioned whether Washington had been the ideal churchman. In his 1903 sermon, Burk declared, "No accusations of the modern self-appointed iconoclast, who would discount the religion of him whom we honor, can make us forget either the evidences of his private devotions nor the records of public worship."[3] In later years, Burk would carefully comb through Washington's writings, picking out sixty prayers and benedictions. Did the spot have to be marked on the Duportail map for people to believe that Washington had knelt in the snow? he would ask sarcastically.[4] Burk would never claim that he knew the precise place or the exact circumstances, but he had faith that, somewhere on the slopes of Mount Joy, Washington had indeed sought God's help for his army.[5]

In early 1903, the wayside chapel at Valley Forge existed only in Burk's mind, but in a memoir she wrote of her husband's work at Valley Forge, Eleanor Burk recalled that immediately after his Washington's Birthday sermon the initial step was taken to make his dream come true. The boys and girls of Burk's congregation took up his cause and pledged the first $100 for the Washington Memorial Chapel.[6]

W. Herbert Burk was born in 1867, son of the Rev. Jesse Y. Burk, who was rector of Old Saint Peter's in Clarksboro, New Jersey. Burk attended the Philadelphia Divinity School of the Protestant Episcopal Church and also received a bachelor's degree in divinity from the University of Pennsylvania. After being ordained in 1894, he became rector of the Church of the Ascension in Gloucester City, New Jersey, then moved on to Saint John's in Norristown and then to All Saints'. He married twice, the first time to Abbie Jessup Reeves, who died in 1907, and the second time to Eleanor Hallowell Stroud.

Photographs and portraits show that Burk had a round baby face, a physical feature that masked the iron determination of this man who met challenges head-on. During a freak snowstorm one Easter Sunday, he forced his car through deep snow on the road from the Washington Memorial Chapel to Port Kennedy, blazing a trail that parishioners could follow to church.[7] After he decided that his parish at Valley Forge needed a cemetery, he was once observed driving a mule team to finish the grading.[8] Sometimes Burk's physical strength failed to match his will—there are allusions in the

parish records to illness caused by overwork and nervous disorders. Some
contemporaries complained that Burk was never fully esteemed. A writer for
the *Norristown Herald* contended, "[Burk] is a lonely figure, in attempting
almost single-handed to do a work every patriot should assist in doing. . . .
His efforts have not as yet been appreciated."[9]

Burk claimed that the initial inspiration for a wayside chapel at Valley
Forge came to him one day when he took his Norristown choir boys there
for an outing. They made their visit in pre-Pennypacker days, when the park
was still forlorn and neglected. They started their tour at Fort Washington—
then an overgrown mound identified only by a signboard. They saw Valley
Creek with its covered bridge, and pushed uphill through thick undergrowth
until they stumbled over the entrenchments on Mount Joy, singing "Onward
Christian Soldiers" to keep their spirits up. Burk decided to make a short
speech but was ashamed to discover that he knew so little about Valley
Forge. He gave the boys Valley Forge's traditional spiritual message, "the
message of Divine strength and comfort, of victory through suffering, of
achievement through prayer" (as he later remembered it).[10] The outing
convinced Burk that Valley Forge was in danger of grievous misuse: it was
well on its way to becoming a picnic ground, a highly inappropriate role for
the place where he believed some 3,000 American patriots had died and lay
buried. He later wrote:

> Their dust makes it hallowed ground, as the blood from their frozen
> feet made the Old Gulph Road, up which the defeated army
> marched to Valley Forge, the Via Sacra of the American people. To
> trample this ground in thoughtless levity, or boisterous sport is a
> desecration of their graves, an insult to their memory, and a crime
> against the Republic which their sacrifices won for us.[11]

Michael Kammen speaks of a trend beginning in the late eighteenth
century in which "nationalism and political ideology started to supplant, at
least partially, a role that religion had customarily fulfilled in our culture."[12]
By the 1880s and 1890s he states, people increasingly turned to history
rather than religion for inspiration, thus blurring the dividing line between
the two. Many sermons used examples from history, while historical pageants assumed religious overtones.[13] In Burk's mind a church at Valley Forge
would make sense as a special kind of memorial emphasizing the sacred
nature of the reserved land and engendering a respect appropriate for the
place. At a time when the park commission was offering no active interpreta-

tion of the Valley Forge experience, a church pulpit was also a vehicle through which that message could be distilled and promulgated in conformity with the tenets of the Protestant religion, then considered the official religion of America by its largely Protestant leaders.

Despite his determination, Burk did not accomplish all that he had planned because most Americans viewed Valley Forge as a place neither completely sacred nor secular. Burk took on his task apparently without the full support of his own superiors in the Episcopal church. An author who knew Burk recalled:

> The bishop of the diocese could see no reason for erecting a chapel in a place where there were few people; and, above all things, a chapel which, before it was finished, might cost—millions. He smiled benevolently, as is the habit of bishops, and put his ecclesiastical foot down. Both feet. So did everyone else whom Dr. Burk consulted, that is to say, everyone who could by any chance have assisted him in this undertaking, among them the writer of this paper. Then people having neither judgement, experience, nor money came to his assistance—and made his work more difficult. It is altogether possible that, without the example of Washington himself, Dr. Burk might never have overcome the obstacles which confronted him. [14]

Burk's efforts followed an earlier attempt to found a church at Valley Forge that had met with even less success. In 1885, Baptist minister James M. Guthrie began raising funds for a new church on the site of an old Valley Forge chapel or meetinghouse thought to have been in use before the Revolution. [15] In July 1886, new foundations were built and a cornerstone was dedicated. Guthrie had plans for a blue marble structure built of blocks cut from the quarries of King of Prussia, Pennsylvania. Every slab would be inscribed with a name. Each signer of the Declaration of Independence, and each Revolutionary hero of Valley Forge, would have his or her name inscribed on a marble block, as would the modern-day schools and teachers who contributed money. [16]

A year went by and no further construction work was done on the church. Within another year, it was reported that Guthrie was leaving the First Baptist Church in Pottsville to dedicate himself to his project at Valley Forge. [17] He raised money, but two more years passed without visible results. A Bucks County teacher wrote:

He sent circulars to the schools of Bucks County as well as Montgomery, asking for contributions, and promising that for $3 contributed by a school, that school should have its name inscribed on one of the marble blocks of the building, and also that the one giving the highest amount should receive the paper of which he was then editor free for one year. My pupils subscribed $3, and each received only one copy of the paper. I have his receipt for the money, dated April 1, 1887. I have written repeatedly to him in regard to it, but have received no answer.[18]

In 1890, the Philadelphia Baptist Association issued a report restraining Guthrie from receiving any more money for his Valley Forge church until he rendered a satisfactory account of the funds he had so far collected.[19] Guthrie had been promising this information for some time but had failed to provide it, and after the Baptist hierarchy got involved he apparently left the area. Grass grew over the church's foundation, and in 1901 a magazine article noted that the site had fallen into ruin, its cornerstone "used as a target by the gunners who traverse the hills."[20]

Only two years later, Burk began holding services at Valley Forge without a church building. The POS of A lent him its Valley Forge meeting hall, and Burk advertised his first service through handbills and notices in the local papers. On May 17, 1903, just a few months after his Washington's Birthday sermon, Burk preached at Valley Forge. Years later he recalled that his first congregation had consisted of "a woman and baby from Valley Forge and a woman and a boy from Bridgeport."[21] After the POS of A declined the continued use of their hall, Burk moved to Blackburn's Hall in Port Kennedy.[22] He soon acquired his own piece of Valley Forge real estate when I. Heston Todd, who had supposedly been inspired by Burk's Washington's Birthday sermon, donated land then located outside the boundaries of Valley Forge State Park.

June 19, 1903, was the 125th anniversary of the evacuation of Washington's army from Valley Forge. Despite a threat of rain, between 5,000 and 6,000 people attended, including Pennsylvania's new governor, Samuel W. Pennypacker, who gave a stirring speech, then retired with his staff to the Washington Inn. Episcopal Bishop Rt. Rev. O. W. Whitaker, presided at the ceremony to lay the cornerstone for Burk's Washington Memorial Chapel. The bishop formally accepted a deed from I. Heston Todd, and the Rev. Dr. C. Ellis Stevens of historic Christ Church in Philadelphia spoke of Washington's earnest Christianity. The bishop ceremonially laid the stone in honor of Washington, and all the "patriot churchmen and churchwomen who served their God and country in the struggle for Liberty."[23] Burk would recall that later in the day he returned alone to the church's foundations to empty the cornerstone of its memorial artifacts and transfer them to a safe deposit box. He had no idea whether he would have any more luck than James Guthrie in completing the edifice.[24]

"I planned to build a chapel; I hoped it might become a shrine," Burk wrote.[25] A competition was initiated to select an architect and a design. Warren P. Laird of the University of Pennsylvania's architecture department judged the entries and selected the work of Milton B. Medary Jr.,[26] who had been born in Philadelphia in 1874 and had practiced largely in the area. Although not that widely known today, his projects included Houston Hall at the University of Pennsylvania, Bryn Mawr Hospital, Saint John's Church in Lower Merion, and the gymnasium at Haverford College. Burk had instructed Medary to plan not just a church but a memorial, a complex of several buildings where a chapel dominated the group without overpowering the other buildings. The chapel would be flanked on its western side by a cloister composed of thirteen bays, each commemorating one of the thirteen original colonies. On the opposite side, the chapel would be connected by a porch to a library, a bell tower, and a hall to be used as a meeting place for patriotic and historical associations.

Medary's plans called for an architectural style known as "Perpendicular Gothic," deriving its inspiration from English Gothic architecture of the fourteenth through early sixteenth centuries and characterized by intricate stonework and an overall linear effect. The choice of this style over the Colonial Revival look so popular in domestic architecture at the turn of the century was puzzling. Medary is remembered chiefly for his Gothic Revival buildings, but he was equally at ease in Georgian styles. Burk could have had a replica of Philadelphia's Christ Church, but he opted for a structure that looked as if it belonged at Cambridge, and one he would also have to defend from time to time. In a magazine article he commented: "Colonial architecture was Georgian; the men at Valley Forge gave their lives in a struggle against the tyranny of a Georgian King. Why mock their memory by building a Georgian Chapel in their honor?"[27]

To house the congregation while the chapel was being built, Burk arranged for construction of a humble barnboard edifice. An early photograph shows it nestled among the trees and identifiable as a church by its arched windows with diamond-shaped panes and the bell on its roof. Burk's wife recalled how

CLOISTER OF THE COLONIES. WASHINGTON MEMORIAL CHAPEL. PATRIOTS' HALL. TOWER AND LIBRARY.

THE DEFENDERS' GATE

Fig. 14. These two drawings show what the Rev. Dr. W. Herbert Burk envisioned at Valley Forge. He planned *(upper)* a complex of chapel, cloister, tower, meeting facilities, and library dedicated to George Washington. West of this complex *(lower)*, he wanted a grand entrance to his churchyard dedicated to "The Defenders of the Union" with an arch memorializing Abraham Lincoln. Only the chapel and cloister were built according to this plan. For years the chapel's rector lived in the west side of Defenders' Gate. (From *Historical and Topographical Guide to Valley Forge* by W. Herbert Burk [Philadelphia, 1910])

she could see squirrels cavorting outside through the chinks in the walls, and that once the rector's warden discovered a fox who had moved inside.[28]

Eleanor Burk also told how her husband's barnboard chapel won national fame and the endorsement of the nation's President. Theodore Roosevelt, she explained, once came to visit the attorney general, Philander Knox, who happened to have a country estate just west of Valley Creek. In conversation, Knox mentioned Burk and the church he was trying to build at Valley Forge. Roosevelt approved of the idea and asked, "How can I help this man?" Knox suggested that the President deliver a speech at the barnboard chapel.[29] Roosevelt, who is known for having described the presidency as a "bully pulpit," took the opportunity to speak from a real pulpit at Valley Forge.

On Saturday, June 18, 1904, the President and Mrs. Roosevelt came by private railway car to Devon, Pennsylvania, from Hyde Park, New York, and were driven to Knox's estate at Valley Forge. On the morning of Evacuation Day they toured the area, viewing the earthworks, the forts, and Washington's Headquarters, where Roosevelt insisted on paying the Centennial and Memorial Association's customary 10-cent fee. After lunch at the Knox mansion, the President set out for the barnboard chapel amid the cheers of Americans lining the roadway. Burk had the honor of introducing the President, who arrived around four o'clock. His presence in the area had not been highly publicized, but the chapel was filled to capacity and surrounded by many more spectators hoping to hear his words through the open windows.[30]

Roosevelt's speech compared two great moments in American history: Gettysburg and Valley Forge. He implied that the fledgling state park was just as important as the far more impressive memorial park at Gettysburg. In fact, the President claimed that Valley Forge had an even more important message for America. Gettysburg, he declared, had been a single heroic effort, while Valley Forge was "what we need, on the whole, much more—much more commonly—and which is a more difficult thing—constant effort." Roosevelt continued, "I think as a people we need more to learn the lesson of Valley Forge than the lesson of Gettysburg."[31]

The President concluded by heartily endorsing the Washington Memorial Chapel:

> I congratulate you that it is your good fortune to be encouraged in erecting a memorial to the great man who was equal to the great deeds that he was called upon to perform, to the man and the men

who showed by their lives that they were indeed doers of the word, and not hearers only. [32]

After the final hymn was sung, the President took his leave, shaking hands with Burk and declaring that it had been his pleasure to come. President and Mrs. Roosevelt left Knox's residence the following morning, again boarding their private railway car for Washington. [33] Roosevelt's presence had enabled Burk to claim a wonderful accomplishment. Theodore Roosevelt had been the first President to visit Valley Forge while in office, and he had come specifically to speak at Burk's barnboard chapel. The structure was renamed the Roosevelt Chapel in his honor.

The barnboard chapel continued to house Burk's congregation while work was begun on the Washington Memorial Chapel proper. Enough money was raised to build the walls of the nave to a height of 10 feet, or up to the windowsills of what would be the completed chapel's stained-glass windows. Then money ran out, and the church was furnished with a temporary roof, but this made the building usable and Burk held his first church service inside it on Washington's Birthday 1905. The barnboard chapel was retained as a Sunday school and as a tribute to Theodore Roosevelt.

Burk began furnishing the half-built chapel by soliciting contributions. Wealthy individuals were encouraged to pay for an article of church furniture in memory of the life of some great American of the Revolutionary period— one of their own ancestors if their roots went back that far. Mary H. Wood provided the church with its pulpit, lectern, and choir perclose in memory of her late husband, Alan Wood Jr., who had been a descendant of William Dewees. [34]

Dr. Burk managed another Valley Forge first at the pulpit's dedication on Washington's Birthday 1909. Because the pulpit honored George Washington's services as a British soldier during the period of the French and Indian War, and particularly the fact that Washington had officiated at the burial of the unfortunate British General Braddock, Burk got a British official to pay homage at Valley Forge for the first time in American history. His Majesty's British consul, the Honorable Wilfred Powell, proclaimed in his speech that Washington had been "the greatest Englishman of the eighteenth century." Powell also had words of praise for the partially completed Washington Memorial Chapel and asked, "Why should not this Memorial Chapel become the nucleus of a Valhalla, a Pantheon or a Westminster Abbey, where the monuments and tombs of the heroes and great men of the United States should find a home?"[35]

Fig. 15. Washington Memorial Chapel during construction, probably between 1905 and 1913. *Upper:* partially completed chapel with temporary roof. *Lower:* interior of the partly completed chapel. (Courtesy, Valley Forge National Historical Park)

The chapel had a long way to go before it lived up to Powell's expectations but it was beginning to turn into a tourist attraction. When Dr. Burk was not available to show the visitors around, his sexton acted as tour guide. Eleanor Burk remembered the first sexton as quite a character, who embarrassed Burk by claiming to know the exact spot at Valley Forge where Washington had knelt in prayer. Once while addressing a group of students from the prestigious Bryn Mawr College, he pointed out an inscription carved in the chapel wall in Old English lettering, saying, "Now gals, I'll just read you these Latin inscriptions."[36]

Dr. Burk was the first to use a museum-style collection of objects in the interpretation of the Valley Forge experience. Burk's father had collected Indian relics, and as a boy Burk himself had roamed the fields of local farmers to see what their plows might unearth. He had long been gathering artifacts associated with Washington and the Revolutionary War, and these were first displayed in 1908 at an "Exhibition of American Wars" sponsored by the Valley Forge DAR. The collection also included an item that continues to be one of the treasures of Valley Forge: the check presented by the U.S. Congress to the Marquis de Lafayette in partial payment for his services during the American Revolution.[37]

Burk opened a museum to house his collection, which was officially dedicated in 1909 and, like Burk's church, was only partially completed at the time. In 1908, Burk's building committee had erected a portion of the chapel complex that would be incorporated into Patriot's Hall, the proposed meeting place for patriotic and historical societies. This second, half-completed steel and concrete structure provided Burk with a room approximately 28 feet by 24 feet in which he could house his precious relics. "The cases were such as I could beg or buy," he wrote, "the relics were few, but as I have already said were of great value." Burk filled in the empty spaces with flags and decorative bunting.[38]

Burk had a vision of what his museum might become, and it was not going to be a small, local museum. He considered Valley Forge the turning point in America's history and therefore believed that his collections should be the basis for interpretation of all of America's history to date. Besides the objects related to the American Revolution and his father's Indian relics, Burk began collecting historical documents and items related to the Civil War and the Spanish American War. He expected to raise $10 million for a complex of museum buildings to be named Pocohontas Hall, Raleigh Hall, Franklin Hall, Washington Hall, Jefferson Hall, Lincoln Hall, and Roosevelt Hall.

As the names implied, each building would be dedicated to a specific period in American history.[39]

As Burk intended, opening the museum encouraged donations of even more artifacts. Mrs. S. R. Bartholomew was inspired to donate the impressive collection of old china her brother had left her. The sexton had just moved out of his room below the museum and into a small house, giving Burk a place to display his latest acquisition. The Thomas H. Schollenberger Collection of more than 4,000 pieces of lusterware, Chinese export porcelain, Staffordshire, and other ceramics remains another one of Valley Forge's treasures.[40]

Burk was probably proudest of another object he personally obtained for Valley Forge. Mary J. B. Chew of Philadelphia mentioned that it might be possible to acquire Washington's marquee—his personal campaign tent. The tent had been passed along by Washington's descendants in the Custis family and the Lee family. It had been seized at the Lee estate known as Arlington during the Civil War, but President McKinley had restored it to the Lee family. Burk immediately reasoned that no matter where Washington had knelt in the snow at Valley Forge, he had certainly made his personal devotions in the privacy of his tent. If patriots revered the pews that great men had occupied in churches, they should also revere Washington's marquee. Since tradition held that Washington would accept no better accommodations than his men enjoyed, and had remained in the tent until huts were built for all the men at Valley Forge, the marquee was also a kind of Washington's Headquarters, and an earlier one than the Potts house. Its thin canvas walls had obviously provided little protection against bitter winter weather, so they clearly evoked the image of desolate suffering at Valley Forge.[41]

Mary Custis Lee, daughter of Robert E. Lee, owned the tent and wanted $5,000 for it, which was a significant problem for Burk. She was engaged in raising funds for her own cause, an "old ladies" home in the South. Miss Lee wrote Burk: "My poor old women want the *money* more than you do the *Tent!*"[42] Although Lee believed she could have gotten a higher price in Pittsburgh or Chicago, she let Burk have the tent for a $500 down payment, with the understanding that he would charge visitors money to view it and send her a percentage of the proceeds.[43]

Once the marquee arrived at Valley Forge, it immediately sparked controversy. When the tent went on display at the chapel complex, someone apparently connected with Burk announced that in 1777 Washington had pitched the tent only a short distance from the Washington Memorial on property currently owned by I. Heston Todd. Valley Forge park officials vehemently disagreed and proclaimed that it had already been established that Washington's tent had stood within the boundaries of the current park. The park already had a marker at the spot on Old Camp Road.[44]

It is interesting to speculate whether the controversy originated after the park declined to give Burk permission to set up the tent on *their* version of its original site in order to photograph it.[45] Burk did eventually erect the tent out-of-doors one winter day after a snowstorm, and arranged for a professional photograph that became a postcard for tourists to buy.[46]

Despite the tent's appeal, Burk had forwarded Miss Lee only $2,397.97 by 1916, which made Miss Lee disappointed in the patriotism of people in the Philadelphia area. She did not want to press, but she still needed the cash for her charity work.[47] When she extended her offer, Burk was finally able to complete the payments. Years later, Burk's interest in history took him to the Library of Congress, where he unearthed the original bill for the tent. Among the items listed on the maker's invoice was a "tickum" lining. Because Burk's artifact had no such lining, he immediately wrote to Miss Lee's heirs, politely explaining that he had paid for the whole tent and felt entitled to have all the pieces. However, Burk never did acquire the lining of Washington's marquee.[48]

Burk recalled that one day while he was showing off his treasure a guest told him, "I saw the flag which belongs to the Tent." The guest revealed that Washington's old campaign flag was then owned by Fannie B. Lovell, a descendant of Washington's sister. A Lovell family tradition identified it as the Washington's Headquarters flag, which had always been used to mark the building where Washington was headquartered during the American Revolution. An image of the blue flag with its thirteen six-pointed stars appeared in Charles Wilson Peale's portraits of George Washington then on display at Independence Hall.[49] Lovell was contacted, and she lent the flag to the museum with the understanding that it would belong to the museum after her death.[50] In order to keep the precious commander-in-chief's flag, Burk later had to fend off Mrs. C. M. Crosby, who claimed that she was the flag's true owner and wanted it back to pass on to her daughter.[51]

Burk retained considerable pride in the important artifacts he had obtained for his museum. He later wrote: "If there was nothing but this old flag and tent in the Valley Forge Museum of American History, it would be the greatest collection of Washington Relics in the world, for these are the two things which were used by him and represented him in the greatest struggle of his life."[52] Burk planned for his museum to incorporate a library and began soliciting donations of books on American history. He moved a bookcase into his museum display room and later began stacking books under the marquee as his collection grew. He was also looking for rare books and hoped eventually to duplicate Washington's library at Mount Vernon by obtaining a copy of every book Washington had ever owned. He designed bookplates that sported a rococo cartouche copied from Washington's personal bookplates.

In 1906, Burk himself wrote a book, among the first of his many publications. He penned a guidebook of Valley Forge designed to connect Revolutionary history with the actual remains to be seen in the valley. Possibly thinking of his own experience on that initial trip with his choir boys, he noted in the preface: "Without some such guidance much of the interest which belongs to the place is lost, as I know from personal experience."[53] Although the park had already produced a similar book, Governor Pennypacker complimented Burk's effort, writing to him: "It is both interesting and useful and will be very helpful to those seeing the locality as well as to the student interested in history."[54]

Burk's congregation grew, and his Valley Forge parishioners organized a number of church groups. As early as 1908, the Washington Memorial Chapel had a choir, a Sunday school, a women's auxiliary, the Washington Memorial Chapel Guild (which raised money for the chapel and published a newsletter called the *Washington Chapel Chronicle*), a Martha Washington Junior Guild, a boys' club, and an organization called the Bartram, which functioned as a baseball club.[55] That same year, the *Washington Chapel Chronicle* lamented that although Valley Forge honored the dead of the American Revolution the Washington Memorial Chapel had no provision for the repose of members of its own congregation.[56] The chapel needed a cemetery, so Burk and his congregation decided on a picturesque slope between the church and the Schuylkill River. The cemetery was estimated to cost another $3,000 but it might actually help the Washington Memorial Chapel financially—money could be made by selling lots.

Naturally the cemetery had to be designed on a scale that would complement the planned chapel and its surrounding complex. Designers were selected to lay out the cemetery's roads and plan its landscaping. In 1911 the *Washington Chapel Chronicle* reported on progress: "The character of the place and the costliness of the development and maintenance make it impossible to compete with the cheaper cemeteries." Although "no member of the congregation will be too poor to find a resting place in God's Acre," wealthier church members were expected to subsidize the cemetery's cost.

The first lots went on sale for a $100 and $200 each, and the prices were expected to increase over time.[57] In 1911, the cemetery had its first interment—the remains of Burk's father, Jesse Y. Burk, were transferred there.[58]

Roosevelt's comparison of Valley Forge with Gettysburg had inspired Burk to consider raising a memorial to Lincoln and the Civil War at Valley Forge, and the addition of the cemetery allowed him to conceive Defenders' Gate. Defenders' Gate was to be a second complex of buildings at the cemetery's entrance mirroring the architectural style of the chapel complex and dedicated to those who had defended the Union in various conflicts. Defenders' Gate would consist of a porter's lodge and a waiting room linked by an arch honoring Lincoln. It was hoped that veterans of the Civil War, many of whom were still alive, would donate funds for the arch. The porter's lodge was quickly built, and on the fiftieth anniversary of Lincoln's first call for volunteers the first stone was laid for the Lincoln Arch.[59] The complex was never completed, and the lodge section looks rather strange today, facing sideways along Route 23 without its arch and adjoining building.

Burk's involvement at Valley Forge took up a good deal of his time and frequently took him away from his official duties at All Saints' in Norristown, where he remained rector until 1910. The wardens and vestrymen of All Saints' asked him to consider whether he was trying to do too much. Burk displayed a little testiness in a letter addressed to them, denying that his mission at Valley Forge had ever been "an incubus." He wrote: "Whatever work I did for the Mission (and I did work zealously for it) was done under the authority of the congregation [at Norristown] which every Easter Monday, from the inception of the work, by a unanimous vote requested me to divide my labors between the Parish and the Mission."[60]

It cannot be a coincidence that around this time the congregation at Washington Memorial Chapel considered breaking away from All Saints' and becoming an independent parish. Burk asked his bishop for his canonical consent. In a letter to the Episcopal bishop, the Rt. Rev. O. W. Whitaker, Burk noted that the closest established parishes in Paoli, Upper Providence, and Upper Merion all approved. He estimated that the Washington Memorial Chapel congregation of forty-five families and seventy-six communicants would be able to handle the expense of the proposed parish.[61] Within a month, Whitaker expressed the consent of the Episcopal diocese of Pennsylvania.[62] The newborn parish was left with the problem of where to house the rector, a problem that resulted in construction of the lodge portion of Defenders' Gate. Burk would temporarily live in what was supposed to become a porter's lodge.

Both before and after becoming an independent parish, Burk and his congregation spent a great deal of time and effort raising money in creative ways for the various building projects. Regular parishioners were expected to fill out pledge cards and make weekly contributions in envelopes provided by the church. On Washington's Birthday 1908, the chapel Guild hosted a "colonial supper" where they recreated Washington's winter camp outside the chapel, complete with men in uniform and horses tethered to the trees.[63] In 1910, the Guild opened a tea room to cater to summertime visitors.[64] The Guild also made frequent pleas for donations, at one point using the pages of the *Washington Chapel Chronicle* to comment on the "trying and transitional period in the growth of the Chapel."[65] Burk made his own pleas and did not exempt the younger generation. He addressed a letter to Episcopalian boys and girls in Sunday school, seeking gifts of cash for the chapel on Washington's Birthday.[66] Burk printed "founder's certificates" for those who contributed to Patriot's Hall. He also published and advertised souvenir books, such as his collection of prayers gleaned from Washington's writings and the text of Roosevelt's speech printed in the same volume with his own Washington's Birthday sermon of 1903.

After it was known that the park would take over Washington's Headquarters, Burk attempted to divert the funds that the park used to reimburse the Centennial and Memorial Association for their buildings. In September 1905, he prepared a form letter addressed to all Centennial and Memorial Association stock certificate holders. "The State will soon return to you . . . the money which you paid several years ago for the preservation of Washington's Headquarters," he explained. "Your money then did good service for Valley Forge and the Nation. Why not devote it again to the same high purpose?" He suggested that these patriotic Americans assign their money to the construction of Patriot's Hall at the Washington Memorial complex.[67] After the park laid claim to the Centennial and Memorial Association's treasury, Burk was able to get two shares of stock transferred to himself, entitling him to attend the sessions at which an independent auditor would decide how to apportion the funds. There Burk also made a claim on Centennial and Memorial Association money. The auditor's report ascribed his action to "purely patriotic motives untainted with a desire for personal profit or greedy gain."[68]

Burk's motives may have been pure, but by the time the fate of the Centennial and Memorial Association was decided in 1912, he was probably feeling desperate. Nearly ten years had passed since his Washington's Birthday sermon, and the walls of the Washington Memorial Chapel still reached no higher than the sills of its planned windows. In 1911 the Guild had used the pages of the *Washington Chapel Chronicle* to discuss whether the money they did have should be used to push the walls a little higher, hopefully priming the pump for more donations.[69] Separate donations were slowly adding bays to the chapel's adjoining cloister and at the dedication of the cloister's Delaware Bay in June 1912, Burk was handed an even more pressing reason to get the chapel done. A wealthy guest had been so moved by the ceremonies that he offered to give enough money to build the chapel's chancel, providing that funds to complete the walls were raised within one more year. The *Washington Chapel Chronicle* hopefully queried: "Another year, and will the Chapel stand forth in its beauty and strength, to challenge the admiration of the visitor and inspire the patriot?"[70]

Exactly one year later, no further work had been done on the chapel, but the *Washington Chapel Chronicle* enthusiastically reported: "The most hopeful sign for the future of this work is the organization of a committee of representative laymen of the Diocese under Bishop Garland for the completion of the chapel."[71] Not to let the chancel challenge grant get away, the Rt. Rev. Thomas J. Garland organized a fundraising committee and asked the wealthy donor to extend his deadline until December 1913. The Episcopal church hierarchy had become involved and would finally complete what Burk had been unable to accomplish alone.[72]

The summer of 1913 was one of hope and tragedy for Burk. On June 19, 1913, on the 135th anniversary of the evacuation of Washington's army, Burk optimistically officiated at the dedication of the New Jersey State panel, the first portion of the "Roof of the Republic," which would someday stretch majestically above walls the chapel did not yet have. The panel was attached to the chapel's temporary ceiling, but it seemed to promise that the building would soon be completed. Even though Burk was no longer alone in his quest, his ten-year struggle took its toll that September. The *Washington Chapel Chronicle* sadly noted: "This summer [Burk] was stricken down, and for months had done his work under conditions which are nearly impossible. A nervous breakdown is not met best in the face of overwork and overdoing."[73]

It soon became apparent that Garland's committee planned to take responsibility for Washington Memorial Chapel away from Burk. Title to the chapel was vested in three trustees, including Bishop Garland, a second Episcopal bishop, and a Charles Custis Harrison. Burk and his vestry were divested of the ability to incur debt or otherwise encumber this property.

The committee would seek out large contributions, which it would spend on the chapel itself rather than on the sum total of Burk's many planned but incomplete projects. Once built, the chapel's ownership would be transferred to trustees of the diocese. Burk, his congregation, and his vestry would merely have the privilege of using it.[74]

Charles Custis Harrison would play a significant role in getting the chapel finished. Harrison had been provost of the University of Pennsylvania and remained a trustee of that institution. His success in raising money had done wonders for the university—nineteen buildings had been constructed during his administration. Instead of writing letters, Harrison made personal appeals. He called on the wealthy and influential of Philadelphia, sending in his card and then making his pitch face-to-face. He also had an interest in history, and his wife had been a founder and president of the Colonial Dames. There is some evidence that he might have been interested in becoming a Valley Forge park commissioner. In 1905, Governor Pennypacker sent Harrison a short note that included a part of a poem: "While the bonnet is making, the face grows old, / While the dinner is waiting, the soup grows cold, / And everything comes too late." Pennypacker commented: "Why did it not occur to me some time ago? The Commissioners have all been appointed."[75]

Harrison visited Valley Forge but was not impressed by what Burk had accomplished in a ten-year period. The Washington Memorial Chapel was a "complete failure" and a "scene of desolation," he wrote, adding, "Nothing of importance had been accomplished there except the endowment of the pews."[76] When Harrison worked his usual magic, the money started rolling in. Once the effort was over and Harrison consulted his ledgers, he recorded: "I find that Mr. Burk has raised $15,000 and I had raised and paid in the sum of $206,000."[77] A contract was awarded for the completion of the building, and Burk's congregation moved the pews temporarily back to the barnboard chapel. Because this displaced the Sunday school, a little log cabin was constructed to accommodate the young people and serve as a new tea room in the summer.

Harrison's involvement helped the Washington Memorial Chapel in more ways than one. Harrison's friend, the Honorable W. U. Hensel, owned the five acres between Defenders' Gate and the chapel but had been unwilling to donate it while Burk was presiding over nothing but an unfinished symphony of projects. However, Hensel agreed to give the land to Harrison and the other trustees as soon as they raised $50,000.[78] Harrison's wife presented Washington Memorial Chapel with elm trees from Mount Vernon that were planted in the shape of a cross 200 feet long and 50 feet wide just west of the chapel, so that within a century or so the Washington Memorial would have a woodland cathedral, the chapel's stone walls acting as its sounding board. Mrs. Harrison also lent the chapel a family treasure—a strongbox she inherited that had once belonged to Robert Morris, known as the "Financier of the American Revolution."[79] Finally, Harrison himself shook loose some additional money so the cloister could be completed soon afterward.[80]

Despite all his work, Harrison felt snubbed by Burk and unwelcome at the Washington Memorial Chapel. In his memoirs he spoke of "disagreeable treatment" after the chapel had been completed. Burk, he contended, was taking credit for his own achievement. He had heard it "spoken within [his] hearing that [he] had practically nothing to do with it." He added: "I am a stranger and no longer wanted at Valley Forge for there are many who have heard both Mr. and Mrs. Burk say that Mr. Burk personally built the Chapel even to the drawing of the specifications."[81]

Harrison may have been overreacting. When Burk won the prestigious Philadelphia Award in 1928, he publicly acknowledged Harrison's contribution to the newspaper reporter who covered the story.[82] In a sermon he preached in 1929 and later published with the title "Valley Forge Miracles," Burk thanked "the splendid efforts of Dr. and Mrs. Charles Custis Harrison, who almost without aid from the Building Committee, had raised the money for this purpose [i.e., completing the chapel]."[83] In an article he wrote for the DAR magazine, he again used the words "splendid efforts" in describing Harrison's involvement.[84]

Regardless what he thought of Burk, Charles Custis Harrison described the Washington Memorial Chapel as being "without parallel in Pennsylvania."[85] On this point he and Burk agreed. Until the dedication of the National Memorial Arch in 1917, the Washington Memorial was the only monument honoring Washington in Valley Forge. In one article about the chapel, Burk commented, "We have used art to glorify religion and to illustrate history."[86]

The building itself contained enough detailed imagery and symbolism to act as an interpretive tool even when no message was being broadcast from its pulpit. Dr. Burk selected the scenes for each stained-glass medallion in the chapel's windows to conform to that window's theme, giving them the same story-telling quality as the windows of Chartres. The window over the altar illustrates the sacrifices of the life of Christ, but all the others reflect the history of the Western world. In the window whose theme is "Patriotism," a viewer can pick out Patrick Henry demanding liberty or death. The window over the front door illustrates the life of Washington and even includes a scene of the hero at prayer in the snow at Valley Forge. Stained-glass artist Nicola D'Ascenzo of Philadelphia produced the windows. In 1925, one writer said of them: "The glowing imagery of stained glass associated with perpendicular Gothic is seen [at Washington Memorial Chapel] in full perfection. In this respect the chapel is comparable to the famous Sainte-Chapelle in Paris but surpasses the European masterpiece in warmth and delicacy of execution as well as in symbolic appeal."[87] According to Burk, they were very simply "the greatest in the world."[88]

American history and the Valley Forge experience were similarly glorified in the chapel's other interior furnishings. Medary, the chapel's architect, designed the choir stalls, each honoring one of the brigades at Valley Forge and each topped by a figure of a Revolutionary soldier in the uniform of that brigade. The prayer desk was provided by the Valley Forge DAR and dedicated to the memory of Anna Morris Holstein and her accomplishments at Valley Forge. Each pew commemorated the services of some important person in colonial or Revolutionary history; descendants of the honored person usually had donated the money for construction of the pew. A pew at the front of the chapel bears the seal of the President of the United States and is reserved for the President's use on visits to Valley Forge. The President's pew is set off by a pew screen bearing the names of all of Washington's generals at Valley Forge. A close look at the name of Charles Lee reveals that it has been defaced by diagonal scratches. Burk believed Lee had planned to betray the American army, and Eleanor Burk recalled that after the wood-carver had finished Lee's name her husband ordered him angrily, "Now draw your chisel across it—the man was a traitor."[89]

Burk's "Roof of the Republic" (the chapel's ceiling) rises so high above visitors that its panels with state seals commemorating each state in the Union are hardly visible without binoculars. But visitors can find their own state panel by consulting the bronze plaques set in the floor of the church's center aisle. Outside the chapel, the cloister is divided by stonework into thirteen bays. Visitors from one of the thirteen original colonies will also find their state seal in the roof of their state's bay, as well as the corresponding colonial seal set in the floor. The cloister surrounds a garth where there is a statue by artist Bela Pratt called *Sacrifice and Devotion*, dedicated to the mothers of America.

When the chapel was completed and World War I loomed ahead, Burk intended to send the nation a message of peace from his pulpit at Valley Forge. In 1915, the *Washington Chapel Chronicle* editorialized on the situation in Europe, saying, "Before the ruthless destruction of women and children, biers heaped with babes, and morgues filled with mothers, the world stands aghast." But should America match crime with crime, the newsletter asked? Surely a quest for peace was a display of sane, moral courage, not cowardice.[90]

Once America was involved in the war, the chapel outshone the park as a source of inspiration to those headed for the trenches. According to Burk, "tens of thousands" of American soldiers visited the chapel to consecrate themselves to God and country before shipping out. Burk compared his chapel to Saint Peter's in Rome and Saint Paul's in London—it was a place people sought out before facing some tremendous challenge.[91] One day while walking outside, Burk heard the distinct sound of someone playing the chapel's organ. On investigation he found a soldier from California at the keyboard while 250 other men were singing a chorus of "America." After a rousing rendition of the "Battle Hymn of the Republic," the men dropped to their knees for Burk's blessing. Later, a few came back so that Burk could bless their swords, one of them remarking, "We are going to give a good account of ourselves there." Burk also recounted how the bereaved mothers of sons who would not be returning came to weep and draw consolation from the statue in the cloister called *Sacrifice and Devotion*.[92] Such stories inspired President Woodrow Wilson to refer to the Washington Memorial Chapel as the "shrine of the American people."[93]

After World War I, Burk added Victory Hall to the list of museum buildings he was still planning for Valley Forge. A handbill declared that Victory Hall would become "Freedom's Greatest Shrine" and tell "the story of the saving of civilization, the extension of brotherhood and the establishment of peace."[94] Burk began collecting artifacts for display and sending letters in an effort to raise money. He thanked Lieutenant Pat O'Brien for the gift of an English penny the lieutenant had carried with him through days and nights of suffering while being held prisoner behind German lines. The humble penny breathed Valley Forge's spiritual message of endurance and sacrifice and was already attracting attention at the museum.[95]

The prospects for Victory Hall did not seem promising because Burk's parish itself was in financial trouble. In 1919, the vestry enlisted the help of a local committee to personally assist in raising $10,000, needed just for operating funds. The committee sent out form letters soliciting gifts to alleviate a growing deficit. Because the Valley Forge area was by then "sparsely populated," the committee explained, it had been difficult to provide appropriate compensation for the rector, the organist, the choir, and the sexton.[96]

Around the same time, Burk was engaged in forming a new Valley Forge organization—the Valley Forge Historical Society. Burk was afraid of what might happen if some successor at the Washington Memorial Chapel lacked an interest in history and failed to maintain what he had worked so hard to establish.[97] On Evacuation Day 1918, he invited a number of friends interested in history to organize this society, which was conceived as national in scope but with state and local chapters, like the DAR. The society would publish a journal and oversee the museum and library. The Valley Forge Historical Society, however, also gave Burk a new vehicle, independent of the Episcopal diocese, which he could use for raising funds for all his other projects.

From his Washington's Birthday sermon in 1903 through his first fifteen years of involvement at Valley Forge, Burk generally had the endorsement of the Valley Forge Commission and got on well with its members. When he opened his museum in 1909 he had said: "There should exist no feelings of jealousy on the part of members of the congregation or of the Commission, as the work of each is distinct, yet complementary."[98] Indeed, the park commission had reason to be grateful to Burk because he was one of the people who had campaigned in Washington for the National Memorial Arch.

Around 1917, a rift began to open between W. Herbert Burk and the Valley Forge Park Commission. While Martin Brumbaugh held office as governor, the park commission was given the mandate to expand to 1,500 acres. Although this was then impossible, given the appropriations, a favorable legal decision empowered them to identify certain properties as future portions of the park, to be condemned at some later date when the park commission had money. Many of the remaining residents in the valley feared that the park commission would drive them from their homes. Burk, who did not have a large enough congregation to pay his operating funds as it was, must have foreseen disaster ahead for Washington Memorial Chapel. He naturally sided with the local inhabitants and against the park commission.

On Washington's Birthday 1918, Burk preached a sermon entitled "Good News for the Home Lovers of Valley Forge," which he later published in booklet form. "Here in Port Kennedy and Valley Forge you have heard the death knell of your homes and the homes of your kindred and your friends," he said. At Valley Forge, "the blinds rattle with the passing winds, the gates creak upon their rusting hinges. No longer can one hear the cheerful farmland voices, the lowing herds, the bleating sheep, the garrulous barnyard fowls, or the barking of the faithful watchdog. These are silent now and one hears only the honk of the tourist's horn." It was a "social crime," he said, to confiscate homes just to add a few acres to a park. He compared it to what the Germans had just recently done in France and Belgium.[99]

But Burk also brought good news. The park commission had asked him to inform residents that no one would be compelled to sell immediately. The commission only planned to purchase the houses of remaining residents when and if they came on the market, and to prevent their sale to outside parties. It seemed that this would preserve what was left of Valley Forge and Port Kennedy as Burk and his contemporaries knew them—at least in the short run.[100]

6

Historical Accuracy vs. Good Taste: Valley Forge in the 1920s and 1930s

In the 1920 edition of his visitors' guidebook, Dr. Burk described a dam near Washington's Headquarters where visitors could rent small boats and row all the way to a scenic bridge some distance to the south. The waters of this dam reportedly covered an older dam, which had been rebuilt, as Burk put it, "in a most substantial manner."[1] In 1896, a newspaper description of the same dam mentioned a white pole and a stone planted on opposite shores of its reservoir marking, "the site of the dam of Revolutionary times, whose exact location was disclosed when a break occurred in the present dam a few years ago."[2] Elsewhere below the water, it was believed, were the ruins of the forge that had given the valley its name.

There would be no more boating on Valley Creek after 1920, when the park commission decided to "restore" Valley Creek and the area around Washington's Headquarters. Silt had raised the valley floor considerably. The commission razed the mill where Ebenezer Lund had conducted his business, removed the tracks and piers from the unfinished trolley, and then demolished the dam. By November 1920, the park commission's Land

Committee reported: "The removal of these obstructions has resurrected the beautiful background of hills along the gorge, and reproduced the wild and picturesque landscape which helped to inspire the courage of the revolutionary soldiers to endure the hardships of that almost hopeless winter."[3]

A number of area residents held a somewhat different opinion and protested the destruction of the dam throughout 1920. Where there had once been a scenic lake much appreciated by the locals for its beauty and the pleasure it afforded, weeds were springing up in an unsightly lake bed. Some even claimed that the park commission had destroyed a relic of Washington's day because, it was believed, the dam's waters once powered a gristmill that ground grain for the Continental army. Charles E. Hires, who owned property in the area, wrote the governor and demanded that the dam be rebuilt.[4]

The park commission was forced to defend its actions. Richmond L. Jones denied the gristmill hypothesis, calling it "a fable, recently invented." This dam, he maintained, had been constructed to serve a cotton mill built between 1812 and 1814 and therefore had only sentimental value.[5] What the park commissioners needed to do, he suggested, was make people aware that the commission was restoring the Valley Forge of the winter encampment.[6]

High above the creek, where the dam had been, visitors could also observe a newly remodeled white mansion with a spacious porch shaded by a two-story colonnade, which had started life as multi-unit tenement housing for mill workers. By the end of 1920, it was occupied by the POS of A—and it was probably no accident that it looked a lot like Mount Vernon. Although such a building might have made George Washington homesick, it had certainly not existed during the winter of 1777–1778, yet the park commission did not object to its sharing the scene with the newly restored Valley Creek.

Washington Camp #150 of the POS of A had previously owned a building in the village of Valley Forge where they held meetings, maintained a library, and housed the village kindergarten. Their hall was a town meeting place, and occasionally others were permitted to use it, the way Dr. Burk been allowed to conduct his first Valley Forge services there. As the park expanded during the administration of Governor Martin Brumbaugh, the commonwealth had condemned and acquired the POS of A hall and demolished it in 1920.

But the park commission was not about to cast the POS of A out of Valley Forge. Members of the Land Committee met with POS of A representatives and worked out an agreement in which the park commission recognized the POS of A as "a patriotic society, organized to disseminate wholesome principles of life and lofty aspirations of government."[7] It further acknowledged that "Patriotic Associations are very helpful in many ways and set an example of reverence for the historic field which is very acceptable and congenial to all the visitors to the sacred shrine."[8] The Land Committee recommended that another park building be placed at the disposal of the POS of A.

The POS of A was granted the right to remodel and use a structure now called the Rogers Building but known then as the Riddle Mansion. The damages they had been awarded for their hall were used for the remodeling effort. The park commission declared that the Mount Vernon–type design they selected was attractive and appropriate for Valley Forge and, at the dedication of the structure, commended the POS of A for "restoring the natural beauty of the field."[9]

In the 1920s and 1930s, visitors to historic sites expected more accuracy and authenticity in what they saw, and restoration was being hailed more than erection of monuments. Attempts at restoration had already been made by the Centennial and Memorial Association and the park commission at Washington's Headquarters, and also by the park commission at the "Letitia Penn Schoolhouse," but these were both interior settings and individual projects. The park commission would now attempt to restore the general configuration of Valley Forge by removing modern structures and preventing any new building. At the same time, park commissioners were loath to give up the pretty park atmosphere that Valley Forge was known for. The quest for historical accuracy sometimes became the strange bedfellow of practical considerations and contemporary upper-middle-class taste, resulting in anomalies like Mount-Vernon-on-Valley-Creek. Though there was no such defined objective, the park commissioners also attempted to rid Valley Forge of outsiders who did not conform to their standards of accuracy or good taste, often leading to turmoil with people, like Dr. Burk, who had been involved at Valley Forge for what was by then a long time and who had different ideas of what visitors should find there. The character of the time as a period of transition can be seen in the interesting controversy over whether Valley Forge should have a restored working forge and, if so, where it should be located.

A good source of waterpower like Valley Creek would have attracted an eighteenth-century industry like iron manufacturing. The swiftly flowing creek never dried up and fell 25 feet in the course of its last mile. In February

1741/2, Stephen Evans and Daniel Walker purchased land in the area and, in partnership with Joseph Williams, operated a forge known as the Mount Joy Forge. In 1757, John Potts of Pottsgrove, a leading Pennsylvania industrialist, became the forge's controlling partner and later its sole owner. Potts expanded operations at Valley Forge, where workers produced wrought iron by removing the impurities from iron cast at other blast furnaces. An industrial community grew up around the forge, and the area soon had a store, a gristmill, a sawmill, a smith, and a wheelwright—businesses that were patronized by local farmers much like a modern shopping center.[10]

The sons and relatives of John Potts joined in management of the forge after 1760, and operations were expanded, probably between 1773 and 1776, under the direction of David Potts and William Dewees. Another sawmill was added, and a second forge was built, on the west side of Valley Creek. Less impressive than the main forge at the mouth of the stream, this forge allowed the Potts family to increase production, and business was good until 1777, when many workers left to take up arms for the cause of American independence.[11]

In the spring of 1777, Thomas Mifflin visited William Dewees at Valley Forge and asked that some of Washington's army supplies be stored there, where they would presumably be safe from the British army that was shortly expected to invade Philadelphia. Dewees reluctantly agreed, and his fears were justified when General Howe sailed to the head of the Chesapeake Bay and encountered the Americans at Brandywine Creek and then at Paoli. This put British scouts in the immediate area of Valley Forge, where a few men were desperately trying to move the supplies to a safer location. The British spied out their activity and sent in their light infantry, which drove off the few American defenders, and burned the forges.[12]

In 1921, while park workers were grading the area where the old mill dam had been, a civil engineer named Jacob Orie Clarke studied the Duportail map and tried to locate the remains of a forge in the area near the mouth of Valley Creek. His complaints that the grading work would prevent proper exploration were brushed aside by the park commission.[13] Grading continued, but in November the park superintendent reported an important find near the breast of the old dam. He wrote: "We [found] an old stone wall about two feet thick and the remains of an old floor built of hewed Chestnut logs, also some lumps of partly reduced iron ore, 'loups' and charcoal dust. Also broken pieces of soap stone, evidently used in a furnace hearth."[14]

The park commission concluded that these were not the remains of the forge the British had burned, but a second forge built sometime after the more important forge had been destroyed. Park Commissioner Richmond L. Jones explained to the superintendent that the ruin had "no historic value," but that it might have been part of the landscape by the time the Continental army marched away.[15] Within a month Jones concluded that it had "no relation to the military camp"[16] and was therefore not protected by the act of 1893 and no concern of the park commission. Workers continued grading the area, and most of the remains were destroyed.

More intensive efforts to locate the old forge began in 1928, when digs were started on both sides of Valley Creek. One dig explored the eastern, or Montgomery County, side of Valley Creek, about one-quarter mile from its mouth at a spot where Duportail had indicated a forge on his famous map. A second dig concentrated on a spot on the western, or Chester County, side of the stream about three-quarters of a mile from the Schuylkill.[17]

Workers made a find at the upper or western site in 1929, where the artifacts were far more exciting than those discovered eight years before. That August they unearthed the walls of what was obviously a forge and found evidence that the structure had once been subjected to fire. They uncovered the remains of a waterwheel 10 feet in diameter and a bar of pig iron marked "Andover." A frame shelter was erected to protect the ruins.[18] The same year, ruins of yet another forge were discovered at the lower site near the breast of the old woolen mill dam near where Clarke had continued investigations on his own initiative and at his own expense some years before, and where he had found traces of a millrace. Here workers found the remains of a stone building, plus a wheel pit and some timbers.[19] There were also more mundane items, such as nails, spikes, and pieces of hardware and crockery.[20]

The park now had two ruins, both thought to be pre-Revolutionary forges. Judging strictly from the artifacts found, the upper site had more to connect it with the business of ironworking. In a recent examination of research done on the ironworking industry at Valley Forge, Helen Schenck speculated that the upper forge might have been a newer forge built by the Potts family so they could experiment in forging steel.[21]

The excavations and the exciting finds prompted the park commissioners to consider locating an old forge somewhere in the park. They consulted with George W. Schultz of Reading, who had long been studying ironworking and old iron plants. Assisted by Charles B. Montgomery of the Berks County Historical Society and a park commission committee, Schultz found a forge in nearby Berks County in a quiet valley south of Birdsboro on Hay

Fig. 16.   Worker excavating one of Valley Forge's eighteenth-century forges in 1929. It is unclear whether this is the upper or lower forge. (Courtesy, Valley Forge National Historical Park)

Creek. The park commission made plans to dismantle this old forge and bring it to the valley for the entertainment and education of park visitors. [22] The park commission established a committee headed by Dr. Albert Cook Myers to decide exactly where the Berks County forge would be erected. [23] Myers produced a report suggesting that the forge be rebuilt at the lower site, near Washington's Headquarters. He did research among deeds recorded in Philadelphia, Montgomery, and Chester counties and found no reference to a forge on the Chester County side of Valley Creek. Myers concluded that the upper site was just a smaller, auxiliary plant and not the forge burned by the British. [24]

At the time, Israel R. Pennypacker was chairman of the park commission. A resident of Ardmore and a former newspaperman, Pennypacker was the brother of Governor Samuel W. Pennypacker and the son of Isaac A. Pennypacker, who had been among the first to recommend the preservation of Valley Forge. Like his brother, Israel R. Pennypacker was known as a historian and had written some works about the Civil War. Pennypacker strongly disagreed with Myers and published his own conclusions in a pamphlet. He maintained that the forge in operation in 1777—the one burned by the British and the one that gave the valley its name—had been located at the upper site. His key evidence was a history of Charlestown Township written by one of his own ancestors, Isaac Anderson, in 1802. Pennypacker attacked the Myers report with stinging words, claiming that it was full of "irrelevant matters" that only "create[d] a wilderness of words and a maze of blind paths none of which leads to a correct destination."[25] He also mentioned the practical consideration that a forge near Washington's Headquarters would clog up that area with too many tourists and vehicles. [26]

When it became obvious that Pennypacker and Myers could not resolve their conflicting views, Pennypacker suggested that the two historians submit their reports to the three lawyers on the commission, who had experience in weighing evidence, to break the tie. Judge Richard M. Koch headed up this new team, which eventually upheld the Myers view that the upper forge had been some sort of appendage to the lower forge. However, Koch concluded that both forges had been burned by the British. Pennypacker, again displeased, produced another pamphlet in which he maintained: "The Report's conclusion is offset by a mass of direct evidence to the contrary such as rarely can be assembled in regard to an historical event pertaining to a remote period of time."[27]

Jacob Orie Clarke believed that the upper forge had been built sometime after the Revolution, and he sorely resented Pennypacker's suggestion that he confine himself to the "physical facts without reference to matters of historical construction." He added, "I must confess my dismay at your evident misapprehension as to . . . the ability of an engineer to function in matters technically historical."[28] In a later letter, Clarke cautioned Pennypacker about embarrassing the park commission with his self-published pamphlets. "Printers' ink will not make authoritative any statement," he warned.[29]

In response to a circular letter from Pennypacker, Schultz questioned the value of arguing over which forge the British had burned. "Really I do not see why we should quarrel about that, because it is clear that the forge on the west side of the creek was burned as well as the one on the east side, but that the one on the east side was older."[30] In 1930, the park commission voted to install the Hay Creek forge at the upper forge site, probably for the practical purpose of spreading out the attractions that drew the tourists. Dr. Myers asked that his negative vote be recorded in the park commission minutes.[31] The project was delayed, however, because the upper forge site was at that time on private property, and it would be 1936 before the park actually acquired the site where they had been permitted to make excavations.

In the meantime, Dr. Myers studied the Hay Creek forge and expressed his opinion that it was not right for Valley Forge after all because it was neither Colonial nor Revolutionary but had probably been constructed in the 1790s or early 1800s. Furthermore, he said, it was not built of stone indigenous to the Valley Forge area—and it was really not a forge at all, but a blacksmith shop with a trip hammer powered by water where scythes and other farm tools had been made and repaired.[32]

The structure was turned over to Pennsylvania's Department of Forests and Waters, then the park commission's parent organization. For a while it was on exhibit at the state museum, but then finally retired and placed in storage, where it probably still remains. No definitive studies have determined exactly what it was, but it might have originally been a forge that was later converted to a blacksmith shop the way old gas stations and school buildings are today made over to serve other functions. Years later, Schultz lamented that his attempt to reconstruct a working forge at Valley Forge had been "blocked by politics and carpers."[33]

The bitter words spoken and written about the forge reflected the park commissioners' desire for historical accuracy, which also inspired some changes at Washington's Headquarters in the early twentieth century. In 1925, Dr. Myers asked Horace Wells Sellers, chairman of the Committee for Preservation of Historical Monuments of the American Institute of Architects (AIA) to study this building, evaluate the restoration work previously done by the Centennial and Memorial Association, and suggest changes that would accurately restore the edifice Washington had known.[34] How extensive Sellers's research was, or what it included, it is unknown today, but his recommendations led to significant changes at Washington's Headquarters. In 1926 and 1927, the reproduction log dining room was removed, a new brick floor was installed in the kitchen, cement pointing was removed from the outside walls, and shingles were substituted for tiles on the hood of the front entrance.[35] Sellers then considered removing the partition that divided the front room from the first floor hall, but Judge Koch, formerly himself a member of the Centennial and Memorial Association, protested angrily that architectural evidence indicated that the layout of the first floor had always been the way it was—two rooms and a stair hall the length of the building (a conclusion upheld by modern research)—and the partition remained in place.[36]

Sellers did succeed in making drastic changes to the kitchen wing at Washington's Headquarters. He examined the earliest available photos and engravings of the building and spoke to a seventy-eight-year-old man still living in the area.[37] In vain, he looked for the records of the previous restoration, searching for some clue as to why the Centennial and Memorial Association restorers had reduced the kitchen wing from two stories to one-and-a-half stories and separated it from the main house by the dogtrot with its arched entry. He concluded that the dogtrot made the kitchen wing unrealistically small, and he wrote Dr. Myers: "I think it is reasonable to assume that the kitchen originally extended over the whole area of the ground floor thus giving access directly from the main house."[38] On the recommendation of Sellers, the work that had been done to the kitchen wing in the 1880s was reversed. The roof was raised and a second floor was reconstructed, while the dogtrot with its arched opening was eliminated. Stairs were built to the new second floor, and a bake oven was added.[39]

In 1933, the park commission also decided that something must be done about the furnishings at the Headquarters, and Sellers advised them to remove "pieces manifestly not authentic as to period."[40] Dr. Myers discovered an inventory listing the personal effects of the husband of a Philadelphia woman named Deborah Hewes, who was related by marriage to the Potts family and who had occupied the structure at the time of the encampment.[41] Antiques dealer Arthur Sussel located objects in the proper style, and when the historic house was reopened it was praised for its aura of realism. One newspaper writer commented: "One of the chief charms of the little house is its air of being lived in. Through the open closet doors of the front ground-floor room, you can see a black Washington tricorn, black cape and sabre."[42] If an inventory was the basis for the furnishing plan, it can be argued that the interior look was indeed more historically accurate, but this praise probably indicated that the interior simply reflected the latest taste in modern conceptions of the past.

The area outside the Headquarters was also transformed. Although the intent was, as Sellers put it, to restore the "original aspect of the house,"[43] the result was more a beautification project. Between 1927 and 1934 a stone wall was replaced by a picket fence, large trellises went up on the sides of the building, and the area was landscaped with boxwood and lilacs. Dogwoods and willows were planted along the nearby creek.

In 1933, a fierce summer storm blew down a tree, damaging the roof at Varnum's Quarters.[44] The DAR members who had renovated and furnished the house and kept it open to visitors sent a check to cover damages. The park commissioners returned the ladies' money, deciding to view their misfortune as a blessing and to restore Varnum's Quarters to its eighteenth-century appearance also.

In 1934, the roof at Varnum's was lowered, eliminating the third floor, the stucco facing was removed, some windows were changed, and a porch on the north side of the house was replaced by a small pent roof.[45] The restorers had studied plans and photographs provided by the Stephens family, previous owners of the house. The park commission claimed another triumph, stating that Varnum's Quarters was "historically faithful, barring perhaps the fireplace in the second story which the architects wished to save, because it is the only considerable part of old woodwork in the house."[46] An incident purported to have occurred in 1937 seemed to confirm this enthusiasm when a couple from Carnarvon in Wales declared the house similar to many old farmhouses in their homeland.[47]

By the end of the 1930s, after work was done at Varnum's Quarters, the park changed its policy on furnishings. Commissioners decided that all objects on display at the park should be owned by the state rather than borrowed from outside organizations, such as the DAR, so commissioners began requesting that the owners of certain loaned objects reclaim them. However, the furniture DAR members had loaned for the decoration of Varnum's Quarters remained in place until the early 1960s, when the DAR donated these objects to memorialize their own role in the preservation of that historic house.[48]

Before the park acquired the house, Varnum's Quarters had been the property of the same William M. Stephens who had protested condemnation of a plot of land to accommodate a prospective Rhode Island monument. The Stephens family had lived at Valley Forge for a long time—in fact, the Stephenses claimed that William Penn himself had deeded their land to a distant Stephens ancestor. The Stephenses still owned about 100 acres around the Star Redoubt flanked by Baptist and Port Kennedy roads and extending down to the railroad tracks that ran parallel to the Schuylkill. In front of the new residence the Stephenses had built when they vacated their old home at Varnum's Quarters, they operated a hot dog stand that did enough business during the summer months to support the entire family. The park commissioners never noted exactly whether they found the modern house or the hot dog stand inappropriate for Valley Forge, but in 1918 this property was condemned. William M. Stephens was paid the purchase money but not the interest on it because his children claimed he was not its sole owner.[49] This enabled the Stephenses to continue living and selling hot dogs at Valley Forge, thanks to a state policy allowing people to remain on condemned property until all moneys due were paid.[50]

Not until the late 1920s was the park commissioners' lawyer able to prepare eviction papers and notify the Stephenses that they would be forcibly evicted if they did not vacate their house. Emily D. Stephens, the wife of William M. Stephens, later published a personal account of what transpired on May 1, 1929—eviction day for the Stephens family. She wrote that she had been at breakfast that morning with her husband and her sister Effie when two moving vans pulled up. Her husband immediately grabbed his hat and ran out to seek an injunction preventing the eviction. He instructed the women to lock the doors and fasten the windows. These precautions did not keep the sheriff out, and the ladies ran downstairs to find him and his moving men on the first floor. Mrs. Stephens wrote:

> The events of that day beggar description. I saw my most cherished possessions, the accumulations of years, handled by vandal hands, as if there was never a possibility that we would behold them again. . . . In a daze I could hear the whining of our little dog, "Lindy." It was pitiful to see how she ran and crouched under chair and table, her big brown eyes so beseeching, only to be sent scurrying hither and yon again by the intruders.

Although the sheriff assured Mrs. Stephens that her possessions would be cared for, she commented bitterly, "we found quite a number of things lying crushed in the mud of the drive that night, such as the pendulum of an antique clock, a quill pen, saucers of glass flower pots, an antique mirror with the glass shattered and a porch chair which had been broken." The family departed sadly with suitcases in hand for a hotel in Phoenixville.[51]

The drama was not over. Mr. Stephens telegraphed President Hoover, and the family appealed the case all the way to the Supreme Court, preventing the park commissioners from demolishing their empty house for another six years. It was not until 1935, two years after the death of William Stephens, that the park commission's position was upheld and the Stephens house was razed, its shade trees left standing to shade the picnic ground into which the site was transformed. The park commissioners could finally congratulate themselves on "the removal of this unsightly encumbrance in the center of the park."[52]

Park commissioners also objected to another food operation in their midst. The owner of the Washington Inn continued to operate within shouting distance of Washington's Headquarters. After Prohibition was repealed and the Washington Inn's owner applied for a liquor license, Park Commissioner Ellis Paxson Oberholtzer wrote the state Liquor Control Board to protest that the inn was "an island in a great Memorial Park, which is visited by hundreds of thousands of people each year." When spirits had been served there before Prohibition, the bar had been "the loafing place for sots," who would find their way back should the inn be granted a liquor license.[53]

The park commission also complained about the Washington Inn's exorbitant prices, prompting a new governor to take action that the park commission would find even less tasteful. The Department of Forests and Waters suggested that the park itself should provide some of the amenities available at the Washington Inn by erecting concession stands like those that could already be found at Washington Crossing Park. In 1935, Pennsylvania's new Democratic governor, George H. Earle, signed a resolution permitting the construction of two refreshment stands at Valley Forge, and by October workers were whacking stakes in at one picnic grove.[54]

A barrage of letters and telegrams immediately made their way to the office of the governor. Members of the DAR, the POS of A, and the Sons of the American Revolution were among those protesting what they considered the crass commercialization of Valley Forge. Some predicted that the governor would award the concessions as political favors for his Democratic cronies. There were also dire warnings about the types of people who would be attracted to Valley Forge. The Department of Forests and Waters blamed the original idea on certain park commissioners who had recently been replaced by Governor Earle for political reasons and who were now among the protesters. The former park commissioners denied all responsibility.[55]

The governor himself entered the "Hot Dog War" with a letter to the current park commissioners.

> There is nothing cheap or degrading about low priced food. Personally I am one of the multitude who like hot dog sandwiches. The "sacred soil" of Valley Forge would not be desecrated if visitors were permitted to purchase cheap and wholesome food in an inconspicuous, but attractive, log cabin. Indeed, I surmise that the Continental soldiers who wintered at Valley Forge would have been thankful had they had an abundant supply of "hot dogs."[56]

The governor backed down, however, and saved face by citing the 1893 resolution and guiding principle of historic preservation at Valley Forge— that the park should be maintained as nearly as possible as a revolutionary military camp. This left the issue up to the discretion of the park commissioners, who quietly voted against it in 1936. Good taste would prevail at Valley Forge, and no cheap hot dogs would entice those who could not afford to eat in a local hotel or restaurant to visit.

The park commission also removed two other private commercial interests engaged in selling other items in Valley Forge. A stand near Washington's Headquarters operated by the Union News Company through a Reading Railroad employee, which had been selling soft drinks and souvenirs, was removed with the cooperation of the president of the Reading Railroad.[57] The park commission closed another shop at the old schoolhouse where a John U. Francis had been selling gum, flags, postcards, tobacco, and the letters of Henry Woodman, which had by then been published as a book. Today the Woodman account is considered a valuable resource, but the park commissioners recorded their current opinion in their minutes with the words "It has little historical value, except as it may suggest the names of the occupants of houses and families in the neighborhood while the army was here and afterward."[58]

Their determination not to tastelessly commercialize Valley Forge backfired on the park commissioners a few years later when they decided to publish a new guidebook. Gilbert Jones, a former park superintendent and then secretary of the park commission, wrote the text, and Karl F. Scheidt of Norristown, who operated a brewery, financed the venture. Trouble arose because Scheidt printed the name of his business in very small type at the bottom of the inside cover. The park commission had to call a special session to counter accusations that the sacred shrine was now advertising beer.[59]

Commissioners withdrew the book from sale at the insistence of the governor. One commissioner blamed the storm of unexpected criticism on members of the POS of A, whose role at Valley Forge had been overlooked by the guidebook's author.[60] Scheidt solved the problem and salvaged a considerable supply of booklets by paying for the printing of little stickers that were then carefully positioned over the offensive words. Jones wrote Scheidt, "The commission always regretted that your generous act should have teen interpreted on a commercial level."[61]

The tendency of the park commissioners in the 1920s and 1930s toward restoring the eighteenth-century scene at Valley Forge placed the commissioners in direct conflict with the Rev. Dr. W. Herbert Burk, who served for a part of this period as a park commission member. Burk wanted to expand his role as chief interpreter at Valley Forge and create a learning center of sorts by making the area a combination of the present Smithsonian Museum complex and a cathedral town. From the outset of this period until his death in 1933, the animosity between Burk and the other park commissioners, especially the outspoken Israel R. Pennypacker, would grow until the issue became exactly who would determine the direction Valley Forge would take.

Early in the 1920s, with assistance from Pennsylvania's governor and attorney general, Burk pressed for legislation authorizing the park to sell him some twenty-seven to twenty-nine acres that had once been part of the Todd family farm, where he planned to erect Victory Hall, then planned as the first of his "Halls of History." He secured the approval and cooperation of the park commissioners, who at the time did not feel they needed all the land they held in the area of the Washington Memorial.[62] Burk was already raising funds to pay for this property by writing form letters addressed to "My dear Compatriot" and seeking donations from Boy Scouts, war mothers, and wealthy individuals in Montgomery County.[63] He also tried to authorize the executive board of the historical society to borrow sums for this purpose.[64]

At the same time, Burk was collecting money to expand his collections. In 1921, Burk appealed by circular letter "to the Student Body" asking for help in purchasing a private collection of Washingtoniana. His letter recommended a suggested donation of 20 cents per pupil forwarded to him by certified check. Schools that could raise $100 would receive a medal.[65] In 1923, another letter to "My dear Compatriot" invited recipients to donate toward the purchase of a "Washington's Birthday Present." The previous year, Burk reported, the society had been able to purchase a cut-glass tumbler reputedly presented by Lafayette to George Washington. Now Burk wanted to do better. He claimed, "The country is more prosperous, our nation is richer," and hopefully thousands could be raised toward the purchase of two silver camp cups, "the only luxury Washington allowed himself in that fierce struggle for freedom."[66]

Unfortunately, the legislation Burk had championed authorized but did not compel the park commission to sell him land, and the park commissioners changed their minds. Burk turned his attention to his temporary museum, where he made many improvements. The sixth annual report of the Valley Forge Historical Society, issued in 1924, took the reader on a tour. Where before there had been a single crowded room, the museum now had two rooms with new, lighted cases. A stairway led down to collections in "Indian Hall" and the "China Room," where a sizable amount of the Schollenberger ceramics collection was on display.[67] Although Burk was proud of the museum's new look, he had not stopped dreaming about Victory Hall. In 1926, he inquired about the price of land near Valley Forge village, where he toyed with the idea of situating Victory Hall on a hilltop above an imposing flight of stairs.[68]

The same year, the park commission finally opened its own museum at Valley Forge by converting the old stable near Washington's Headquarters to a display area for relics unearthed in earlier excavations and other objects. Burk protested bitterly in a letter to the chairman of the park commission, accusing the commissioners of purposely setting up a competitive museum. "Money is needed everywhere," he complained, "but at Valley Forge, it can be used to create a useless and hopelessly petty museum merely to establish a rival to a Museum known all over the Nation for its educational and inspirational service."[69] Burk publicly expressed his anger in the 1928 edition of his guidebook to Valley Forge with the statement "The Valley Forge Historical Society offered the Commission a room in the Valley Forge Museum of American History, rent free, but unfortunately this generous offer was rejected for reasons too unworthy to mention."[70]

The park commission was not likely to build a rival church at Valley Forge, but around that same time Burk was beginning to consider dwarfing his wayside chapel with a structure patterned after York Cathedral in England that would seat 5,000 people. He may have been motivated by the reluctance of his own church hierarchy to transfer title to the Washington Memorial Chapel to him. In a 1926 letter to his bishop, the Rt. Rev. Thomas

Garland, Burk questioned whether the previous transfer of title to three trustees—which had been done when funds were raised to complete the chapel—was contrary to state law.[71] Burk stated his official justification for the cathedral in a pamphlet in which he observed that the Washington Memorial was mobbed each Sunday when "hundreds of thousands press to its doors, to catch something of its service of prayer and praise." His brochure challenged the American people to donate enough money to open the new cathedral by the bicentennial anniversary of Washington's Birthday, in 1932.[72]

Burk acquired land for his cathedral when a house on land east of the Washington Memorial burned down and its former owner sold him approximately fifteen acres. On Washington's Birthday 1928, Burk broke ground in a ceremony that attracted more than 500 spectators, including many members of historical and patriotic societies. Followed by his choir and his color guard dressed in the uniforms of Washington's Life Guard, he led a procession from the chapel to the site planned for the new edifice. Shovel in hand, Burk proclaimed, "We touch this soil in the belief that we can build here a house to the honor of God and the glory of a Nation and the memory of Washington and his patriots of the Revolutionary Army."[73] Around Evacuation Day of the same year, the Free and Accepted Masons dedicated the cornerstone for Burk's Valley Forge cathedral.

Burk's plans for a cathedral came as a surprise to Bishop Garland. In the Episcopal church, a cathedral was defined as the church of a bishop, and only a bishop was entitled to erect one. What was more, the Pennsylvania diocese of the Episcopal church had already selected a site for a cathedral in Roxborough, not at Valley Forge, where, Garland believed, the weekly congregation was made up of tourists and sightseers. A park commission report quoted Garland as saying that at Valley Forge "all the church had ever desired was a little shrine in the woods, more ambitious plans being without the church's sanction."[74]

Even the little shrine irked Israel R. Pennypacker of the park commission, who expressed his own view in print, as usual, in a 1926 article written for *American Mercury* magazine. Pennypacker claimed that the presence of any type of church was "unhistorical" because there had been no church at Valley Forge in Washington's time. He further maintained that Burk's church did not serve the community of Valley Forge, where most of the remaining residents were not Episcopalians. Burk, Pennypacker charged, was drawing his crowd from the wealthy Main Line suburbs of Philadelphia and giving local people the impression that "their presence would be more welcome at the 'cathedral' services if they could afford to drop five or ten dollar bills into the collection plate."[75]

Pennypacker's feelings about Burk and his operations were echoed by others, including H. W. Kriebel, whose letter to the editor of the *Philadelphia Bulletin* was reprinted as a handbill titled "Valley Forge, a National Problem." Kriebel accused Burk of forming a holding company for his various enterprises, competing with the park for land, and filling his museum with objects of questionable authenticity and his property with inappropriate memorials. "The very presence of the chapel," Kriebel wrote, "is an affront to American citizens whose religious convictions are not in accord with the sentiments this organization represents."[76]

An ongoing feud arose between Burk and some of the other commission members, with bitter battles over such tangential issues as where Burk's parishioners were supposed to park their cars. Many people visiting the Washington Memorial and the nearby 1901 monument to the unknown dead customarily parked on the grass outside the chapel or across the road from it. This land belonged to the park, and the park commissioners established a Parking Committee, which resolved that the state had no obligation to provide facilities for a private institution. The committee also suggested that the cars were tearing up what might well be the graves of Revolutionary soldiers.[77] Burk had tried to counter by proposing a resolution that research be done to document the existence of these supposed graves, and that the park commission "place a permanent stone marker at every grave found in this tract."[78] Burk stated in no uncertain terms to members of the press that the park commissioners were actually opposed to the very existence of his chapel. He was quoted as saying, "One of the investigating committee I know would like to take down the edifice and throw it into the Schuylkill River, stone by stone."[79] In another article, appearing on the same day, Pennypacker was quoted as replying: "Oh—Dr. Burk! I'd prefer not to go into personalities. Dr. Burk has had fourteen nervous breakdowns and it is hard sometimes to follow just how his mind does work."[80] Burk petitioned the governor, but in the end the area opposite the Washington Memorial was planted with grass, and parking there was prohibited by signs.[81]

The key issue underlying the years of conflict between Dr. Burk and some of the park commissioners was whether the park would swallow up what was left of the two communities of Port Kennedy and Valley Forge and all the territory between them, transforming the area according to their conception of the eighteenth-century Valley Forge and necessarily quashing Burk's plans for the cathedral. By the mid-1920s, park commissioners were aware that builders were planning residential communities at Valley Forge like the one called "Valley Forge Manor" touted in a brochure as a "sportsman's paradise" and an "ideal home community."[82] The park commission used such schemes to justify additional condemnations in the area of Valley Forge village, warning that building developments would "destroy with commonplace houses the natural and beautiful surrounds and make forever impossible the preservation of what now can be preserved."[83] Pennypacker expanded on this statement, speaking of "the menace of bungalow development, of booze parties, of a litter of cans and refuse."[84] By the late 1920s the park commissioners sought sizable appropriations with the objective of new expansion for the park.

As a park commissioner, Burk was consistent in his opposition to park expansion plans. At one point he asked that his vote against plans of the park commission's Land Committee be recorded in the minutes because, he said, their program was "unhistorical and unsocial."[85] He could not see why the park should be any bigger than the winter encampment appeared to have been according to then available documents. He expressed this opinion in a pamphlet titled "What Shall We Do With Valley Forge?" which he personally distributed to members of the state legislature in Harrisburg. Washington, Burk wrote, "never placed any of his men in a swamp. Yet a swamp, filled in with cinders, was part of the ground purchased for Valley Forge Park." Burk came close to making charges of graft with the words "Shall [Valley Forge] become a thin excuse for a raid upon the treasury of the Commonwealth, or shall it be kept as a sacred trust for the Nation?"[86] The park's planned expansion led to Burk's resignation from the park commission early in 1929.

Burk faced his greatest challenge from the park commission later that year when the park commissioners voted on whether to condemn the very land he had already purchased for his cathedral and where he had erected its cornerstone. Park commissioners were divided on the issue, 6 voting yea and 6 voting nay. This meant that the resolution did not pass, and Burk expressed his gratitude in a sermon titled "Valley Forge Miracles," in which he thanked his saviors by claiming, "They stood out against the enemies of religion and patriotism." He went on to state that all the land connected with the Washington Memorial was dedicated to the American people and that "only eyes blinded by jealousy, greed and bigotry have failed to see this."[87] Around the same time, Burk found himself fighting a more personal battle when the park commission condemned property belonging to his wife plus another parcel owned by Frank Quigg, a member of his vestry. The park commission did not object when a jury of view awarded more for these properties than they wanted to pay.[88] Settlements were made, and by the end of 1931 structures on these two properties were razed.[89]

The same year, conflict arose over who would get to host President Herbert Hoover at Valley Forge: the park commission or Dr. Burk. Roosevelt's 1904 visit had attracted a good deal of attention for Burk's little chapel, and in 1921 President Harding had visited the Washington Memorial where he spoke at the dedication of the Rhode Island bay in the cloister. In 1929, the Valley Forge Historical Society voted to make President Hoover an Honorary Perpetual Life Benefactor of the society and invited him to visit the Washington Memorial to receive this honor.[90] In the spring of 1931, while President Hoover was actually planning such a visit to Valley Forge, the park commission voted to invite him to inspect Washington's Headquarters while he was in the area.[91] Somehow the President changed his plans, and his visit to the Washington Memorial became a visit to the park.

Israel Pennypacker was delighted to receive the President's acceptance and the news that Hoover would deliver a Memorial Day address at Valley Forge.[92] In preparation for the visit, the park commission erected a platform near the farmhouse now known as Huntington's Quarters, literally across the road from the Washington Memorial, and furnished a parlor there for the President's use.[93] Burk complained, "The Valley Forge Park Commission has found some way to have it act as his host in spite of the fact that he is an Honorary Perpetual Benefactor of our Society and was to have received his gold insignia here on Memorial Day."[94] The final insult came when Burk received a letter from a park commission member saying that officials in Washington had already been assured that he would not even ring the church bells at the Washington Memorial before and after the President's speech, as he had been planning to do.[95]

A special train brought President Hoover to Valley Forge, and a motorcade conducted him along Outer Line Drive to the National Memorial Arch and finally to the speaker's platform. The President's speech remains one of the strongest and best ever delivered at Valley Forge, skillfully linking the Valley Forge experience to America's then very depressed economy. "The American people are going through another Valley Forge at this time," he said. "To each and every one of us it is an hour of unusual stress and trial." Stressing a point he would make many times in his administration, Hoover observed that there were no panaceas, and that the American people did not collectively owe each individual a living. At Valley Forge, Washington and his men too might have surrendered to despair, but chose instead to conserve their strength and husband their resources. Similarly, America now depended on "the inventiveness, the resourcefulness and the initiative of every one of us. . . . God grant that we may prove worthy of George Washington and his men of Valley Forge."[96] Dr. Burk did not have a seat on the speakers' platform, and the invocation that day was delivered by the Episcopal bishop, the Rt. Rev. Francis M. Tait. Before the President departed, however, Burk did manage to present him with a bouquet of thirty red roses, which was enough to get his own name in the news.[97]

The American people would survive the depression, but Burk did not. He died on June 30, 1933, and was buried in the churchyard behind the Washington Memorial. The president of the American Friends of Lafayette condoled the officers of the Valley Forge Historical Society with the words "It is a distinct loss to those who are interested in keeping alive the traditions of our Country, when a real enthusiast falls out of the ranks."[98] Burk's cathedral essentially died with him. The few physical remains of his ambitious plans include the cornerstone now hidden by thick undergrowth in a wooded area of the Washington Memorial property, and a statue Burk intended for cathedral decoration.

In 1931, Burk had obtained permission from the governor of Virginia to make a bronze cast of the famous statue of Washington by Jean Antoine Houdon in the state capitol at Richmond. Burk had hoped that President Hoover would dedicate it during his visit to Valley Forge that spring— another dream that never came true.[99] This statue was still standing at the cathedral site in the 1940s when the park commissioners considered acquiring their own statue of Washington for the park but doubted that funds could be secured for this purpose.[100] Burk's statue apparently fell into park hands when the commissioners purchased a few acres of Washington Memorial land.[101] It was placed at Huntington's Quarters, but in 1957 plans were made to move it to Washington's Headquarters, where it was mounted on a base and attractively landscaped and considered quite tasteful, until it was removed in the interests of historical accuracy. It is now in the park's Visitor Center.

Until his death, Burk optimistically continued collecting artifacts and hoping to expand his museum operations. In 1930, the volunteer firemen of Pennsylvania were raising money for a museum of fire-fighting apparatus, to be located on the Washington Memorial grounds.[102] The following year, the historical society purchased another of its treasures, the 1883 painting titled *Washington Reviewing His Troops at Valley Forge* by W. T. Trego. The directors of the society, however, soon felt the effects of the depression and had to call special meetings to determine what could be done when people began

Fig. 17. Valley Forge's replica of Jean Antoine Houdon's statue of George Washington. Burk hoped it would adorn the cathedral he planned for Valley Forge. For a number of years, the statue was placed outside Washington's Headquarters. Today, it is located in the Visitor Center. (Courtesy, Valley Forge National Historical Park)

neglecting to pay their membership dues, causing debts to mount. A few months after Burk's death, the society sent a form letter asking recipients to donate money for coal to heat the museum.[103] As the difficult 1930s continued, without the enthusiasm and leadership of Dr. Burk, collecting virtually ceased. In 1938, the historical society reported a lack of funds for the purchase of artifacts, "owing largely to the depression."[104]

Burk did live long enough to see the demise of the expansion plans proposed for the park between 1927 and 1929. In the summer of 1929, Pennsylvania's governor informed the park commission that no funds were available for extending the park,[105] and they were not forthcoming two years later when the park commission sought $100,000 to purchase land.[106] As a result, the Land Committee considered raising its own funds "from the general public for the acquisition of land needed for the proper completion of the park."[107] They even took a lesson from Dr. Burk, contemplating the sale of certificates to public school students.[108] But neither scheme was carried out.

Dr. Burk also lived long enough to see his old enemy, Israel Pennypacker, removed from the park commission. When Governor Gifford Pinchot took office, he decided to purge the appointed officials and state employees he had inherited from the previous administration of rival Republicans. Early in 1932, members of the park commission got letters asking them to continue to serve but demanding that they sign a loyalty pledge to the governor's platform. Most refused, and Governor Pinchot named newcomers to the park commission. Pennypacker later lamented those who had been replaced, describing them as "a number of the most interested, best informed and most diligent of the members of the Commission."[109]

By the end of the transition period of the 1920s and 1930s, the evolution thus far of Valley Forge as a historic site had created a strangely eclectic landscape. In a 1936 book called *The Blue Hills*, Cornelius Weygandt wrote:

> The hills of Valley Forge were far more beautiful in my youth than they are to-day. Then there was no intrusion of a Gothic church, of an architecture alien to eighteenth century America; and then the countryside was still a typical stretch of Pennsylvania farm country. Now large portions of the park look like a cemetery without graves. Gettysburg has been preserved as Pennsylvania farm country. Valley Forge has suffered the indignity of being transformed into a "park."[110]

Unknown to the author, the park commission was formulating plans that would transform it even more.

Fig. 18. Dr. Burk's grave, behind the Washington Memorial Chapel. The marker lists his many accomplishments.

7

The "Complete Restoration" of Valley Forge

"All roads will lead to Valley Forge," the local newspaper said on June 21, 1935. The story described yet another dedication ceremony that would transpire the following day. Once again guns would boom and patriotic speeches would be delivered. Those attending would also witness a high-tech tribute to Valley Forge when the National Guard piloted a squadron of fighter planes overhead.[1]

This time, the structure being so honored was not a historic house or an imposing monument, but a small log hut built by the Pennsylvania Society of the Sons of the Revolution based on considerable research by architect D. Knickerbocker Boyd. Boyd was then near the end of his career, and today is remembered primarily for the private homes he designed on the Philadelphia Main Line. Under Boyd's direction but without the involvement of an archaeologist, a still-visible hut hole had been cleared of its accumulated debris, and an original hardpan dirt floor had been uncovered. The reproduction hut had been constructed according to George Washington's express orders and positioned precisely over this floor; the hut's replica fireplace stood exactly where deposits of charcoal had been found.

Optimistically calling it "Valley Forge Hut No. #1," the Sons hoped it would inspire other patriotic groups to erect additional huts, eventually creating "an entire 'company street' of Revolutionary huts on the sacred ground where Washington's men bled and starved during the severe winter."[2] Its dedication marked the outset of a new phase of historic preservation roughly from 1935 through the 1950s, when the park commissioners would institute a major development program known as the "complete restoration" of Valley Forge. Actually, the complete restoration was a mixed bag of projects, but strategic groupings of log huts constituted a key component.

Years later, once the building program was under way, editor Gilbert Jones made several comments in the Valley Forge Historical Society's journal indicating why log huts were so important to Valley Forge at that time. Jones congratulated the park commission on its efforts to construct a "living re-creation of this historic scene" so that "the future may learn from the past."[3] Jones later commented that visitors in the past had been disappointed to find so little to see at Valley Forge. He wrote: "A marker is not graphic enough for the average person and he carries away only a hazy idea of Washington's historic Encampment."[4] Jones observed that recent visitors had been considerably more inspired by that original dirt floor in the 1935 hut. Jones's language linked the floor to one of Valley Forge's sacred symbols when he spoke of its being "trod by many bleeding feet that historic winter."[5] In the same article, Jones mentioned the historic sites of Williamsburg and New Salem Village. Surely Valley Forge too could transport the visitor back in time. This would be "the finest of all tributes to the free men who fought not with weapons of warfare, but in the Spiritual battle at Headquarters, in Huts, on Parade Ground and behind Entrenchments at Valley Forge."[6]

His key word was "Williamsburg," the extraordinary project directed and financed by John D. Rockefeller Jr. mainly during the late 1920s and into the 1930s. With the help of experts and considerable archaeological and documentary research, Williamsburg went far beyond the restoration of a single house or building; it was the attempted re-creation of an entire colonial town. The project had been started in secrecy when Rockefeller authorized a local minister to begin buying up property anonymously. Buildings that predated the late eighteenth century were restored, but a far greater number of more recent origins were summarily demolished.[7] The result was a kind of movie set peopled with costumed guides performing the

Fig. 19.   One of the first replica huts at Valley Forge. In the absence of surviving structures, such reproductions were meant to give visitors something tangible to see. This one was constructed in 1905 by the Daughters of the Revolution and can be seen today near the Washington Memorial Chapel. (Courtesy, Valley Forge National Historical Park)

crafts of a bygone era. Visitors were literally drawn into the past, and America's imagination was truly captured.

In his book *Preservation Comes of Age*, Charles B. Hosmer Jr. writes of the enormous influence that Williamsburg had on historic preservation. By the 1930s it was considered a national trust and a place where those administering other sites could come for ideas and advice. It got a great deal of exposure in newspapers and magazines and was considered a success by every standard.[8] In more recent times, however, Williamsburg has been criticized. In an article titled "Visiting the Past," Michael Wallace contends that it did not show a visitor a true cross section of society. "Rockefeller was not the least bit interested in recapturing the culture of 'the folk,'" he writes. "This town commemorated the planter elite, presented as the progenitors of timeless ideals and values, the cradle of that Americanism of which Rockefeller and the corporate elite were the inheritors and custodians."[9] In a recent article in the *New York Review of Books*, Ada Louise Huxtable criticizes the use of an arbitrary cut-off date at Williamsburg. She writes:

> Once a "cut-off date" has been chosen for a project, the next step is to "restore it back"—to use preservation-speak. "Restoring it back" means re-creating the place as someone thinks it was, or would like it to have been.

The "selective fantasy" that results she links to the birth of theme parks: "Certainly it was in the restoration of Colonial Williamsburg that the studious fudging of facts received its scholarly imprimatur and history and place as themed artifact hit the big time."[10]

In the 1930s, however, such voices were not being raised against Williamsburg or Henry Ford's Greenfield Village. Greenfield Village was another attempt to re-create the past on a large scale, but one that would illustrate the lot of the common man: the blacksmith, the farmer, or, as Wallace puts it, "the sturdy pioneers."[11] Greenfield Village profited from the populist tendencies of the 1930s, a time when the lesser figures of American history, such as Paul Revere, were being rediscovered, and when less emphasis was put on the deeds of heroic individuals—while collective group efforts were increasingly glorified.[12]

Valley Forge could perhaps not aspire to the architectural magnificence or genteel lifestyle that had been re-created at Williamsburg, but it was believed to be a place where a great many sturdy, common soldiers had collectively developed as an army. In the late 1930s, the time was ripe for Valley Forge to move beyond the relatively conservative, piecemeal restoration projects of the recent past with a single, coordinated project designed to actually re-create the winter encampment the same way that towns had been re-created at Williamsburg and Greenfield Village. In 1936, the commission finally sounded the death knell of the era of monuments by resolving that no additional monuments would be erected in the park, although those already in the park would be maintained and their landscaping improved. In the words of the commission report for that period, "The Commission did not approve any suggestions for the erection of monuments and expresses its opinion that restoration, where possible within reasonable historical accuracy is the better plan for memorializing the Valley Forge encampment."[13]

Park commissioners needed no new mandate or legislation to justify their plans. They reinterpreted the language of the 1893 legislation creating the state park, which charged that future custodians maintain Valley Forge as nearly as possible in its "original condition as a military camp." This mandate would now be taken literally by park commissioners, who believed that they were finally doing what Pennsylvania's lawmakers had envisioned more than a generation earlier.

The "complete restoration" began with yet another attempt to enlarge the park. In November 1936, Governor George H. Earle announced intentions to finally acquire the entire area believed to have been occupied by the Continental Army, plus surrounding parcels of land, increasing the park's size by some 3,500 acres. The governor revealed that the Pennsylvania legislature would be asked for $350,000 immediately and $1,050,000 over a period of three years. Earle explained, "The land itself not only will be cheaper now, but we will be saving the cost of any buildings erected in the meantime. Building here is advancing with recovery."[14] The governor's plans were considerably scaled back by his successor.

Governor Earle wanted the federal government to foot the bill for the "complete restoration," which initially called for reconstruction of miles of entrenchments and the building of hundreds of soldiers' huts. The governor explained: "I hope the CCC, meanwhile, will be able to restore the old camp to its Revolutionary character. I will confer Monday with James F. Bogardus, Secretary of Forests and Waters, preparatory to asking CCC aid."[15] The Civilian Conservation Corps (CCC) was part of the U.S. Department of the Interior and one of the many job-generating programs of President Franklin Roosevelt's "New Deal." The CCC placed individuals in state and national parks and sites of historic interest under the supervision of the National Park Service. The governor's initial plans for federal aid fell through, however. In December 1936, Conrad L. Wirth, chief of the CCC, reported that current regulations forbade the opening of any additional CCC camps. If, however, the CCC was reorganized the following year, a Valley Forge camp might be considered.[16] This opinion was echoed by Emergency Conservation Director Robert Fechner, who also urged Earle to enlist the aid of the National Park Service.[17]

As soon as the governor's plans were made public, they came under fire from the same element that had so loudly protested a perceived commercialization of Valley Forge in the governor's hot dog stands. Though some of the protesters had previously been proponents of individual restoration projects, they did not like the sound of this larger-scale effort and they used the same reasoning that can be found in Huxtable's modern criticism of Williamsburg—that such a project would re-create too arbitrary a vision of the past, perhaps at the expense of genuine artifacts. Former Park Commissioner Dr. Ellis Paxson Oberholtzer used the words "desecration" and "abomination" to express his opinion. "To touch the inner line entrenchments as they stand would be a crime," he said. "They are the only untouched thing of camp days in the park." As for the log huts, Oberholtzer commented:

> About them there is scanty knowledge at best. The whole thing would be unhistorical. This chaste, simple landscape, the ideal which we have had before us for years, would be marred by ugly structures. Valley Forge would be an exposition instead of a beautiful piece of Pennsylvania countryside. Every historical and patriotic association in the States should rise up in protest against such desecration of an American shrine. [18]

Dr. Albert Cook Myers said, "The data is insufficient to do as the Governor proposes. It would be much better to leave such restoration alone. . . . Let them protect and preserve what they already have."[19] Lawrence C. Hickman, president of the Sons of the American Revolution, professed himself to be "bewildered":

> Even if they had sufficient data, I don't see how the reconstruction could be done with thousands of dollars' worth of monuments and the Washington memorial arch already standing. How could they do it? It would certainly be incongruous to put up huts around the modern monuments. Or would they tear down these expensive markers put up by various States and organizations?[20]

The "complete restoration" never did get off the ground in the 1930s, for lack of funds, not because of philosophical opposition. Valley Forge had no John D. Rockefeller Jr., nor was money forthcoming from the CCC, the National Park Service, or the Department of the Interior. From June 1935 through June 1937, the state legislature also slashed Valley Forge's maintenance appropriation from its previous level of $60,000 to $25,000. Between June 1937 and June 1939 it was raised, but only to $35,000.[21]

But the people serving as park commissioners during this period would not let their idea die. They continued to develop plans, sketches, and man-hour estimates. Gilbert Jones kept mentioning restoration plans on his extensive rounds as public speaker, and he was often quoted by the local press. In 1938, he spoke before the Pottstown National Guard Unit, saying, "Valley Forge Park is a shrine, not a cemetery, and it should be restored to its original condition instead of erecting tablets and monuments."[22] In 1939, Jones spoke to the Norristown Kiwanis Club and commented on the difficulty of securing funds: "Everyone wants to wave a flag at Valley Forge but very few want to pay for the flag."[23] In a book on Valley Forge published in 1938, author Harry Emerson Wildes mentioned that plans for the restoration were still alive and that Williamsburg was evidence of what could be done.[24]

In 1941 and 1942, the park completed a few scattered restoration projects with its meager funds. Several replica fortifications were built, including the structures then known as Fort Mordecai Moore and its two flanking redans; the Stirling Redoubt; two redans flanking Fort Washington; and a rifle pit on the inner line entrenchments. These projects were done without significant preliminary archaeological research and are now considered questionable, but at the time the park commission saw that public interest was high, which encouraged the commissioners in their determination to do more at Valley Forge.[25]

In 1942, the park commission drew up a new resolution to restore Valley Forge as a military camp as soon as "the general conditions permit." This resolution included plans to complete all entrenchments and forts and to plant ten log huts on each of four sites where four different divisions had camped. In the area where the Continental Army had massed their artillery, visitors would find a colonial blacksmith shop and stable. General Von Steuben's Quarters would be restored. Guardhouses and picket posts would be added to the scenery. Field ovens would be built. The "lost redoubt" known as Fort John Moore would be located and restored. Known redans, lunettes, and abatis would rise at their original locations. Two projects that had interested former park commissions would finally be completed: a working forge would be built, and the Washington Inn would be restored to its colonial appearance with the hospital quarters and bake ovens it had supposedly housed during the encampment. For the practical convenience of twentieth-century visitors, there would be new parking places, latrines, and recreational areas, as well as improvements to the roads. The park would have a new administration building and a new observation tower built of stone. The total cost was estimated at a whopping $500,000.[26]

The resolution was presented to Pennsylvania's Governor Edward Martin late in 1942. No immediate action was taken, and the commission renewed its recommendation in 1943. At that time, the state was planning the re-employment of its men and women once the war was over. The park commissioners hoped to do their part by finally making available the jobs

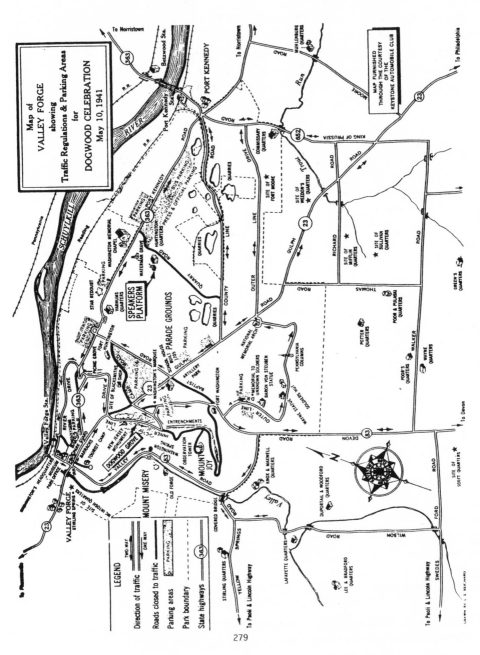

Fig. 20. Map of Valley Forge in 1941. (Courtesy, Valley Forge National Historical Park)

279

that they had so long wanted to create at the park. While Governor Martin promised that the matter would receive attention, again nothing was done, causing the park commission to wonder whether Valley Forge had become the commonwealth's stepchild.[27] It was May 1944 before the state's postwar planning commission finally considered the park commission's extensive plan. In July 1944, General Shannon of the park commission met with the chairman of the postwar planning commission and returned to report: "It is likely this important work will be accomplished under the present administration if the war emergency shall be terminated."[28]

The war ended in 1945, and Valley Forge finally got some money. In May 1946, Governor Martin visited Valley Forge to confer with the park commissioners, and in July word was received that Governor Martin had approved $135,000.[29] This was good news, but $135,000 was only a fraction of what it would cost to complete all the projects in the 1942 resolution, which by then carried a price tag of $650,000. After James H. Duff was elected governor of Pennsylvania in November 1946, he was quickly invited to Valley Forge to reaffirm the state's commitment.[30] Early in 1947 Duff appropriated $140,000. The governor made available an additional $271,500 from postwar appropriations under Act 83-A.[31]

The restoration at Valley Forge could at last proceed, but it would not be quite as "complete" as originally intended. Plans were scaled down to include a new observation tower built of stone, the rediscovery and restoration of Fort John Moore, a blacksmith shop in the artillery park, plus seventy-four log huts. Plans for the tower were subsequently scrapped to release funds for other projects. The number of huts was later reduced to thirty, and the project of acquiring the Washington Inn and restoring it to its colonial appearance was again added to the list.

In October 1946, Norris D. Wright, chairman of the Park Commission, received a letter from George Edwin Brumbaugh acknowledging his appointment as architect for the "improvements to Valley Forge Park." Brumbaugh wrote: "During the coming week I shall telephone in order to make an appointment at your convenience for our first conversation. It will be a real pleasure to work with you to secure the best results of which we are capable, for this most important historic spot."[32] Brumbaugh was one of the nation's best-known preservation architects. He had restored or reconstructed many historic sites throughout the Delaware Valley. Coincidentally, his father, Martin Brumbaugh, had been one of Valley Forge's first park commissioners, and later the Pennsylvania governor who had delivered the acceptance speech at the dedication of the National Memorial Arch. During George

Edwin Brumbaugh's childhood, his family had rented a summer house on Gulph Road, not far from Washington's Headquarters. Together with the young son of the caretaker at the Headquarters, Brumbaugh had amused visitors with informal tours, which he conducted for a nickel tip. He and his father had often roamed over the remaining entrenchments and wandered along Valley Creek to the site of the old forge.[33] If any architect had a personal interest and a commitment to Valley Forge, it was Brumbaugh.

At the time Brumbaugh began his work at Valley Forge, there was little evidence indicating exactly what the soldiers' huts had looked like. Washington's hut specifications were a key source and had been used when the 1935 hut was built. On December 18, 1777, Washington had written:

> Soldier's huts are to be of the following dimension, viz: fourteen by sixteen each, sides, ends and roofs made with logs, and the roof made tight with split slabs, or in some other way; the sides made tight with clay, fire-place made of wood and secured with clay on the inside eighteen inches thick, this fireplace to be in the rear of the hut; the door to be in the end next to the street; the doors to be made of split oak-slabs, unless boards can be procured. Side-walls to be six and a half feet high.[34]

Brumbaugh studied both Washington's orders and a poem that had appeared in an 1863 issue of *The Historical Magazine*. The poem, supposedly written by the camp surgeon, Albigence Waldo, was titled "Valley Forge" and dated April 26, 1778, a time when surviving muster rolls show that such a person was indeed at Valley Forge. The original copy has never been located, however. Among the poem's sentimental and florid words, there was a forty-four-line description of a hospital hut at Valley Forge, but one that had many comfortable features never specified in Washington's orders, including an oak floor, three windows, and a separate kitchen.[35]

As for actual physical evidence, there was none. By the late 1940s, even the structure in ruins on the old road to the river ford Dr. Burk had named the "last hut" and pictured in his guidebooks published early in the century was gone. All that remained of the huts at Valley Forge was, perhaps, a single log. In 1935, the Pennsylvania Society of the Sons of the Revolution acquired a seven-foot log that was purportedly part of one of the huts at Valley Forge. It too had inspired poetry. Frank E. Schermerhorn had written an ode to the log and the things it had "seen," concluding, "You listened, high in eery-raftered poise / To starving-tales with deeds of courage done /

That turned the storm-wind's ghostly, rumbling noise / To chants of God who gave us Washington."[36]

Besides tradition and documentary evidence, Brumbaugh studied the several log hut replicas that Valley Forge already had, in addition to the 1935 model. The National Society, Daughters of the Revolution of 1776 had led the way back in 1905 by building a replica near the Washington Memorial on the site of an actual hut originally built by soldiers of the Fourth Connecticut Regiment. In July 1905, newspapers reported that the structure had been "dedicated in the presence of a few persons, no public notice having been given of the event."[37] This organization restored their hut in 1945–1946 and again in 1968. Few records regarding the replica of a hospital hut built by the park commission around 1910 near the Wayne statue exist. Even this date is suspect, because the *Philadelphia Record* carried a story about it in September 1909, describing its popularity with visitors when park guard James McGroury played surgeon there.[38] In 1922, the Washington Memorial acquired a second log structure built by the World War I survivors of the 314th Infantry of the 79th Division. This was not really a hut, but rather the regiment's old recreation hall, originally constructed at Camp Meade and moved to Valley Forge to house the mementos of these men, most of whom had come from Pennsylvania. Dr. Burk had welcomed this mini-museum, hoping eventually to incorporate it into Victory Hall. He patriotically charged the veterans a ground rent of only one red rose a year. Until death claimed most of the men, the log structure served as their weekend gathering place.[39] The park also had its guard huts, small log cabins built as field bases for park guards on patrol. Ten or eleven of these had been constructed between 1906 and 1911; others were added in 1939 and 1946.[40]

The 1905 hut, the circa 1910 hospital hut, the 1935 hut, and a copy of the 1935 hut built in 1946 as a guard hut were all supposed to be replicas of what American soldiers had spent their famous winter in. These huts all looked very different, however, and the authenticity of each interpretation had or would come under attack. The 1909 newspaper story about the hospital hut quoted one woman's remark that this hut was a better replica than the daughters' 1905 model, "as the latter smacks of a darkey's cabin."[41] The hospital hut would later be criticized for having too many windows and too tall a door. Brumbaugh would criticize the 1935 hut for its low walls, windows, and iron hardware. Washington's orders, which seemed so precise, left a good deal of room for interpretation.

In response to the park commission's exhortation that the "huts should be authentic in every particular,"[42] Brumbaugh drew largely on Washington's orders and his own considerable knowledge of early American log construction and local precedents. He employed John J. Rogers as a general foreman and set up a log hut workshop in the former dining room of the old Washington Inn, which had finally been acquired by the park in the late 1930s. There Brumbaugh designed a sample hut to teach his twentieth-century workers some long-forgotten skills. His original plan was to build each hut in the dining room, then knock it down and rebuild it on site. His first huts were to be erected near Washington's Headquarters, where the commander-in-chief's guards had been housed. All workers were ordered to inspect these initial huts frequently.[43] Brumbaugh's specifications, including requirements for wooden hardware, handwrought nails, and fireplaces made of irregular local stone, showed his mania for detail. Logs were to be cut from trees in the park and to be "handled and shipped carefully to ensure minimum damage to the bark."[44]

The huts were to be located throughout the park at the places where soldiers had originally built them. A few huts each would mark the positions of General Maxwell's New Jersey Brigade, General Varnum's Rhode Island Brigade, General Woodford's Virginia Brigade, General Poor's New York and New Hampshire Brigade, General Muhlenberg's Virginia and Pennsylvania Brigade, General Learned's Massachusetts Brigade, and General Wayne's Pennsylvania Brigades. Muhlenberg's Brigade would have the largest number of huts, and it was hoped that eventually some officers' huts, a hospital hut, and a shop could be added at this location. The huts were to be positioned according to the Duportail map, which implied that eighteenth-century soldiers had neatly aligned their huts in orderly company streets.

As the first huts began to appear, they generated much public excitement—evidence of America's continuing interest in the history of the common experience. Previous generations of visitors to Valley Forge had been greatly moved by Washington's Headquarters; modern-day visitors found the huts where ordinary soldiers had been quartered equally inspiring. Valley Forge even made the *New York Herald Tribune* when a reporter mused, "The visitor wonders what the ragged troops, as they erected their huts in the snow of 1777, would have thought if they were told that some day men would build a monument to them—not of stone, or bronze, but of the same rough local tree trunks, shaped to form reproductions of those crude shelters they were building."[45]

Hut-building went slowly, causing Brumbaugh to feel some pressure from the park commission. Brumbaugh reported delays in getting good labor, and in May 1947 the park superintendent, Milton Baker, expressed his concern that if the huts were not erected quickly enough the state government might take the park's appropriation away. "I am certain that Mr. Brumbaugh is a well qualified architect and will do a fine piece of historical research but I am fearful that he does not recognize the importance of the time element in this project," Baker wrote.[46] Brumbaugh's difficulties continued, and by July only one complete hut was visible on the site of Washington's guards' quarters.[47] In October, Brumbaugh reiterated his labor problems and also mentioned problems getting materials and equipment. Other, more interesting delays were encountered. Bones were found at the excavation for one hut foundation, which stalled the job until they could be examined by an anthropologist to determine whether they were human remains. They were not, and building continued.

In November 1947, Milo F. Draemel, then secretary of Pennsylvania's Department of Forests and Waters (the park commission's parent organization), stated Harrisburg's desire to see "some real accomplishment on the Restoration Program." As a result, the park commission awarded Edwin H. Hollenbach a contract to build twenty of the log huts.[48] Brumbaugh's painstaking technique of building and rebuilding each hut was abandoned. By December, huts were finally appearing, and by July 1948 they were completed. The park had its monuments to the common man.

The techniques Brumbaugh instituted resulted in uniform huts, regularly placed. While Brumbaugh built the huts, Americans were rushing out to purchase new tract houses of uniform design in planned suburban subdivisions. It almost seems that Brumbaugh was unconsciously creating a "Log Levittown" for the ghosts of Valley Forge. Naturally, this was nothing remarkable to Brumbaugh's contemporaries. Only after look-alike tract homes went out of style and were attacked as symbols of the stifling conformity of suburban life would Brumbaugh's huts be criticized.[49]

In fact, the park commission wanted to go Brumbaugh one better in copying suburbia by landscaping the huts. In July 1948, at the suggestion of Norris Wright, Park Commissioner Norman Randolph and George Edwin Brumbaugh met with a landscaper to obtain an estimate. Although Randolph strongly felt that military exigencies would have made the eighteenth-century encampment a very barren place, he described what General Washington *might* have wanted "had it been possible." This included stone walks to the entrance of each hut, shade trees between the huts, and low shrubs around each hut "to keep down the dust in dry weather."[50] Fortunately, these highly inaccurate finishing touches never materialized.

Once the huts were well on their way to completion, Brumbaugh was

Fig. 21.   Replica hut built in 1935 by the Pennsylvania Society of the Sons of the Revolution, who hoped to inspire other groups to erect similar huts. (Courtesy, Valley Forge National Historical Park)

instructed to begin another phase of the "complete restoration"—the rediscovery of Fort John Moore, popularly known as the "lost redoubt." Fort John Moore would have been an earthwork fort or redoubt surrounded by an open ditch or moat created by the digging of soil to form its walls. Tradition had it that Fort John Moore was one of two redoubts that would have been located at the northern extremity of the outer line, completing the chain of forts surrounding the encampment. Antiquarians referred to it and its sister earthwork as Fort John Moore and Fort Mordecai Moore, after the owners of the farms on which these structures had been built. Fort John Moore had been built shortly before Washington marched his men out of Valley Forge, and it had long since been plowed under by local farmers. Author Henry Woodman mentioned Fort John Moore in his 1850 history of Valley Forge, and the fort appeared to be indicated on some early maps of the encamp-

Fig. 22. Replica hut designed by George Edwin Brumbaugh for the "complete restoration" of Valley Forge. It is located near the 1935 hut and shot from a similar angle, but is significantly different from that hut. (Courtesy, Valley Forge National Historical Park)

Fig. 23. Brumbaugh's huts were later criticized because they were too uniform and too regularly spaced. In this photo, they resemble cookie-cutter tract houses built in suburban communities of the same era. (Courtesy, Valley Forge National Historical Park)

ment. The park commission found the documentary evidence "contradictory and confusing" and in the instructions to Brumbaugh emphasized the importance of accuracy and authenticity.[51]

Attempts were made to locate the fort using mine detectors to find metal relics that might be hidden beneath the soil. The Pennsylvania National Guard Military Engineers looked for the fort in February 1948, and the Second Army looked again in May. Neither came up with positive results.[52] Brumbaugh had heard that air photography was being used to locate Roman ruins in Britain and was eager to apply this new wrinkle in scientific archaeology at Valley Forge. Consequently, the Eleventh Air Force flew a mission for Valley Forge the week of May 11, 1948, and provided the architect with photographs of the suspected terrain. One picture showed a short and faint line in the grass indicating subsoil disturbances. Brumbaugh and Park Commissioner Norman Randolph, a former brigadier general, carefully located the spot in the fields at Valley Forge by relating it to trees visible in the pictures.[53]

The next step was conventional field archaeology. Military archaeologist J. Duncan Campbell was engaged to dig an exploratory trench. Right away he found "disturbed earth," which everyone interpreted as the ditch that would have been outside the fort. Dr. J. Alden Mason of the University of Pennsylvania became interested and cooperated with Campbell. The actual diggers were high school students on vacation, and when it became clear that they would have to report for classes before the excavation was done, Brumbaugh rounded up construction workers from another Valley Forge site and put them under the supervision of Mason and Campbell. Within a few more exciting days, the walls and moat of Fort John Moore were either uncovered or clearly indicated.[54] In all the digging, only one disappointing eighteenth-century relic was found: a small hand sickle. No other remains were unearthed except for some layers of charcoal and more suspected human bones. Fort John Moore was reconstructed entirely on the evidence of "feature archaeology," or the subsurface remains of a long-buried structure.[55]

No one knew what eighteenth-century soldiers would have called this particular earthwork, but Brumbaugh suggested that the fort's name be changed to Fort Muhlenberg because Muhlenberg's troops had been encamped closest to it. The Pennsylvania Historical and Museum Commission named it Fort Greene after Nathanael Greene, one of Washington's major-generals. It is now known by the unsentimental name "Redoubt #2."

Having reconstructed the log huts and located the lost redoubt, the commission would take one more step toward re-creating the winter encampment with the construction of the Knox Artillery Shop. According to tradition, there had been such a shop somewhere near the old road running through the camp's artillery park (now Baptist Road Trace), a central location where the Continental Army's artillery was thought to have been collected so that cannon could be quickly dispatched in any direction in case of attack. The shop replica would be built near the artillery park's replica cannon and would be equipped with period tools. Demonstrations could be staged to show visitors how camp horses had been shod and gun carriages repaired.

Construction of the Knox Artillery Shop went fairly smoothly. The Second Army again used mine detectors to try to identify the shop's original location, but found nothing where this shop had supposedly once been. Although elsewhere they identified possible submerged metal within a 50-foot radius of a deposit of charcoal, their results were inconclusive, so Brumbaugh was instructed to erect the shop at its traditional site. Based on his knowledge of colonial blacksmith and wheelwright shops, Brumbaugh designed a building with wide doors and a wheelwright's bench appropriate for the operation of these crafts. The shop's equipment was donated by the director of the Fort Ticonderoga Museum in New York.[56]

The fourth jewel in the "complete restoration" crown was to be the drastic renovation of the Washington Inn, where hotel and restaurant operations had always been such a thorn in the side of the park commission. With its tall, round cupola and fancy balconies and ironwork, the Victorian Italianate Washington Inn also visually overpowered nearby Washington's Headquarters and dominated the park's major intersection. To tourists it had always been a landmark; to the park commission it was an eyesore. Park Commissioner Norman Randolph used that very word, calling it "an eyesore in grotesque contrast with one of the principal restorations designed to enhance the beauty and dignity of the Headquarters area."[57] Brumbaugh agreed. Like most disciples of the Colonial Revival Movement, he was devoted to the merits of seventeenth-, eighteenth-, and early nineteenth-century architecture. Brumbaugh referred to the renovation that had given the Washington Inn its Victorian Italianate features as "vandalism."[58]

In 1947, Brumbaugh began carefully peeling away the layers at the Washington Inn. When the cupola was dismantled, he encountered one interesting message from the past. On the back of an arched spandrel over one of the cupola's windows, a nineteenth-century worker had penciled the words "May 5, 1854—The son of a bitch that takes this down will remember Garrett Snyder, the son of Harry Snyder, Roxborough Town Ship, Philadelphia —G. Snyder foreman for Sam Rau, Wages $2 per Day."[59] Undaunted,

The Washington Inn
at Valley Forge, Pa.

supposed to have been built prior to 1768, owned by the Potts estate, and occupied by Colonel Dewees, who built large ovens in the cellar to bake bread for Washington's army. To the soldiers it was known as the "Bakehouse." It was not made the headquarters of any general, but within its walls some of the courts martial were held.

The Inn is now a Licensed Hotel
owned by
DANIEL J. VOORHEES
and is conducted as one of the most up-to-date Inns in the country.

Cuisine First Class
Private Dinners a Specialty
Large Dining Porch Always Open

Motorists Accommodated
Automobiles and Teams to Hire
Fishing, Boating, Batoing

Steam Heat   Acetylene Gas
Two Blocks from P. & R. Station

Fig. 24.   Advertisement for the Washington Inn before Brumbaugh's restoration. The park commission considered the Victorian Italianate inn an "eyesore" and directed Brumbaugh to restore it to its eighteenth-century appearance. (Courtesy, Valley Forge National Historical Park)

Brumbaugh proceeded with his careful demolition and eventually identified six or seven stages in the structure's history. He concluded that an original log cabin had been rebuilt as a stone dwelling, which was subsequently expanded into a long, two-story house around 1758. Later a rear wing had been added, which Brumbaugh interpreted as an adaptation that converted the house for the simultaneous use of two different families. A major reconstruction had occurred sometime after the encampment around 1790. This had been followed by the "vandalism" of Garrett Snyder in 1854, which had been further adapted about twenty years later to transform the house into a hotel.[60]

The history of the house made its restoration particularly problematic. So great were the changes made after the encampment that exactly what the house had looked like to Washington's men could not be determined. Brumbaugh found better clues to its appearance in its postencampment incarnation, including some attractive wall paneling and markings on the plaster walls indicating the position of chair rails and baseboards. Other marks, on the floorboards, clearly showed where fireplaces had been.[61] It was decided to make the Washington Inn look like it had shortly after the encampment, when renovations had transformed it into what is known as the Federal style.

As with Brumbaugh's other projects, work went slowly. In January 1948, Brumbaugh wrote Norman Randolph: "This house has been one of the most difficult I have ever worked upon. Changes were made so often and so well in its history, that traces and clues have been obscure and contradictory. But the mystery is yielding to patient research, and I am growing more enthusiastic as we proceed."[62] By the end of the year, Brumbaugh was again dealing with labor problems and late deliveries, while Randolph expressed his concern at the slow progress on this project. In the interest of speed, Randolph suggested that Brumbaugh eliminate the flues leading from the restored fireplaces to the house's central chimney, because these fireplaces would no longer be used. Brumbaugh reacted strongly, citing his "reluctance to build shams in as important a building as this." His letter promised more speed without sacrifice to authenticity.[63]

Brumbaugh was apparently willing to compromise on the porch. The Washington Inn once had large porches, but such porches were very uncommon in Federal-style houses. Brumbaugh found evidence on the exterior walls that the porch foundations of the house had been added sometime after the Federal renovation but before the 1854 renovation. It is now believed that the porches were added between 1825 and 1850, so they should have been omitted from Brumbaugh's Federal-style restoration. However, the park commission wanted porches for the convenience of visitors, and Brumbaugh included them.[64]

There had long been a tradition that somewhere in this structure bread had been baked for Washington's army. The legend had originally been inspired by a letter dated August 30, 1777, from Richard Peters, secretary of the Board of War, to Pennsylvania's then chief executive officer, Thomas Wharton. This letter recommended that six militia bakers be sent to Valley Forge, where supplies were hidden, to take care of "a large quantity of Flour spoiling for want of baking." In her history of the Potts family written in 1874, Mrs. (Isabella) Thomas Potts James claimed that this baking had been done in ovens located in the cellar of the Washington Inn. She was probably just guessing based on the wording of some of Washington's orders, in which the general referred to the "Bake-House by Headquarters."

For weeks, Brumbaugh eagerly sought evidence of these ovens. He found it entirely conceivable that ovens might have been constructed in the cellar just before the encampment so that large-scale baking could be done for the army in secret. However, he found nothing in the cellar except a "curious curved wall, one brick in thickness, surrounding a depressed, brick-paved pit, 27 inches below the earth floor of the basement." The pit had an equally curious terra-cotta pipe leading out of house through the west wall. At the time, this reminded Brumbaugh of a kind of oven used by the Pueblo Indians, but the architect had no way of telling whether the unusual structure had been used for baking bread in 1777–1778. There was no evidence that it had ever been subjected to heat.[65]

Brumbaugh recommended that no oven replicas be constructed in the cellar until more evidence was uncovered. Instead, Brumbaugh suggested that a more typical oven be built outside the house. Brumbaugh was not consulted in 1963 when the park commission decided to go ahead and build oven replicas in the cellar anyway, even moving the cellar entrance to a new location to accommodate their construction.

The current version of the bread-baking story holds that the house *was* the site of production-scale baking as early as the 1760s. It is believed that the owners of the house wanted to enter the flour trade, as well as provide supplies for the workers at the old forge. During the encampment itself, bread was probably still baked at this general location for the use of those quartered at or near Washington's Headquarters. But the house had in no way served as a central bakery for the whole Continental Army, nor were there ever any ovens in the cellar. Any old-timers who remembered "ovens" in the cellar may have been thinking of the brick structures incorporated into some houses during the 1830s and 1840s, which retained hot air and acted as a kind of central heating system. As Brumbaugh suspected, the ovens the house had possessed had probably been conventionally located outside the house somewhere near the kitchen. Brumbaugh's clay pipe leading out of the basement pit is currently believed to have allowed the pit to fill with cool water so the basement could function as a spring room for the preservation of food. Unfortunately, this unusual eighteenth-century architectural feature was obliterated by the inaccurate oven reproductions built in the cellar in 1963.[66]

While Brumbaugh was being goaded to hurry along with work at the Washington Inn, the park commission was also deciding what to do with the building once Brumbaugh was done. This restoration had not been undertaken to add anything to the headquarters area, but rather to rid the park of the objectionable architecture of the Washington Inn. In 1949, it was decided to use the building as an administrative headquarters because at

Fig. 25. The bake ovens that never were. It was once thought that bread had been baked at the Washington Inn in ovens hidden in the cellar. Though Brumbaugh found no traces of such ovens, replicas were installed anyway in the 1960s. (Courtesy, Valley Forge National Historical Park)

that time it seemed unlikely that the park would ever get the funds for a separate administrative building.

The old Washington Inn was first renamed the Bake House. Once it was no longer being interpreted as the bakery for the Continental Army, its name was changed to "Colonel Dewees Mansion," after William Dewees— the name Brumbaugh had also used for it. It is now called the "David Potts House," after Dewees's cousin David Potts, who is believed to have owned and lived in the house at the time it was renovated in the Federal style after the death of Dewees in 1782.

When the park's "complete restoration" was nearly finished, a "gala occasion" was planned for its dedication on Evacuation Day, in June 1949. The park commission gratefully received the governor's congratulations for their efforts. The park commission's official published report for this period applauded the entire project and its potential value to the education of visitors at Valley Forge. The report said: "Not only do visitors get a better understanding of the appearance and layout of the Encampment but each restoration, according to their reactions, symbolizes one or more of the qualities of the men of Valley Forge which sustained them through their crisis."[67]

This period of celebration and self-congratulation was short-lived. As early as 1951, it was noticed that the huts at Muhlenberg's Brigade were deteriorating. Early in 1952, Brumbaugh was called back to inspect them, and he reported on their problems in a letter to Norman Randolph. "I was shocked and surprised at the extent of decay in certain locations," he wrote. The problem might have been traced to Brumbaugh's craving for authenticity. He had reasoned that in 1777–1778 the soldiers had not taken time to hew their logs (remove the bark). Now Brumbaugh's logs were rotting under their bark. The park superintendent had already begun removing bark and scraping away soft, rotted wood. It would be more difficult to remove the rot where it had crept across the intersections of logs at corners. Brumbaugh obtained a price of $275 each for the repair of the huts from contractor Hollenbach. He offered his own services as supervisor free of charge.[68]

In the early 1950s, Governor John Fine placed the park on an austerity program so no major project was initiated to save the huts. By 1955, the park commission reported that the huts were in "deplorable condition," posing a real problem for the park superintendent.[69] Again Brumbaugh was consulted and this time he investigated the efficacy of available surface treatments. At the May 1956 commission meeting, the minutes stated: "Mr. Brumbaugh had no plan to offer covering the repair of the huts in a practical manner with a reasonable outlay of money." In Brumbaugh's opinion, repair was "practically a hopeless task," and he suggested tearing the huts down and rebuilding them. This was naturally not in the budget, and the park superintendent was merely instructed to do the best he could.[70]

Other references to the sad condition of the huts can be found in the commission's minutes for the following three years. Washington's log huts had been built to last one winter. Brumbaugh's huts lasted a little over ten years. By the end of the decade, they were decayed beyond repair, and the issue became how to completely replace them. This would have to be done economically, using park labor. At one point, the commission considered using "discarded electric poles" in their reconstruction.[71] Brumbaugh's thoughts on authenticity were not solicited at that time.

The following decade would see a major hut-rebuilding program, during which eighteen of Brumbaugh's huts would be taken down and rebuilt and the rest of them removed. When the park reconstructed its reconstructions, many of Brumbaugh's meticulous details were omitted and the huts became almost indistinguishable from the remaining park police huts. In a 1966 letter, Brumbaugh wrote about these "huts of sad memory, because, in recent years, their roofs have been altered, with complete loss of authenticity." In this letter he added, "However, I have been accused occasionally of being a perfectionist, and proudly accept the accusation."[72]

In the years leading up to America's Bicentennial, there was one more phase of hut-building at Valley Forge. This time the work was done by the Schnadelbach-Braun Partnership working with the park staff. By that time, archaeological investigations had failed to provide evidence of a single hut matching Washington's instructions exactly. Instead, archaeologists had found traces of crude shelters that differed from one another considerably in the location of chimneys, the construction of joints, and in wall and roof treatments. The collective evidence led to the conclusion that the urgency with which shelters must have been constructed during the winter of 1777–1778 would have prevented the army from building huts as uniform and neatly lined up as Brumbaugh's. Accordingly, new huts completed in 1976 would be arranged in random patterns and would reflect the wide variety of designs and building techniques used in early log construction all along the eastern seaboard. Brumbaugh would believe that this project went much too far.[73]

An interesting postscript was added to the "complete restoration" when the park commission reconsidered a project that had been previously dropped from the list—the restoration of Von Steuben's Quarters. In 1955, when this subject came up, tradition held that Von Steuben had been quartered in a remote building far up Mount Misery called the "Slab Tavern," which was then in deplorable condition. The proposed project languished for several years until the Steuben Society of America agreed to lend financial support.[74]

In 1960, Brumbaugh examined the old Slab Tavern, but to the dismay of the park commission he proclaimed that it had been built around 1850 and therefore could never have been Von Steuben's Quarters at Valley Forge.[75]

Because the Steuben Society had already publicized through its state and national agencies its intention to restore this building, one official wrote the park commission that, despite Brumbaugh's findings, "traditional facts have so long been accepted that there could be no grave error in doing a restoration job."[76] In a special report written for the park commission, John Reed, a historian and author long associated with the park and other Valley Forge associations in many capacities, seconded Brumbaugh's opinion based on his own inspection of the Slab Tavern. But Reed was not an architect, so his findings led officers of the Steuben Society to demand still more research. The park called on another outside expert, John F. Heyl of Allentown, who confirmed the findings of Brumbaugh and Reed. This led the park commission to definitely conclude that the Slab Tavern had "no historical value."[77]

In a book on historic houses occupied by Washington's generals, in which he had described the Slab Tavern as "an ancient cripple, the plaster covered stone structure . . . in sad squalor in the arms of Mount Misery," Edward Pinkowsky had already stated the opposite.[78] Pinkowsky visited Reed to argue his point, but revealed that he had based his assertion on the strength of local tradition alone. Nevertheless, he questioned Heyl's findings, which prompted the park to solicit yet another expert opinion, this time from S. K. Stevens of the Pennsylvania Historical and Museum Commission, who upheld the positions of Brumbaugh, Reed, and Heyl.[79] Pinkowsky's arguments brought considerable delay, but the park commission finally razed the Slab Tavern in 1965, which by then had become a safety hazard.

Around the same time, the park commission considered giving Valley Forge's other Victorian hotel building, known as the Mansion House, as drastic a renovation as that given the Washington Inn. This building would once again look colonial, and it would be furnished to suggest a camp hospital—its supposed function during the winter encampment (although archaeological investigations in this area have yet to confirm this). In 1965, after he discovered a vague statement in the 1778 journal of Von Steuben's aide-de-camp, Peter S. Duponceau, Pinkowsky began insisting that the old Mansion House had been Von Steuben's Quarters. At Pinkowsky's suggestion, Pennsylvania Representative John Pezak introduced legislation that the Mansion House be called the "Adjutant General's and Steuben's Quarters."[80] S. K. Stevens agreed, provided that building's use as a hospital be emphasized in its interpretation.[81] The building was dedicated by the park commission in 1966 and by the Steuben Society in 1968. The society expressed its pleasure in the cooperative effort and apologized to the park commission for Pinkowsky's involvement. Pinkowsky, they wrote, had not always obtained their approval for everything he had said and written—and besides, he was Polish.[82]

Today the building is considered an unfortunate restoration. It is speculated that it might have had some kinship with Washington's Headquarters in that some of the same eighteenth-century craftsmen may have worked on both dwellings. While the building's exterior may have regained an eighteenth-century look, its restorers came up with a highly unlikely interior plan. Furthermore, during the time when the building was open to the public, the furnishings on view had a distinctly German flavor, and whether they were typical of what would have been found inside such a house at such a location in Washington's day is questionable.[83]

In 1962, the "complete restoration" nearly had a second postscript from the original wish list when Waters Dewees Yeager, a great-grandson of William Dewees, began a letter-writing campaign to restore the old forge.[84] The findings of the excavations done some thirty-three years earlier were

Fig. 26.   Postcard depicting the Mansion House, another former Valley Forge landmark. In the 1960s, this building was also remodeled in Colonial style and promoted as Von Steuben's Quarters. (Courtesy, Valley Forge National Historical Park)

still visible in a clump of weeds off the trail running alongside Valley Creek. Lack of funds put this suggestion on hold until 1966, when an archaeologist was employed to reexamine the remains.[85] This project finally fell by the wayside in the summer of 1968, when a freak storm raised the level of Valley Creek to its roadbed and showed that any reconstructed structure located where the forge had once been would be swept away in another such storm.[86]

The purpose of the "complete restoration" had been to re-create the military camp and suggest the activities of people during the winter of 1777–1778. Though they still did not give up the park's attractive landscaping, the park commissioners had attempted to re-create the Williamsburg experience at Valley Forge by establishing new points of interest so visitors could literally see where men had been quartered, where bread had been baked, where a blacksmith had operated, and where the sick had been treated. Today, however, the Knox Artillery Shop is boarded up and there is talk about demolishing it, the Steuben Memorial is closed, and signs warn visitors to keep their distance from Fort John Moore, Redoubt #2. Sometimes the David Potts House is open, but the building itself is usually not interpreted on those occasions. The replica huts were perhaps the most successful part of the complete restoration. Although they require a great deal of ongoing maintenance, they still form a stage setting or backdrop for reenactments and costumed interpreters.

Perhaps the real lesson of the "complete restoration" is that one cannot completely re-create the past. Certainly there was no lack of emphasis on historical accuracy in the work of Brumbaugh, but re-creations reveal only the extent of knowledge at the time, the styles and the attitudes of those who do the re-creations, something that becomes readily apparent as soon as a generation passes and more is learned or styles change. Unless re-created structures can be continually updated, they soon cease to be of interest—until enough time has passed for them to become appreciated as artifacts of their own era, a stage that has not yet been reached by the projects constructed during the "complete restoration" at Valley Forge.

While some were trying to remake the past at Valley Forge, others were hoping that the Valley Forge story could be used to shape attitudes and create a brighter future for their own troubled times.

8

New Uses for an Old Story

"We ought to make this Society a real power for Americanization and I am doing all that I can to bring it to the attention of the people," Dr. Burk wrote his wealthy neighbor E. B. Cassatt in 1920.[1] To another contact, Burk spoke of the importance of Valley Forge "with its history, traditions and ideals in the development of the American citizen" and his expectation that his museum could foster "the development of a truer spirit of patriotism and devotion to the ideals of America."[2] In yet another letter, he referred to his museum as a school, calling it "a school of history and patriotism for the American people."[3] Dr. Burk was among the first to suggest that there might be new uses for the old Valley Forge story. Motivated by the nationalistic spirit of the 1920s and 1930s, a time when loyalty to the state was considered vital to America's interests, Burk echoed the voices of many other administrators of museums and historic sites in proposing that these institutions could be used to Americanize immigrants and their descendants, then sometimes derogatorily referred to as "hyphenated Americans."

It was one more thing that put Burk at odds with the park commission and other influential groups involved at Valley Forge. These people had developed a proprietary attitude about the place, and their actions reveal a kind of fear that such outsiders would somehow harm Valley Forge. In 1926, Israel R. Pennypacker wrote:

> Just as many Negroes, migrating to the North and finding that their conduct has a wider latitude than in the South, pattern their behavior after the lower class whites, so the recently arrived Hebrews, Greeks and Italians outdo the older stock of Americans in their lack of decent respect for the associations of Valley Forge. The young orator of the 1878 celebration said, "Americans, take your shoes from your feet, for the spot where you stand is holy ground!" But that it is not holy ground to large groups of newly-made Americans may be inferred from their disregard of warnings not to leave behind their paper boxes, newspapers, stuffs for the garbage pail, and other such evidences of their picnics.[4]

In 1928, the POS of A complained to the park commission that a group of Italians was holding an annual picnic at the park. Burk was on the commission at the time, and the minutes record his statement that the Italians were there at his invitation. The minutes also indicate that the suspicions of the other commissioners were not allayed. They directed the superintendent to arrest any "disorderly persons" at the next Italian picnic.[5] That same year, the Italian Federation of the Sons and Daughters of Columbus was grudgingly allowed to use the park, provided they abide by the law.[6] In 1933, the request of another Italian group was "granted after discussion, subject to inquiry by the Superintendent as to the nature of this Society, and the observance of the visitors of the rules of the park."[7] In 1934, the fact that a member of a Polish women's alliance had placed a wreath at Washington's Headquarters was remarkable enough to be recorded in the park commission minutes.[8]

Besides immigrants, Burk extended his Americanization program to younger Americans. In 1926, a teacher wrote to him when she discovered a form letter composed by Burk inviting youngsters to join the "Valley Forge Legion" and form "camps" at their schools. Burk described this organization as a junior branch of the Valley Forge Historical Society and called it "America's Americanization Association." The teacher objected to the group's badge of membership and its requirement that members pledge their allegiance to it. Such emphasis on uniforms and badges, she contended, had "an insidious and unconscious effect upon our children in the direction of making war a glorious thing."[9]

This teacher's pacifist attitude was shared by many others as World War II loomed ahead in the late 1930s and Burk's successor, Dr. John Hart, attempted to use the Washington Memorial to further his own interpretive program, which was initially one of promoting peace. He established a peace committee and hoped to associate with other international peace organizations, such as that at Westminster Abbey.[10] Hart's attitude changed dramatically after Hitler's blitzkrieg and the occupation of France by Germany. In 1941, he mounted a paper on the church bulletin board enumerating the faults of Hitler, and when a parishioner objected he publicly addressed his congregation—denouncing the Hitlerization of Germany, which had "destroyed the home, breaking every sanctity and tradition. Why do we wait?" he asked. "Why are we uncertain? Why does America not enter the war?"[11]

Once America was at war, Hart used his position to drum up support. Volunteer workers gathered at the chapel to knit and sew garments for distribution by the American Red Cross. British comedienne Gracie Fields was invited to the chapel, where she sang "The Lord's Prayer," "Ave Maria," "God Bless America," and "There'll Always Be an England." In 1943, Hart dedicated an honor roll of parish men and women who had joined the armed forces.[12]

Unlike the first two rectors at the chapel, the park commission did not consciously use Valley Forge as a soapbox before America's entry into World War II and were anxious that no other outside groups be permitted to do so. In 1939, a league of German war veterans in the United States planned to convene in Philadelphia and asked for permission to hold a memorial service at the Von Steuben statue at Valley Forge.[13] The chairman of the park commission wrote the governor suggesting that he talk to the state department, saying, "We are loathe to permit a display of swastika flags, under existing circumstances, the nazi salute, heils, etc."[14] The organization was informed that the park commission would not even permit a furled German flag, and in the end the German war vets simply drove around the park and conducted no ceremonies of any kind.[15]

After America entered World War II, the park did join the Washington Memorial in making material contributions to the war effort. Reproduction cannon that had been cast in 1918 were donated to the nation's scrap metal drive. The commissioners put some of the park's acreage under cultivation but found that the state would not finance a project to raise beef cattle.[16]

The park became a training ground for the 102nd Artillery Brigade, the 59th Hospital Unit, and a group of cadets from Valley Forge Military Academy.[17] The 601st Anti-Aircraft Corps of the Coast Guard Auxiliary used the park's observation tower as a lookout.[18] The park struggled along with a reduced staff as employees resigned to enter the armed forces or essential war industries. Those who remained dutifully purchased war bonds and stamps.[19]

There was no question that the park's administration supported the war effort, but at no time did those associated with the park use Valley Forge to actively promulgate a point of view. Instead, they cooperated in allowing the Valley Forge experience to be drawn on as a source of inspiration for Americans in crisis. A Valley Forge flagpole was formed from a red cedar that had stood near where the Virginia troops had camped. It was presented to President Franklin Roosevelt, together with a flag hand-sewn by the Betsy Ross Seamstresses of Philadelphia.[20] The park commission honored the request of an army private that some ivy from Washington's Headquarters be sent to a cemetery in the Philippines so American soldiers from the Philadelphia area who had died there could be honored with a living link to Valley Forge.[21]

On Evacuation Day in 1944, a radio program originating at Washington's Headquarters included an interview with Sergeant Al Schmid, a Marine who had distinguished himself at Guadalcanal. A script listed the questions Schmid would be asked and suggested how he might want to frame his answers. The replies were to be generally upbeat regarding military progress, but he was also to remind Americans that the struggle was not over and encourage them to make their own sacrifices by purchasing more war bonds. Dr. Hart connected the interview with the Valley Forge experience when he spoke of how Washington "gave unstintingly to the task of wresting independence from tyrants, often suffering hardship and calumny."[22]

The huge number of visitors who trooped through Washington's Head-quarters around V. J. Day was evidence that Americans found inspiration in the Valley Forge experience during World War II. The park superintendent reported that on August 15 and 16, 1945, some 3,500 people visited this historic house. Around Labor Day the same year, he recorded 8,700 visitors on a weekend when the site usually accommodated around 1,100.[23] Valley Forge continued its inspirational role after the war's end when the name "Valley Forge" was given to a 27,000-ton aircraft carrier that went into service in 1946. Park officials attended its commissioning at a ceremony where Dr. Hart gave the invocation. Park commissioners also presented the Navy with a Revolutionary cannonball and a piece of iron that had been excavated from the forge site on Valley Creek so that this vessel could have a constant symbolic link with Valley Forge.[24]

Dr. Hart was no doubt thinking that the Valley Forge experience could inspire the whole world when he suggested in 1945 that Valley Forge become the site of the new United Nations. In a letter to London, he mentioned the architectural element at his own chapel called the "Porch of the Allies," which he said had foreshadowed the current trend toward peace and unity. Hart contended: "An invincible inspiration awaits the United Nations on this ground. . . . Valley Forge is the place for the Parliament of Man."[25] Hart's suggestion was rejected when the Philadelphia area in general was eliminated as being too close to Washington, D.C.

The end of World War II severed the tenuous alliance the United States had enjoyed with the Soviet Union, and America entered a period now known as the Cold War. The establishment of satellite states in Eastern Europe by Joseph Stalin, Soviet Premier and General Secretary of the Communist Party, pitted the Soviet Union against America and her Western allies in imposing a system of values on postwar Europe. Americans began to view Stalin as an aggressor bent on world domination. Fears were heightened when the Soviet Union developed the atom bomb in 1949, and many Americans came to believe that a vast, unseen conspiracy threatened their freedom and way of life. Americans grew even more fearful when the Soviets launched their satellite Sputnik in 1957 and there were widespread feelings of panic during the Cuban Missile Crisis in 1962, followed by a wave of national pride when the Soviets backed away from a confrontation with the United States.

Because communism was regarded as a radical break with the past, Americans increasingly glorified their own history during the Cold War period. In his *Mystic Chords of Memory*, Michael Kammen speaks of Americans in the Cold War era drawing on history to teach democratic beliefs and thus enhance national security.[26] Aggressive programs to bring visitors to places like Williamsburg, where they could appreciate the origins of modern concepts such as self-government, individual liberty, and opportunity, were established.[27] The Cold War raised the question of whether Valley Forge park should also play a more active teaching role, and whether those in charge of the park should utilize the Valley Forge experience to foster patriotism and combat the threat of communism. A 1951 park commission report read:

> We are at another Valley Forge. . . . Today there remains no doubt that the sinister forces of Communism are intent on world

domination either by psychological aggression or armed aggression or both. Nor is there any doubt that the purpose of their psychological aggression is to destroy Freedom by creating among free peoples confusion, disunity and frustration so as to break their will to resist.

The report mentioned the "educational value" of Valley Forge, describing it as "one of the best—if not the best—means at our disposal for neutralizing the insidious methods of Communism in the psychological war it is waging on us."[28]

When the park hosted National Boy Scout Jamborees in 1950, 1957, and 1964, park commissioners probably believed they were advancing such laudable goals. Groups of Boy Scouts had been camping in the park on Washington's Birthday since 1913, and in 1950 officials of the Boy Scouts of America requested the use of Valley Forge for the first national jamboree to be held since 1937, when the approaching war had limited such activities. Although this would constitute the largest gathering ever held in Valley Forge up to that time, the park commissioners welcomed the Boy Scouts, acknowledging in the commission minutes their expectation that a stint at Valley Forge would be good for the general development of American youth.[29]

Between June 30 and July 6, 1950, more than 47,000 Boy Scouts camped in the park, some directly on the sites of the eighteenth-century brigade encampments from their home states. They built "gateways" to serve as entrances to their sections, each one symbolizing something about the boys' geographic regions, such as the gateway replica of the Empire State Building built by Scouts from New York, and the gateway replica of the Golden Gate Bridge, identifying a California group. The boys attended classes on scouting skills and mounted massive pageants. They cooked their meals over charcoal burners, set up their own telephone system, post office, and bank, and dug holes for underground sewers and water pipes. Their presence at Valley Forge attracted an overwhelming number of sightseers and created bumper-to-bumper traffic when visitors stopped to photograph Valley Forge's second great encampment.[30]

John M. McCullough reported daily on the gathering for the *Philadelphia Inquirer*, and his articles clearly reiterated that the jamboree really served the national cause of freedom. It was the largest youth gathering in the Western world to date, and a "ringing challenge and rebuttal to the appeal of Communism to world youth."[31] It was not to be compared with a recent "sordid" Communist youth rally in Berlin, McCullough claimed. The American boys had come together voluntarily, and no one was making them goose-step.[32] McCullough wrote: "American youth took up the challenge flung down in Berlin by the rejuvenated panoply of East German youth at the behest of their authoritarian masters—and hurled it back with a spectacle that had even veteran newspapermen and State Police clearing suddenly husky throats."[33] He was particularly inspired by hearing thousands of Scouts pledge allegiance in unison, and by the spectacle they made one evening when they each lit candles honoring their freedom of worship and symbolizing enlightenment in a dark and frightening world.[34]

The world became a little more frightening that very week when North Korean forces crossed the 38th parallel, an issue that the jamboree's principal speakers, President Truman and General Eisenhower, both addressed. McCullough wondered whether Truman would use the occasion to make a policy speech, but his message was a cautious one advocating fellowship and human brotherhood and building a world of good neighbors.[35] Eisenhower damned the invasion, to a roar of applause. Hinting at U.S. military intervention, he asked, "How can we doubt eventual success if we meet these issues firmly?" Yes, there would be a cost in the lives of young American men just like those gathered before him, but the alternative was an "enslaved world."[36]

Once the jamboree was over, each boy took home some souvenirs: the candle he had lighted, a Valley Forge guidebook, and a package of dogwood seeds. About half the boys also took home a case of poison ivy. After the boys were gone, Pennsylvania's civil defense organizers studied photographs of the jamboree taken from the air to determine how well Valley Forge would serve as an evacuation area in case of atomic attack by the Soviet Union.

When the Boy Scouts held another national jamboree in Valley Forge in 1957, the intent was again to allow each boy to draw inspiration from the setting and learn to appreciate his freedom. A map issued to Scout leaders said: "It is the earnest desire of all jamboree leaders that each boy should go home inspired and filled with a deep appreciation of what this historic setting means to every American. Make it live in the hearts of your boys."[37]

President Eisenhower, then in his second term, was unable to attend, and Vice President Richard Nixon arrived to address the boys. The Scouts cheered when the president of the Boy Scouts of America accidently introduced Nixon as President of the United States rather than Vice President. Nixon's theme was civil rights, not the Cold War. He stressed equal dignity among Scouts regardless of color or creed, and the importance of valuing an individual's achievements rather than his background.[38]

The 1964 jamboree brought the Scouts back to Valley Forge for a third and final time. The purpose was once again to show the world a grassroots youth gathering in a free society. This time one of the points of interest was a pageant with a history lesson where a fictional Scout patrol took a trip through time, witnessing the Boston Tea Party, Paul Revere's Ride, the battles of Bunker Hill and Trenton, and finally the arrival in America of an ethnically diverse group in the shadow of a 20-foot Statue of Liberty.[39]

By the mid-1960s, liberal intellectuals together with certain members of Congress and the media were questioning the old Cold War agenda, and the question at Valley Forge became whether the inspiration to be gained there was worth the trouble of letting nearly 50,000 young men live in the park for a week. A reader wrote to the question-and-answer column in the Valley Forge Historical Society's journal, asking, "Is not a Jamboree a desecration of Valley Forge? Is not the ground too sacred, historically, to be tramped upon by thousands of careless youths?"[40] The park commission also recognized that the jamborees essentially closed the park to other visitors and created a "disturbance of turf" requiring major rehabilitation projects to bring the park scene back to normal.[41] Indeed, a study done in 1979 reported that, more than any other postencampment park activity, the Boy Scout jamborees had had the greatest impact on subsurface remains. The Scouts had created their own remains, which would have to be differentiated from earlier artifacts in all subsequent research. In 1979, one test pit was dug because a sensing device had been attracted by the presence of Boy Scout tent pegs. Further research revealed that these particular young men had pitched their tent directly on the fill of a genuine hut hole, which might have been truly inspiring to them had they only known it.[42] The Boy Scouts were invited in 1969 but chose to convene elsewhere.[43] And in 1971, a directive from the park commission's parent organization made it clear that Valley Forge was no longer considered appropriate for Boy Scout jamborees.[44]

The jamborees were one way in which park administrators fostered Americanism, but the more successful purveyor of the Valley Forge story during the Cold War era was located just west of the park on Route 23: a new organization called the Freedoms Foundation. Among its founders in 1949 were Don Belding, of the Los Angeles advertising firm of Foote, Cone & Belding; Edward F. Hutton, of E. F. Hutton & Company in New York; and Kenneth D. Wells, another advertising executive then serving as director of operations for the Joint Committee on Economic Education of the American Association of Advertising Agencies and Association of National Advertisers. Their cause attracted a high-profile and enthusiastic supporter in Dwight D. Eisenhower. At a Freedoms Foundation ceremony in 1952, Eisenhower said: "This is one engagement I requested. I wanted to come and do my best to tell these people who are friends, who are supporters of the idea that is represented in the Foundation, how deeply I believe they are serving America."[45]

There are several conflicting stories on exactly how and why the Freedoms Foundation got its start. In a 1965 edition of the organization's newsletter, one version tells how Belding found himself in Europe with the Citizens' Food Committee, which had been established to prevent riots and Communist takeovers. In response to the questions of Europeans, Belding realized that the world needed a good definition of the "American Way of Life."[46] This version is repeated in a 1983 article for the *Philadelphia Inquirer Magazine* by Chuck Bauerlein, together with an alternative version the author found in an out-of-print Freedoms Foundation pamphlet. In this second version, Belding visits Wells and is asked by one of Wells's young sons to define the "American Way of Life," prompting a discussion that lasted well into the night. After the boy had retired, Belding reportedly concluded: "I think we've got something."[47] A third and much earlier version appeared in 1949 in a small Chester County newspaper that printed a story telling how Wells's son had sought help with a school paper. To Wells's surprise, the teacher had supplied both subject and outline, "which read like something out of Karl Marx's 'Das Capital.'" Upon questioning his son, Wells discovered that totalitarianism had entered his own home when he realized that the boy and his whole class had been indoctrinated with the teacher's views.[48]

The motivating reason for the formation of the Freedoms Foundation was probably the genuine fear that its founders shared with many others that the freedom of America's citizens was gravely at risk, not only from the threat of communism but also because Americans took their freedom for granted. At an early foundation event in 1949, Hutton remarked, "Present events in the world and on the domestic scene make it quite clear that our American heritage of freedom and the good life which such freedom makes possible are now in perhaps their greatest jeopardy since 1777, when Washington's army occupied the very site on which we stand."[49] In one of the organization's first published reports, Wells spoke of the nation's "apathy" and the need to rededicate Americans to the American Way.[50] In a 1949 letter to Wells, Hutton defined the Freedoms Foundation as "the quickest and most dynamic means by which we can bring the great value of the freedoms philosophy before the man on the street."[51]

Property purchased by Edward F. Hutton and donated to the Freedoms

Foundation gave that organization a Valley Forge address, although it is still unknown whether this particular piece of land played a role in the winter encampment of 1777–1778. Hutton's comment above about the "very site on which we stand" would indicate that he, at least, thought so. To date, no primary source material confirms this, although it would have made military sense to secure the high ground on which most of the foundation's buildings are now situated. Current officials at the Freedoms Foundation speculate that the ground may have been occupied by the Continental Army's artificers (those responsible for the upkeep of military equipment) or by men dispersed to cleaner and healthier sites once spring arrived at Valley Forge. Tradition holds that two structures still in use at the Freedoms Foundation predate the Revolution, and one of these, popularly known as the "Powder House," is supposed to be where General Lord Stirling had explosive powder blended and stored.[52] It would now be difficult to determine whether this property had been part of the Valley Forge encampment. Though the founders of the Freedoms Foundation revered history, they were not professional historians or preservationists, so significant changes were made over the years without any formal documentary, cartographic, archaeological, or topographical studies being done beforehand. The changes began when a number of buildings were remodeled for use in 1949, including a barn that became the foundation's operations building.

Once they had a headquarters, the Freedoms Foundation's founders began to pursue their agenda. They intended to foster the American Way of Life through an awards program that would recognize Americans who promoted the cause of freedom by word or deed. Citizens could nominate themselves or any other citizen. An entry might consist of a sermon, a commencement address, a film, an editorial, a company publication, an article, or a radio program, among other means of expression. Entries were initially screened by patients at a nearby veterans' hospital, then formally judged by an independent award jury, whose members are selected anew each year. E. F. Hutton described the awards program as a "good sized group of big prizes for the defense of our liberties and freedoms," which he hoped would excite Americans as much as the popular television quiz shows of his day.[53] Don Belding described the awards program as "an effective device of continuously selling the American system to its people."[54]

Awards decisions were based on how well these entries embodied the "Credo," a summary of basic freedoms intended to distill the essence of the Constitution and the Declaration of Independence. The Credo had been drawn up by Belding, Wells, Hutton, and Eisenhower and then reviewed and endorsed by a number of state supreme court justices.[55] Each article of the Credo was brief and easy to understand; some were obviously drawn from the Bill of Rights (like "Right to free speech and press" and "Right to assemble"), while others had an economic bent (like "Right to bargain with our employers"). The Credo was originally graphically represented as though the articles had been carved on twin tombstones vaguely resembling the tablets of Moses. On other stones, forming a kind of foundation for these uprights, were the words "Fundamental Belief in God" and "Constitutional Government designed to *Serve* the People."[56] The Credo grabbed media attention and was reproduced on the covers of *Reader's Digest* and *Atlantic Magazine*, which described it as "as concise a statement of what the United States of America is as has been our lot to see."[57] The Freedoms Foundation made it known that the Credo was not copyrighted and could be reproduced by anyone.

The foundation planned to hold the first awards ceremony on the grand parade at Valley Forge[58] but decided instead on an auditorium newly completed in their barn. Eisenhower attended the ceremony, where a number of Americans from all walks of life were honored with cash awards and medals. The event was attended by members of the press from all over America and broadcast throughout the nation on radio and television.[59]

Through the years of the Cold War, Freedoms Foundation awards ceremonies brought many famous people to Valley Forge either to give awards or to receive them. Herbert Hoover returned in 1958 and delivered much the same speech he had made in 1931.[60] Vice President Richard Nixon made a trip to the flag-draped barn to present awards in 1953.[61] Among those honored that year was Cecil B. DeMille, who in his acceptance speech delivered a message to John Waterman, the one man whose grave had been marked at Valley Forge. The Soviet Union, he warned, planned to conquer the world with its ideas and doctrines. "Is this true, John Waterman?" he rhetorically asked. Or would others be willing to die as Waterman had to keep America strong and free?[62]

Although big names ensured generous press coverage, a person did not have to be famous to win a foundation award. Prizes were allotted to both the great and the humble. In 1949, Mrs. Ruth Mills of Merion, Pennsylvania, won $1,500 for her "Credo Freedom Cookie Cutter" and her "Recipe for America."[63] The foundation also made awards to public, private, and parochial schools for programs that taught good citizenship, although this program did not capture as much media attention. Winning schools received a medal and a collection of materials for the use of students and teachers.

The principal of each winning school also selected a teacher and a student for an expense-paid "pilgrimage" to Valley Forge, where they were taken on various inspirational outings to historic sites in the Philadelphia area.[64]

Apparently the foundation encountered little opposition to its programs. A survey of articles indexed in the *Readers' Guide to Periodic Literature*, as well as those published by Philadelphia-area magazines and newspapers, reveals none critical of the organization before a *Philadelphia Magazine* article published in 1968, a time when this magazine was publishing a great deal of material with an iconoclastic slant. Greg Walter, who wrote the article, questioned the institution's then status as a tax-free organization, which meant that it was really subsidized by all taxpayers while representing the ideal of only an ultra-conservative segment of society. Its Credo, he noted, "does not concern itself with civil rights or any other such mundane matters."[65] This dearth of early criticism probably reflects the political correctness of that day. As Walter also writes: "Senator Joseph McCarthy, by this time, was at the height of his power. The American superpatriot was having his field day. Who in high office would have the guts to stand up and refuse to allow his name to be associated with any organization designed to 'fight Communism'?"[66]

There is some evidence that the organization did not enjoy full support from organized labor. One award winner in the local area returned a $600 prize and medal after consulting with the president of his labor union, the United Paper Workers. This prompted a series of letters to the editor of an area newspaper, in one of which the union leader declared, "Freedoms Foundation is very much out of order in appointing itself judge and jury over standards of 'Americanism.' It has announced itself as a forum of Americanism. Actually behind its star-spangled front lies a network of greed, hatred and self-interest shocking to any fair minded American." The award, he charged, was just a subtle way of obtaining a union endorsement for an organization where one of the founders (Hutton) was a known strikebreaker. It is interesting that this writer used the language of patriotism to criticize Hutton and Belding, stating, "They are the leadership of what can become totalitarianism in America—and I'm not kidding—it can come from Wall Street as sure as the Kremlin."[67]

This isolated protest was easily lost among the voices of those who supported the Freedoms Foundation. Americans like Kate Smith went on the air describing the foundation as something that put America's competitive spirit to work for the American system. Sure, some people would question whether the Freedoms Foundation put a price on American loyalty, but this she claimed was not so. Americans were simply recognizing the good done by other Americans and saying thank you.[68] Other stars with recognizable voices recorded spot commercials for the foundation. Jimmy Durante, Frankie Lane, Bob Hope, and John Wayne could all be heard urging Americans to join the foundation and send for their Freedoms Handbook,[69] a brochure that illustrated the articles of the Credo with photographs of Americans enjoying their freedoms and suggested programs that communities and corporations could organize to promote the cause of freedom.[70]

The radio spots certainly suggest that the foundation came to Valley Forge mainly for its name. In the days before nine-digit zip codes, the address "Freedoms Foundation, Valley Forge, Pennsylvania" was very easy for people to remember when they heard it on the radio. In his 1984 article, Chuck Bauerlein cited a Freedoms Foundation official who said a 1949 public opinion survey had been conducted to find "the most patriotic spot in America," resulting in the selection of Valley Forge.[71] When the Valley Forge property was dedicated, Hutton remarked that the ceremonies should serve to "remind our fellow citizens that Valley Forge is still there and that the freedoms which were defended here are still ours to enjoy and defend."[72]

"We do not presume to put ourselves or our programs on a plane with Washington and his Valley Forge soldiers," Hutton continued,[73] and indeed his speech said little about the winter encampment. The founders did not sponsor research at Valley Forge that would have contributed to any new interpretation of what had happened in 1777–1778. Instead, they and their staff would simply invoke the Valley Forge story, linking it with the abstract concept of freedom. This link was made in simple language on a foundation souvenir, a small envelope filled with dirt and printed with the rhyming message "A bit of soil, some dogwood seed / From Valley Forge, where men were freed."[74] Ken Wells used more florid terms in 1949 when he said:

> [Americans] revere the historical background of Valley Forge be-
> cause it was here that the decision was made as to whether this
> nation would be a free nation or a slave nation. Now that America
> is at the crossroads it is only proper that our nation make up its
> mind in Valley Forge again as to whether we continue as a free
> nation or become a totalitarian state.[75]

In a 1957 issue of the Freedoms Foundation newsletter, Wells questioned whether Americans could keep the faith of George Washington and his men at Valley Forge, where, Wells contended, although one-third of the soldiers had gone home and one-third had died, the rest had "turned the feeble spark of freedom into the torch of liberty."[76] These statements always sounded good, although a historian might have questioned Wells's statistics and whether anyone had been literally "freed" at Valley Forge, especially in light of the fact that a great many African Americans had been no more free after the Revolution than they had been before it.

In his remarks of 1949, Hutton promised that there would be "no impressing granite buildings" at the foundation, but rather "ideals which will have endured far longer than granite."[77] In the early years, the foundation was run from its adapted farm buildings, but a building program in the 1960s provided the foundation with more appropriate housing and the look of a small college campus. The foundation's new structures were brick, not granite, and built in the Colonial Revival style. They provided the foundation with room for seminars and meetings and a place to store the awards entries that had been gathered over the years. The contributions of individuals and organizations made possible structures that had such names as the Martha Washington Building, the Ben Franklin Building, and the Faith of Our Fathers Chapel. In 1965, the foundation opened a unique library in one of the buildings containing, among other holdings, a collection of materials on totalitarianism, on the communist movement, and on American radical movements, as well as works on U.S. history. This material was intended to support graduate seminars, history workshops, and youth leadership programs.[78]

We do not know today whether the building program unearthed any significant artifacts of the Revolutionary era, but the foundation did acquire some artifacts when the widow of Charles F. Jenkins donated her late husband's unique collection. Jenkins had collected bricks, cobblestones, stepping-stones, and flagstones, each associated in some way with a signer of the Declaration of Independence. With the help of donations, these were arranged at the Freedoms Foundation to form the "Independence Garden," consisting of thirteen sections representing the original colonies.[79]

The Freedoms Foundation's Medal of Honor Grove was dedicated in 1964 on fifty acres donated by a resident of Phoenixville. This added a memorial park atmosphere to the campus and honored those who had been awarded the Congressional Medal of Honor. The grove was also divided into sections, and citizens of each state were encouraged to raise money for an obelisk of native stone to replace a temporary fiberglass obelisk provided by the foundation.[80]

Over the years, other monuments have been erected at the Freedoms

Foundation, by far the most impressive being the monumental statue of Washington kneeling in prayer, dedicated in 1967. Back in 1918, the park commissioners rejected a proposal for a statue of Washington at prayer when a POS of A camp had requested permission to erect one. The commission secretary quoted a letter he had received from the chief of the manuscript division of the Library of Congress:

> If the prayer story can ever be authenticated, there could be no possible objection to a marker on the spot, but . . . it cheapens Valley Forge, and tends to destroy the atmosphere of the place when mere tradition is monumented with all the solemnity of established fact. [81]

However, it is said that the monument at the Freedoms Foundation was not intended to illustrate the Weems story about Washington being observed at prayer at Valley Forge, but rather to symbolize the role of religion in the foundation of America. [82] The foundation accepted this statue as a gift from the Free and Accepted Order of Masons of Pennsylvania. Wilbur M. Bruker, a former Secretary of the Army, was the principal speaker at dedication ceremonies and invoked the Valley Forge experience as inspiration for America's crisis in Vietnam when he said, "[Washington] didn't cringe during eight long years of warfare. Instead of listening to impatient counsel of defeat, America should tighten its belt and resolutely turn again to the grim task of destroying Communist aggression." [83]

The few references to the Freedoms Foundation among the minutes of the Valley Forge Historical Society indicate that relations between these two organizations were fairly good. The historical society initiated a "good neighbor policy" and several times allowed the foundation to commemorate Pearl Harbor Day at the chapel. Dr. Hart was among those presenting foundation awards in 1952, [84] and in 1958 the Washington Memorial Chapel, as an institution, received a Freedoms Foundation award. [85]

Similarly, there are few references to the Freedoms Foundation in the park commission minutes, but there are some hints of early friction. Ken Wells set up an office in the waiting room at the old Valley Forge train station, property the park commission wanted for its own use. [86] At one point, the foundation acted without the park commission's knowledge in generating a press release containing information about the graves of 120 soldiers on park land; the park commissioners had no idea what they were talking about. [87] In 1964, one park commissioner mentioned that in chatting with friends he had become "greatly distressed with the fact that many persons do not realize the difference between Valley Forge State Park and the Freedoms Foundation in Valley Forge."[88]

In a way, Burk's attempt to use the Valley Forge story to package and sell a program of Americanism was carried out during the Cold War, and most successfully by the Freedoms Foundation. It is interesting that this new use for the old story resulted in Valley Forge's acquiring a lot of new artifacts. The Boy Scout remains—now just a nuisance to archaeologists—may one day be of interest to the interpreters of material culture in the mid-twentieth century. And the Freedoms Foundation itself is an interesting artifact. Its buildings, monuments, records, and publications may one day be employed to interpret the thinking of one segment of American society in the doomsday atmosphere of the Cold War.

9

The Siege of Valley Forge

The late 1930s and early 1940s saw the first manifestations of real crowd-control problems at Valley Forge, particularly in the spring, when the impressive concentration of flowering dogwood trees dedicated to Washington and his army drew almost a million visitors annually. A 1936 memo decreed: "We cannot allow visitors all the time they may desire. They must be satisfied with such view as they get moving along or else our physical task will be too difficult."[1]

How to deal with the hordes of visitors as well as people who wanted to locate permanently at Valley Forge became a key park issue between the 1950s and 1976 as the general area became increasingly developed. Concurrent bad press, financial problems, and trouble between the park commission and its parent organization caused individuals involved at Valley Forge and concerned members of the community to develop a kind of siege mentality. When the National Park Service took over Valley Forge on July 4, 1976, its uniformed rangers were welcomed like the cavalry arriving at a besieged frontier town.

An era of highway-building opened immediately after World War II, soon bringing a modern high-speed artery to the very edge of Valley Forge State Park. In 1944, land in Upper Merion Township was condemned to make way for the Pennsylvania Turnpike. A local editorial titled "A Threat to Hallowed Acres" acknowledged that highways were necessary but protested that "few persons are of the opinion that these adjuncts of the twentieth century should be permitted to disfigure those shrines which are a part of this nation's glorious past."[2] For almost a year, the park commissioners had been trying to second-guess what effect the turnpike would have on Valley Forge, but they made no official protest.[3] And indeed, other than making the park more easily reached by travelers from distant parts of the state, the new road brought no real changes to Valley Forge.

Change would come once the Schuylkill Expressway provided a high-speed route from the turnpike's Valley Forge exit directly to downtown

Fig. 27.   Valley Forge in the spring during the 1940s. Flowering dogwood is one of the park's attractions. (Courtesy, Valley Forge National Historical Park)

Philadelphia. The expressway had evolved from plans for a "Valley Forge Parkway," proposed as early as 1930 to link Valley Forge and Fairmount Park.[4] After World War II, the expressway was again proposed as an alternative to widening existing roadways. Its planned route was to follow the Schuylkill River to Gulph Mills, where it would join a yet-to-be-built Route 202 near Valley Forge State Park. Construction began in 1950, and the Schuylkill Expressway officially opened in 1958. On the very first day, traffic became snarled, but the road system then in place made it inevitable that the village near Valley Forge with the peculiar name "King of Prussia" would become a major hub of commercial and industrial development, a kind of satellite community outside the city of Philadelphia.

As the King of Prussia area was developed, still more highways were needed to handle the traffic, and the impact of development on Valley Forge increased. Park commissioners voiced concern that highways would "strangle" the park[5] and unsuccessfully protested the building of a giant cloverleaf near the park's eastern entrance.[6] In 1965, another highway called the County Line Expressway (Route 422) divided what little remained of Port Kennedy, leaving nothing but a church, a deteriorating mansion, and a few structures near the old railroad station, all of them strangely separated by roads that were almost impossible for pedestrians to cross. The volume of traffic through the park also increased, posing new threats to some well-known landmarks. In 1967, the one-lane covered bridge spanning Valley Creek, which had been built in 1865 and restored as recently as 1960, was closed for several weeks after an overloaded tractor trailer attempted to cross it, almost completely knocking out one of its sides.[7]

Businesses hastened to locate at this new, convenient thoroughfare, and many of them wanted the cachet of a Valley Forge address. Around 1960, efforts were made to build a new post office in Valley Forge village, which would also accommodate tourists who wanted a Valley Forge stamp cancellation. Kenneth D. Wells of the Freedoms Foundation protested, expressing in a letter his desire that the proposed post office would not serve the new industrial areas of King of Prussia, or make a Valley Forge address available to those outside the "confines of the reservation."[8] Nevertheless, the new post office was dedicated in 1964, a Colonial-style building designed to blend tastefully into its noble surroundings.[9]

In 1962, the Freedoms Foundation approved plans for commercial development on property just west of Valley Forge. These plans would have enabled a builder to erect a concentration of shops, a restaurant, "sleeping units," and a theater.[10] Park commissioners joined with others involved at

Valley Forge in protesting what they considered an attack on the park's still-undeveloped western border. Historian John Reed protested to Schuylkill Township supervisors: "Freedoms Foundation, by its own admission, chose to site itself at Valley Forge because of the historical allusions of the place. It seems to me that it is a shame that the Foundation should be allowed, or should even wish, to pervert those allusions by selling property for the proposed use."[11] The proposed shops never materialized.

Certain members of the local community reacted to the threat of development with a plan to surround Valley Forge with a buffer circle of land divided into fifty parcels on which each state could erect a building of Georgian design that tourists could visit and that could provide housing for visiting students. The plan may have been inspired by world's fair structures or perhaps by the Colonial-style campus being erected at the Freedoms Foundation. A 1967 pamphlet titled "Valley Forge Crisis" proclaimed that the shrine was "threatened by a booming urban build-up that is taking place in the King of Prussia area."[12] Joseph Perron, whose name appeared on the pamphlet, presented the idea to the park commission in 1968. The DAR had already introduced the plan to the director of the Pennsylvania Historical and Museum Commission,[13] and there were other supporters too, including renowned novelist James Michener.[14] The park commissioners withheld their support, claiming that such plans were out of their purview, but commission minutes suggested hope that the same effect could be achieved if Montgomery and Chester counties would each locate a community college on the park's perimeter.[15] Without the park commissioners' active support, the grassroots buffer plan was abandoned by the end of the year.[16]

The park commissioners continued to deal with each new development project bordering the park as a separate issue. The park commission deemed plans for a Dutch Inns Motel adjacent to the park "undesirable," contending that such an establishment would sell liquor and create additional traffic problems.[17] Park officials contacted local residents and other interested parties to oppose the zoning changes that would allow such a motel.[18] They succeeded in quashing plans for the motel, later opposing a second motel plan and a youth hostel as "not in keeping" with Valley Forge Park.[19]

The commissioners' opinions were initially divided when plans were presented for the Sheraton Hotel and Convention Center, a much larger operation than anything previously proposed, but one that would be located a bit southeast of the park's main entrance.[20] Citizens protested what was rumored to become a complex of high-rise buildings almost overlooking the park. One couple objected to the encroachment of commercialism on a "national treasure" where "peace and beauty refresh the spirit; its very existence remind[ing] us of a proud moment in our nation's history."[21] Park commissioners declared that they would not oppose zoning changes if the Sheraton would be no taller than six or seven stories.[22] The Sheraton, of course, eventually stretched much higher than that; it was and is visible from Outer Line Drive. Once the Sheraton complex was completed, the park commissioners were more vocal in resisting another affront, a proposed 15-foot-high rotating sign on top of the building.[23]

In the late 1960s and early 1970s, many Americans became more politically aware as a result of America's involvement in Vietnam, and Valley Forge began attracting people seeking a place to make a political point. In 1969, park commissioners recorded no objection to a request from a group that wanted to hold a patriotic rally at Valley Forge. They replied that Valley Forge was at the disposal of the people and merely asked that park regulations be followed and confrontations avoided.[24] However, the commission was called into special session when the Vietnam Veterans Against the War asked to stage a demonstration in the park on Labor Day of the following year, when they planned to march to Valley Forge from Moorestown, New Jersey, and listen to speeches by peace advocates. Although commissioners felt they could not deny access to the park even though they found the group's beliefs distasteful, they were chagrined to find themselves burdened with an extra potential problem on a weekend when the park was normally mobbed. They offered the group certain conditions, including the requirement that they obtain insurance and provide their own toilets and parking attendants, and these conditions set a precedent and were later applied to all groups that wanted to stage demonstrations at Valley Forge, regardless of political viewpoint.[25] Let 'em come, said fundamentalist preacher and conservative spokesman Dr. Carl McIntire. "The more they talk, the more people will turn from the defeat and surrender they champion and demand that the Nation win the peace by victory and honor."[26]

There was no violence at the Labor Day demonstration, but the park superintendent did receive several anonymous threats to bomb Washington's Headquarters and other Valley Forge landmarks. Park police were issued shotguns and put on extra duty. That Saturday, when one officer saw a car being driven in a erratic manner near Washington's Headquarters, he repeatedly ordered the driver to halt, then fired on the vehicle. The driver kept going until he reached the Valley Forge Soda Shop about half a mile away, where he was intercepted by local police. The terrified driver identified himself as a rabbi recently transferred to the area who had become lost. Both the rabbi and his wife had suffered injuries from shotgun pellets.[27]

The Montgomery County district attorney ordered an investigation into the unpleasant encounter. The incident became more unpleasant when the rabbi received two traffic tickets for swerving his vehicle from side to side and going through a stop sign—after he had been wounded and while believing that he was fleeing for his life.[28] On the recommendation of State Attorney General Fred Speaker, the park guard responsible was finally suspended. Quoting a state Justice Department report, Speaker said: "In the opinion of this department, if the facts as described by the shooting victims are ultimately established, they constitute a gross and unprovoked attack by an employee of the Commonwealth."[29]

Fortunately, there were no problems in December 1971, when 100 Vietnam veterans came back for "Operation Winter Soldier," even though Dr. McIntire led his own followers to protest the protesters.[30]

Young people looking for a place to hang out were more of a problem than political demonstrations. "Valley Forge bears too honorable a name in our history to permit hoodlum gangs to disgrace it," stated a 1969 editorial in the *Philadelphia Inquirer,* complaining of the trash they left behind and the limbs they broke from the flowering dogwoods.[31] Shortly afterward, the park commission issued a press release firmly denying "the possibility of marijuana growing in abundance in this park."[32] Philadelphia's other major daily newspaper, the *Philadelphia Bulletin,* quoted a park commissioner's allegation that "an army of young drifters, supplemented by commando squads of older undesirables, has turned the historic park into a No Man's land." This article told of young people riding motorcycles across the grass, urinating on monuments, and romping about unclothed.[33] The commissioner in question later claimed that the reporter had exaggerated his statements.

While such allegations were being made and denied, the park commission launched an investigation by its new "Subcommittee on Sex, Hippies, and Whiskey Swillers," which issued a report in 1969. The investigation uncovered "no evidence of widespread violations of park rules" but admitted, "There are scattered whiskey and beer swillers, there are heated love scenes being enacted on blankets here and there in view of the moving traffic and there are groups of hippie-like characters who can be observed doing their 'things' (mostly sitting around in circles)."[34] The park commissioners proposed to solve what problems they admitted the park had by printing and enforcing all park regulations and preventing parking or stopping except in designated areas. Arrests would be made if warnings were not heeded.[35]

Real trouble came with the real criminals who began to make their way to Valley Forge. The Valley Forge Historical Society reported a theft of guns and Washingtoniana in 1968.[36] About the same time, vandalism resulted in $75,000 worth of damage when some young people camping near the Washington Memorial filled a trash barrel with rocks and wedged it between the rails of the train tracks, seriously damaging an oncoming train.[37] A brazen scam was perpetrated at the park in the early 1970s when people posing as "maintenance volunteers" removed seventeen valuable mature walnut trees from forested areas.[38]

The 1970s also brought confrontations and violence, prompting S. K. Stevens of the Pennsylvania Historical and Museum Commission to write to an official of the Boy Scouts of America discouraging the use of the park for a jamboree in 1973. Stevens reported: "There most certainly has been a tremendous increase in urban tensions in the Philadelphia area."[39] He may have wanted to avoid incidents like one reported by a teacher who took her eighth-graders to the park and had some of them confronted by students from another school who beat two boys and demanded money from some of the girls.[40]

In 1976, when Meade Jones had been president of the Valley Forge Historical Society for just five days, she took a guest to the historic house in the park known as "Maxwell's Quarters," where some of the society's treasures had been on display, and was shocked to find smashed cases and all the evidence of a major, professional heist.[41] About 100 items then valued at $250,000 were gone, including historic Blue Staffordshire china, lusterware china pieces, oil paintings, pewter, and some tableware that had seen use in the White House. The FBI was called in, making a total of eight federal, state, county, and local law-enforcement agencies cooperating in the recovery of these irreplaceable antiques. After six months of intensive investigation in a three-county area, most of the objects were recovered, having been found wrapped in newspaper in fifty-five-gallon drums at the bottom of an embankment in a Phoenixville landfill.[42]

The increase in crime coincided with allegations of corruption among Valley Forge employees. Robert Fowler, who had covered the story of the accidental shooting of the visiting rabbi for a Philadelphia newspaper, soon followed up with another story reporting that state employees who conducted tours in the park were pocketing tips while collecting state salaries. In an interview, the park superintendent admitted to Fowler that he had been aware of what was going on and that the practice was fairly widespread. He revealed that some park employees had even complained of being deprived of this moneymaking opportunity. The park commissioners and the park's then parent organization—the Pennsylvania Department of Forests and Waters—denied knowledge of the practice, and one guard was ordered to repay the state what money he had collected.[43]

About a month later, Fowler was back at the park interviewing the superintendent about allegations that he had taken kickbacks. It had been reported that the superintendent had paid a park policeman for ten days' work during a period when the man had actually worked only four days. When the officer returned the money, the superintendent used it to create a kind of petty cash fund which enabled him to bypass the inconvenient state requirement that he get bids even for small purchases.[44] The superintendent was suspended and later fired when he failed to appeal his suspension.[45]

At the same time that the park commission was dealing with this bad press, they were also getting used to a new parent organization following a major reorganization of commonwealth government offices. Since 1923, the independent park commission had operated under the Department of Forests and Waters, which had acted as a kind of middleman between the park commissioners and the state legislators. An act signed by Pennsylvania's governor late in 1970 abolished this department and transferred the park to the Pennsylvania Historical and Museum Commission (PHMC).

An ongoing controversy that quickly emerged between the park commission and the PHMC centered on appropriate uses for the park. By 1970, Valley Forge had evolved into a community greenspace: most visitors came to pursue some recreational activity that had nothing to do with the history of Valley Forge. The prevailing mission of the PHMC was to preserve historic resources, and among its leaders there was a distinct feeling that there was a right way and a wrong way to use those resources. A new park superintendent appointed by the PHMC angered commissioners who thought he had his own agenda and withheld support for the projects they endorsed, such as the making of a film on Valley Forge by the publisher of *Screen News Digest*.[46] Commissioners were equally annoyed when they learned that the PHMC had contemplated adding the word "historical" to the name "Valley Forge State Park" without so much as notifying them.[47] Such incidents accounted for some unpleasant language in the park commission minutes, including this statement by one commissioner: "For too long has the Valley Forge State Park been the mistreated child of the parent organization."[48]

The park commissioners considered breaking away from the PHMC and operating as an independent state board. A committee was formed, and early in 1974 its members issued a special report complaining: "The role of the Park Commission has been greatly diluted since the State Legislature transferred its direct Harrisburg affiliation to the PHMC in 1970. . . . The Commission's status in this setup has gone from the governing and policy-making board of the Park to that of an advisory unit. And, even the advice presently offered is shunned or ignored." The report suggested that park commissioners contact local legislators and initiate a bipartisan legislative study "to resolve the current crisis at Valley Forge."[49]

Animosity deepened that year when the PHMC published its "master plan" formally defining the park's problems as it saw them, proposing solutions, and determining how the park would be developed and used for the nation's Bicentennial and in the future. As the report neared completion, the park commission minutes revealed the park commissioners' "alarm" that the planners had spent so little time in the park.[50] They were also miffed to learn that Park Superintendent Horace Willcox had been working with the planners, something they had decreed was not to interfere with the regular duties of his position.[51]

The master plan, finally published in 1975, declared the intent of the Pennsylvania Historical and Museum Commission (PHMC) to transform the park from a recreational area to a real historical site, to "return the park to the mood, pace, spirit and appearance of the eighteenth century."[52] The report proposed that "vehicular intrusion" be curtailed by turning several modern roads into dirt-road traces, including fairly busy Gulph Road and Baptist Road.[53] These modern road surfaces would be covered with a hard-packed soil mixture in which old wheel ruts might even be simulated.[54] New huts would be built, and Washington's Headquarters would be restored one more time, its Colonial Revival landscaping finally replaced by the kinds of plants and shrubs that would have grown in the area during the eighteenth century.[55] There would be "living history" programs at Artillery Park, near the blacksmith shop, and eventually at one of the park farms, which would be developed as a working farm of the appropriate era.[56] Area residents who used the park as a place for picnics and recreation could continue to so do, but primarily in the area north of the Schuylkill River, which was not thought to have been part of the winter encampment.[57]

The park commissioners believed that both the writers of the master plan and the key members of the PHMC were ignoring many nuts-and-bolts issues. In their minutes, they derided the master plan as a "mini-plan" that did not go far enough and examine the park's needs up to the year 2000.[58] One park commissioner went on record saying, "The proposed master plan is a public rip off. I have no doubt that the plan itself was honestly written—under specific direction given to the Planners as to substance and content. I do not believe Phase I was written with the idea of serving the People of the Community or the State but rather, to foster and further nurture the 'Ivory Tower' concept of its directors."[59]

The commissioner went on to identify rest-room facilities and drinking water as amenities that had not been given adequate consideration.[60] Other notes in the park commission minutes stressed the need for more police[61] and money to clean up the picnic areas.[62] The park commissioners also voiced concern over the deteriorating condition of Valley Forge's famous dogwood groves, where dying trees were not being replaced.[63]

Other issues widened the rift between the park commission and its parent organization. For literally as long as anyone could remember, no admission fees had ever been charged at Valley Forge State Park. In 1973 the PHMC proposed a 50-cent fee for entrance to the historic buildings at Valley Forge. Annamaria Malloy, the park commission's first female chairperson, immediately protested, noting that if an entrance fee were imposed it should be a general park entrance fee, because many visitors never entered the buildings. She was also quoted as saying: "If we are going to charge, let's charge enough to embarrass the legislature. Let's not put a charge on historical buildings. Do you want me to put fifty cents in a box to look into my mother's grave?"[64] The park commissioners also wondered whether the funds collected would be used at Valley Forge or would enter some slush fund and be spent at other sites.[65] As if fees were not distasteful enough to the park commissioners, they were coupled with the proposal to close the park on Mondays, holidays, and Sunday afternoons.

The years of contention over park uses and procedures coincided with plans for the largest development to date on a tract just south of the park that had long been the property of the University of Pennsylvania. This piece of land had been donated to the university in 1926 by Henry F. Woolman, a Penn alumnus. At that time it was known as Cressbrook Farm, and part of it was supposed to have been occupied during the 1777–1778 encampment. A building now known as the Duportail House was located on the property, named for its famous guest, Washington's chief engineer. The university had been considering moving at least some of its operations from its West Philadelphia location ever since the early 1920s when a huge new railway terminal and post office threatened increased development in this area, and the Woolman gift seemed to provide a good suburban site. Valley Forge, it was believed, could be a very uplifting place for an Ivy League university. One pamphlet proclaimed that the location "would send forth men of higher ideals of service and patriotism than could be acquired anywhere in the country."[66] Another pamphlet noted: "This American shrine is watched over by the spirits of many distinguished alumni who suffered there," including Anthony Wayne, Class of 1765.[67]

Penn never did build its suburban campus, and the old farmland had long remained undeveloped. In the 1930s, a university study noted that relocation "at the present time would not be welcome to the management of the University."[68] It was speculated that the plans for the move might incur increased financial burdens and detract from the "support" the school then enjoyed.[69] The university's president had indicated opposition to the project,[70] causing the group of alumni who had supported the move during the 1920s to scale back their plans and by the end of the 1930s finally abandon them.

The open, rolling farmland held by the University of Pennsylvania was finally purchased by developer Richard Fox of Jenkintown. A planner worked up a development plan for a community to be named Chesterbrook that would combine commercial buildings, single-family and cluster housing, apartments, recreational facilities, and planned open space. Area residents and the media used the adjective "high-density" to describe it, and there were estimates that it would bring at least 10,000 and perhaps as many as 12,000 to 14,000 new residents to Valley Forge.

Local residents united with the park commissioners in opposition. Five hundred people cheered at one meeting held late in 1971 when Tredyffrin Township delayed the zoning decision that would have enabled development to start.[71] The park commission protested that Chesterbrook would encroach on yet another park border and perhaps bring the same type of undesirable scenery that Valley Forge now had to the east. New residents were expected to burden the park with recreational demands, while Chesterbrook office workers would put more commuter traffic on the roads running through the park. There would also be pressure for new utility easements, like the one already under consideration for a pipeline running through the park itself from a sewage-pumping station south of the park to a disposal plant on the Schuylkill.[72]

Many people began asking why the Chesterbrook tract could not simply become part of the park. Pennsylvania's Governor Milton Shapp asked the Pennsylvania Historical and Museum Commission to investigate the feasibility of acquiring at least enough of Chesterbrook to prevent potential flooding on Valley Creek.[73] Annamaria Malloy kept the governor apprised of the opposition of area residents, reminding him that the Chesterbrook tract could give the park more recreational area and thereby take the pressure off the park's historic core.[74]

Two local groups were organized to oppose the development of Chesterbrook. The Citizens Organization to Reclaim Chesterbrook (CORC) studied the ecological and environmental aspects and predicted dire consequences for the park itself.[75] In 1973, concerned citizens organized the Chesterbrook Conservancy to obtain pledges toward the actual purchase of Chesterbrook. Their initial goal was to raise commitments for $100,000—not nearly enough for this valuable real estate, but seed money that might attract state, federal, or foundation funds.[76]

In 1975, the specter of Chesterbrook was suddenly overshadowed when a retired brigadier general informed the park commission that the Veterans Administration was considering Valley Forge as the site of a 500-acre cemetery that would stretch from the park's eastern entrance along Outer Line Drive to the National Memorial Arch.[77] Local newspapers were joined by publications as national in scope as the *New York Times* in suggesting that the veterans consider another site. Annamaria Malloy cooperated in supplying information to journalist Colman McCarthy for a two-part article that was published by the *Washington Post*'s wire service in many other papers, including the *Philadelphia Inquirer*. "With the nation braced to celebrate the bicentennial," McCarthy wrote, "Valley Forge is enduring a new crucible." He quoted Malloy's statement that there were 4.5 million veterans in the district, 60 percent of whom were age sixty-two or older, making it likely that headstones would soon dominate the Valley Forge landscape. Mrs. Malloy was also quoted as saying, "I know already that we have a beautiful burial ground. We have revolutionary soldiers out there." A Veterans Administration official whom McCarthy asked whether new graves might desecrate the unknown resting places of Revolutionary patriots answered, "We would hope we wouldn't do that, but I suppose when you start digging anything might happen."[78]

By that time, however, the Victorian concept of Valley Forge as the burial place of hundreds, even thousands, of soldiers was no longer so widely supported. Historians were speculating that relatively few men would have died *in* the camp, because the sick would have been removed to outlying hospitals. The graves that had been found were identified by brass markers provided back in the 1930s by the "Veterans Graves Registration Division of the WPA."[79] These were so few and so isolated that visitors often misunderstood them. One tourist who came across one of these markers wrote the

Fig. 28.   Grave marker on Mount Joy. Today, some members of the park staff question the authenticity of these markers. (Courtesy, Valley Forge National Historical Park)

park commission that he had been dismayed to see "that the grave of the Unknown Revolutionary Soldier is almost lost in the woods, marked by a very small sign and outlined with a few pieces of rotted logs." The park commissioners sent a letter back explaining that the unknown soldiers were collectively honored by two other monuments.[80] The old Victorian ghost stories had been largely forgotten, as if even the spirits had found their newly developed surroundings less desirable than lonely, rural Valley Forge.

The Pennsylvania Historical and Museum Commission consented to exploratory testing to determine the suitability of the park's soil for veterans' gravesites. Malloy objected strongly and sought an injunction as a private citizen.[81] After a commonwealth judge overturned the injunction, Valley Forge park staff members, some of them attired in Revolutionary garb, watched helplessly as Veterans Administration engineers dug sample graves on park soil.

Most of those opposed to the cemetery at Valley Forge shared the argument that a modern cemetery would "superimpose" one national shrine on another. The U.S. House Committee on Appropriations made this point as it too entered the fray, noting, "There is no justification for developing national shrines as cemeteries or overly concentrating activities in such locations." The committee then denied funds and thereby thwarted plans for a veterans' cemetery in the park.[82] The dead, at least, would not be allowed to move in on Valley Forge.

As the publicity over the cemetery had mentioned, America's Bicentennial was quickly approaching, bringing up the critical issue of whether Valley Forge would have sufficient funds to receive all the Americans who were expected to spend some time there in 1976. An editorial in the *Philadelphia Bulletin* stated: "The park also has suffered from a lack of funds for preservation of historic sites and construction of adequate visitors' facilities. Some 1.7 million people now visit the park annually. An estimated 5 to 15 million are expected in 1976."[83] On July 4, 1975, Valley Forge was officially granted the honor of flying the American flag twenty-four hours a day, but later that year the park commissioners lamented that they did not even have enough money to purchase an adequate flagpole.[84]

State Representative Peter Vroon introduced legislation for emergency bicentennial relief money for Valley Forge. He attended a park commission meeting and explained how two house bills would allocate $600,000 for the fiscal year ending June 1976, and $500,000 for the fiscal year ending June 1977. The park commission immediately passed a resolution urging the PHMC to support a campaign for the passage of this legislation that would provide the funding needed so desperately to handle the expected bicentennial crowds.[85]

All the trouble Valley Forge had endured from the beginning of intensive commercial development in the area again raised the issue of whether the cause of historic preservation at Valley Forge would be better served if the state park became a national park. Following the bad press of the early 1970s, many local residents and groups began writing letters to their congressmen, seeking creation of a National Park at Valley Forge. The executive director of the PHMC, S. K. Stevens, announced his support for this grassroots movement, yet progress remained slow because the Nixon administration had adopted a policy against federalizing state parks, instead advocating a return of excess federal lands to local control.[86] A turning point was finally reached in late 1974 and early 1975 when several key political leaders including Pennsylvania's Governor Milton Shapp, took up the issue.

Governor Shapp approached the secretary of the interior and Congressman Dick Schulze, who together with various co-sponsors introduced a bill in the U.S. House of Representatives authorizing the interior secretary to establish Valley Forge National Historical Park. While Pennsylvania Senator Hugh Scott introduced an identical bill in the Senate, Pennsylvania state legislators worked on bills that would allow the transfer of Valley Forge from the commonwealth to the federal government.[87]

The position of the park commissioners had gradually changed from opposition to endorsement. In June 1974, a park commission resolution recorded in the minutes read: "Let [Pennsylvania] meet its obligations by making adequate provisions for [the park's] operation instead of relinquishing to the Federal Government."[88] A vote taken in the fall of 1975 showed that at that time nine commissioners favored the transfer while only four still opposed it. One member of the remaining opposition questioned whether the federal government had done so well at Gettysburg. Valley Forge already had an absentee landlord in the PHMC, he maintained. Would the park now become the "stepchild" of Independence National Historical Park in Philadelphia?[89]

A hearing was convened on Monday, September 29, 1975, in Washington, D.C., to consider legislation that would finally create a national park at Valley Forge. The Honorable Roy A. Taylor, who presided at the meeting, opened with the remark that the Valley Forge experience was a story "known by every school child, and the ordeal endured by Washington and his army is seen as one of the key turning points in our struggle for independence."[90] Dick Schulze, in whose district Valley Forge was located, spoke of the hallowed ground being under siege, surrounded by commercial development, its landmarks sorely in need of attention.[91] Vroon also mentioned urban sprawl, lamenting that lack of vision years before had allowed the Pennsylvania Turnpike to come too close to Valley Forge.[92] Malloy commented on the park commission's difficulties in dealing with the PHMC, calling the parent body "an ineffectual commission."[93]

Malloy and several other speakers raised the issue of proposed development on the neighboring Chesterbrook tract. Malloy identified the Chesterbrook property as an "integral part" of Valley Forge and called on the federal government to acquire it and make it part of Valley Forge National Historical Park.[94] Developer Richard Fox, who did not oppose the creation of a national park, did insist that the economic, social, and environmental impacts of the planned community of Chesterbrook would not be as dire as predicted.[95] Nathaniel Reed, the assistant secretary of the interior, questioned whether the acquisition of Chesterbrook would be worth the expenditure of an estimated $22 million for land with limited historical importance that would essentially serve the park as a buffer zone. [96]

Chesterbrook continued to be an issue as the bill made its way toward becoming law. The Senate Committee on Interior and Insular Affairs also considered the bill, and Senator Hugh Scott continued to press for the inclusion of the Chesterbrook tract in the proposed park, suggesting that the National Park Service chip in $12 million, the remaining cost to be borne by township, county, and private contributors. When the committee voted in the spring of 1976, however, it approved an amendment precluding the acquisition of Chesterbrook, stating that this issue should not interfere with the goal of nationalizing the park, and soon afterward the bill making Valley Forge a national park was passed. [97]

President Gerald Ford signed the bill into law at a special ceremony held at Valley Forge on July 4, 1976. He congratulated the legislators who had worked long and hard to get their legislation through. He thanked Pennsylvania Governor Milton Shapp, pledging, "And so, Governor, we are delighted to take over and make certain that the good work of the State of Pennsylvania is carried out and that this historic site will become another in the complex of national historic sites for the preservation of these things that mean so much to us—those sites that contributed so significantly to our national history and our national progress." [98]

Within another month, the transition was well under way. H. Gilbert Lusk, a New Jersey native who had been with the National Park Service since 1962, was appointed the first National Park Service superintendent at Valley Forge. [99] Meetings were conducted with Valley Forge's other associations, such as the Valley Forge Historical Society. National Park Service officials admitted there would be changes, generally emphasizing historic preservation and discouraging some recreational uses of the park, but these would be gradual and would be made after discussions with interested groups and individuals. [100] Annamaria Malloy made it clear that her interest in the affairs of Valley Forge would not cease with the demise of the park commission. [101] Special ceremonies were held at the National Memorial Arch on March 30, 1977, to formally transfer the administration of Valley Forge to the National Park Service. [102]

The talk of change was all rather vague, making it clear that no one was certain exactly what the new era opening at Valley Forge would bring. In the meantime, another struggle and another transition was taking place among the successors to the Rev. Dr. W. Herbert Burk.

10

A Struggle for Growth and Professionalism at the Washington Memorial

Much of the early literature generated by Dr. Burk emphasized that the Washington Memorial had been founded for "religious and patriotic purposes."[1] The American flag flew when services were being conducted in the chapel, which occurred not only on Sundays and religious holidays, but on national holidays as well. In Burk's mind, his parish, his historical society, and all the other projects he originated fit logically together. Yet the Washington Memorial was also the creature of Burk's era and of the force of his own personality. Would it survive intact after his death, while attitudes of Americans toward religion and patriotism underwent considerable change?

In 1937, several years after Burk died, the Rev. Dr. John Robbins Hart became rector at the chapel. Hart was a Philadelphia native educated at the University of Pennsylvania, where he had also served as chaplain. He had been a columnist for the *Philadelphia Public Ledger* and was active in many Philadelphia area upper-crust organizations, such as the Union League, the Penn Athletic Club, and the Philadelphia Optimist Club, among many others. During the course of his life he would make headlines by preaching before the British Royal Family at the Royal Chapel in England.[2]

At the time he took over, the Washington Memorial was probably best known as a charming little chapel just perfect for weddings. Its popularity as a place to tie the knot had been on the rise since about 1919. In 1935, it was reported that 283 weddings had taken place there, 66 of them in June. That year, couples came from eighteen different states, and a local paper speculated that more marriages occurred at the Washington Memorial Chapel than in any other church in Pennsylvania.[3] The chapel employed a "directress of weddings," charged a fee of $5.00, and required a waiting period of three days, something that not all the happy couples were aware of. It made the local news in 1937 when one couple drove with their wedding party from Reading in Berks County but were turned away from the chapel because they had not notified the chapel three days before. They headed for a telephone and got in touch with a Lutheran minister in Phoenixville, begging him to marry them "somewhere in Valley Forge" be it under a tree or out on the "battlefields." The minister had no way of getting to Valley Forge, so the couple and their friends came to get him. He then convinced them to be married in his own Phoenixville church. It was not Valley Forge, but apparently for this couple it was close enough.[4]

Hart wanted to complete the building complex at the Washington Memorial according to Burk's original plans, and by 1941 he was collecting funds for a bell tower. The tower would house the National Peace Chime, a collection of bells that Dr. Burk had begun to accumulate. Originally there had been thirteen bells (one for each original colony) and a "national bell," giving Burk enough notes to play the National Anthem. Gradually other bells had been funded, and by the time Dr. Hart took over at the chapel there were forty bells hanging in a wooden structure behind the chapel. Hart wanted to move the bells into a stone tower that would adjoin the temporary museum, and he began writing letters to individuals and organizations describing the bell tower as "a memorial to a Free American People by a Free American People."[5] One recipient discouragingly complained about rising taxes and the huge number of appeals one received, replying, "I should think this would be about as bad a time as one could choose to raise money for the belltower."[6]

A fortunate connection with the DAR enabled construction to begin. Various state DAR chapters had already raised money for some of the bells, and one DAR member, inspired by Hart, established a committee to secure funds for the tower.[7] Construction began in the fall of 1941 according to plans drawn up by the Philadelphia firm Zantzinger & Borie.[8] The tower would be called the "Robert Morris Thanksgiving Tower," and while construction continued, Hart planned its dedication for Thanksgiving Day 1942.[9] The demands created by World War II for money and labor slowed this project down considerably, but the pace picked up once again as the war ended. The Valley Forge Historical Society's journal reported regularly how much the daughters had collected for the project—more than $61,000 by the fall of 1946,[10] some $85,000 by the spring of 1947,[11] and finally $122,941 (enough to complete the tower) by May 1947.[12]

Construction began again in 1949, and the tower's cornerstone (originally laid in 1944) was relaid on Evacuation Day 1950. At an elaborate ceremony an additional box of memorial contents was added to the one already sealed inside the stone. Speeches were made by the proud rector of the Washington Memorial Chapel, various DAR members, representatives from the Sons of the American Revolution, and members of an organization called the Children of the American Revolution. The hymn "Faith of Our Fathers" was played on the carillon bells, still housed in their old wooden frame.[13] During the postwar era, the exciting project of building the tower got so much attention that few people remarked on the demolition of the small, original frame chapel, which was removed in 1947.[14]

Hart also had plans for the Valley Forge Historical Society, and in 1939 he made public his intent "to get it back to the prominence it gained under the late Dr. W. Herbert Burk," a scheme that included a large, new museum.[15] In 1941, it seemed that the Washington Memorial would soon have a new place to house the society's collections when the National Sojourners (an Army and Navy officers' division of the Free and Accepted Masons) announced plans to sponsor a new structure called "Patriots Hall," which would be wedged between the chapel and the new bell tower.[16] The National Sojourners pledged $100,000, plans were drawn up, and an architectural model was constructed. In 1942, the historical society minutes noted that "war conditions" might incur delays, but members remained optimistic.[17] Their hopes faded within a year when they learned that the National Sojourners had not even started a fundraising campaign.[18] By the end of 1944, the society got the bad news that the organization had withdrawn its sponsorship of the building project.[19] Once the war was over, the society hoped that the parish vestry could help raise funds, but as the years went by and the project's estimated price tag rose from $350,000 in 1947[20] to $1,000,000 in 1957,[21] the prospect of a new museum became more and more remote for the historical society.

Hart and fellow members of the historical society turned their attention to the contents of the museum building they already had. Burk's collection policy had been all-encompassing, but Hart recognized the need to refine and limit the scope of the collection. Besides their excellent examples of Washingtoniana and objects with Revolutionary War associations, the historical society had a mismatched assortment of donated objects. For example, among their holdings was a piano Queen Victoria had presented to the famous midget Tom Thumb.[22] And in 1945 one donor was assured that the statue of Humpty Dumpty he had given the society would not be removed from display. An officer wrote him: "As a matter of fact just this week we placed Humpty Dumpty at the entrance to one of our rooms in a more prominent position that [sic] it had been placed."[23]

A 1951 cleanup effort unearthed some real treasures that current members of the historical society did not even know were in the museum. Several women volunteers decided to clean the display room where Washington's marquee was set up, the area concealed by its canvas walls having long been used as a catchall. One participant was put to work sorting through an old cardboard box that had not been opened in years, and she immediately found a collection of signatures of signers of the Declaration of Independence. The ladies pulled other treasures out of the tent, including several letters of George Washington, Washington's vest and gold seal ring, and Martha Washington's "shawls."[24]

Hart and his officers decided to weed out inappropriate objects from the collection and do a better job of displaying the remaining ones. Relics with no real connection to the encampment or the Revolutionary War would be disposed of, perhaps by loaning them to other museums.[25] Objects associated with the Civil War or the Spanish American War might be traded for objects with Revolutionary associations.[26] It was also decided that the exhibit rooms needed to be arranged with more purpose and that the museum overall "must not present the atmosphere of a funeral parlor."[27] By 1950, a portion of the museum had been transformed into one of the then very popular period room settings, and the historical society named it the "Gallery of Home Decorative Arts and Crafts."[28]

In the early 1960s, the Washington Memorial Library, little used since the death of Dr. Burk, also received some attention. Books were sorted and cataloged, while others were disposed of, making the library at least accessible to users. It was optimistically hoped that the library collection, though it would necessarily remain small, would attract theological scholars and historians and become "a memorial to God and the American Revolution, the freedom of soul and the freedom of man."[29]

While Dr. Hart's efforts generally had the effect of carrying out Burk's program, a change would come in the mid-1960s when Hart retired and Sheldon Moody Smith became rector at Washington Memorial Chapel. Hart remained connected with the Washington Memorial, residing at Defenders' Gate and continuing to act as president of the historical society, while Smith focused on the project of developing a parish of the Episcopal Church.

Smith, who came with the highest recommendations as priest, parish worker, and scholar,[30] had been warned by church officials that the parish had been going nowhere and was in danger of disbanding. When he arrived for his first interview at the chapel, he was shocked at what he found. There was not so much as a sign identifying the building as a church, and in its vestibule a lady in colonial dress was selling little brass cannon. In speaking with the vestry (the decision-making body of a local Episcopal church) Smith also discovered that the choir and acolytes were paid for their services and that there was no altar guild and no Sunday school classes to speak of. Smith made it clear to the vestry that if he became rector of Washington Memorial Chapel, his mission would be to keep the parish alive and nurture its growth. He announced he would accept the appointment as rector only if he had the unanimous support of the vestry.[31]

Some of Smith's changes effectively downplayed the role of the Washington Memorial Chapel as a national shrine. He drastically limited the "State Sunday" services that had been initiated by Dr. Burk to honor a different state each week with a special service and perhaps a guest speaker. Smith restricted the eligible states to the thirteen original colonies and then those states contiguous to Pennsylvania. He also drastically limited the number of weddings performed at the chapel, which in Hart's day had increased to 500 per year. "I could see them in the pews," he said, "an anxious young couple just waiting to pounce after the service." Smith can still recall how in 1974 he was contacted by a young woman who wanted to be married in the Washington Memorial Chapel on July 4, 1976. This was not possible, he explained, because the day was a Sunday, when weddings were not conducted. "Besides," he asked, "are you sure your fiancé will want to wait that long?" Oh, she was not yet engaged, she replied, but by that time she was sure she would be and she already knew that she wanted to be married in the pretty little chapel at Valley Forge.[32] Smith made it clear that wedding ceremonies would be conducted primarily for members of his parish, and by

1968 Frank Law, who played the carillon in the Washington Memorial's bell tower, reported that the chapel was down to about two weddings a month.[33] Smith's action had the interesting effect of raising the number of requests received by the park for outdoor weddings at Valley Forge, a practice discontinued in 1976 in anticipation of the nation's bicentennial.[34]

If the parish were to grow and attract more families as members, the chapel would need more space, especially for the expansion of its Sunday school program. Within a year of Smith's institution as rector, he and other members of the vestry were wondering whether it might not be best for all concerned to have the historical society move its collections to other facilities, an idea that was once again being discussed by officers of the historical society. At the end of 1967, the society's minutes noted: "In the spirit of partnership we suggest to the Chapel Vestry that a joint meeting be arranged with our building committee so that the Vestry might be educated as to the purposes of the Society as founded by Dr. Burk, as well as the present goals of our Society."[35] Meetings were held, but it could not be decided exactly where to erect a new museum building, what kind of structure it would be, or how much money to allot for it. In the meantime, the historical society relinquished to the chapel the rooms in which its china collections had been displayed.

Both organizations aimed for a spirit of cooperation, but it seemed that they were entering into a kind of competition over which had the more important objectives. One vestry member expressed his opinion in a letter to a historical society officer, saying, "The housing and display of, say, a china collection is less crucial to the proper exercise of the corporate purpose and commitment of the Valley Forge Historical Society than the need for spiritual guidance to the youth of Washington Memorial Chapel is to its function and being as a church."[36]

The historical society tried to initiate a transfer of real estate between the chapel and the state park that would have given the society a desirable piece of property for a new museum. However, Smith and the vestry declined to make the swap until the historical society was firmly committed to erecting a building. Members of the historical society did not believe they could begin to solicit funds until they had secured their land, so by 1970 this plan had also fallen by the wayside.[37]

A locked door came to symbolize a growing enmity between the church and the historical society. In 1969, Smith locked the door that led from the chapel directly into the vestibule of the museum, where the society's gift shop was located. Smith did not like tourists loudly tramping in from the museum, often leaving behind candy wrappers and other litter. He had also discovered that some visitors mistakenly assumed that the museum entrance fee also purchased admittance to the church. If visitors came to the chapel by the front door, he reasoned, they would approach the building with the reverence proper for a functioning house of worship and also realize that admission was of course free.[38] Society members viewed the locked door as an inconvenience, particularly in bad weather, and their minutes noted this "discourtesy to visitors."[39] The subject was discussed, but the door remained locked.

After the land swap had been considered, the park commission discussed the prospect of building a museum on state park land and simply leasing it to the historical society. In 1972, the historical society's president, Howard Gross, requested the vestry's forbearance, informing them that Pennsylvania Bill 562 had been introduced by a state senator and if passed would allocate $1 million for such a building.[40]

The rector and the vestry had already asked that the historical society move out of the Washington Memorial by that fall, and Gross's letter did not move them. The vestry replied that they indeed wanted to solve material problems but that the chapel absolutely needed the space the museum areas would provide. Only if the room the historical society used as its office and gift shop could be vacated would the society be permitted to stay beyond the autumn of 1972.[41] New pressure was brought to bear after the Upper Merion Township building inspector reported problems and code violations in virtually every room of the historical society's temporary quarters.[42]

While plans for a new museum building for the historical society on state park land languished, some individuals long associated with the park began to question the advisability of this idea. Margaret Roshong, a former park employee, wrote an open letter to the park commissioners reminding them that in 1929 Dr. Burk had been the park commission's bitter enemy. She charged that in the past the society had irresponsibly "lost" certain donated artifacts, and observed that admission to its museum required a fee, which had long been against park policy.[43] In a second letter to Park Commissioner Charles E. Mather she declared, "After 77-years of hard-and-fast rules covering non-commercialization of *our* sacred shrine, it is fantastic to believe that this administration would so far reverse the policy as to not only permit the practice but to *tax we citizens* to erect a $1,000,000 building for a competitive group to have the sole right to the privilege. AS BUSINESS PEOPLE, would you provide funds and land to promote the welfare of a business competitor?"[44] By 1973, the park commissioners were considering their own plans for a new museum at Valley Forge and had begun to share Roshong's view that the historical society museum on state land would be a kind of competitor.[45]

The park commission considered adopting the historical society as an associate group, an arrangement whereby the society would retain its identity and ownership of its collections. The professional staff at the park commission, however, would determine how the society's artifacts would be displayed in a new museum, developing a story line for their interpretation, and special programs to attract visitors.[46] These plans fell through just before the nation's bicentennial, when the state park's own future as an organization became uncertain.

The bicentennial year brought the historical society a new president, Meade Jones, wife of its former president L. Davis Jones, who had resigned for health reasons. Mrs. Jones, originally from Virginia, was enthusiastic, dedicated, deeply interested in history, and an excellent organizer who had been on the board of the historical society since 1967. As president, Meade Jones would set the tone for the society's relationship with the new national park created at Valley Forge in 1976. The national park's new superintendent did not want the society's small museum to compete with displays planned for their own new reception center, nor did he want the society to build elsewhere in the park the new museum they had long been discussing. He suggested that the society consider a long-term loan of key encampment and Revolutionary artifacts to the park. Meade Jones considered this proposal and summed up the society's plight as she saw it: The Valley Forge Historical Society was now being pressured to vacate current quarters by the chapel and give up the best of its collections to the park. Would it be left with no space in the park and no source of income? Would the organization even continue to exist?[47]

Friction between the chapel and the historical society came to a head in 1979. Under Smith's guidance, the parish continued to grow despite the decline of both Valley Forge and Port Kennedy as communities and the need to attract members from a wider area. In 1978, Smith reiterated his problems to the historical society, pressing hard to gain space for classrooms and meetings.[48] In the spring of 1979, the historical society was presented with a report listing code and safety violations in their building. Its members also learned that the oil stored in tanks in their boiler room had been drained, reportedly for reasons of safety, and they were ordered by the chapel to vacate the Washington Memorial by the end of that September 1979.[49]

Following Jones's leadership, and believing they were fighting for the very existence of their organization, the directors of the historical society turned to the law for protection, petitioning the Orphans Court of Montgomery County for a judgment protecting the organization's interests and removing the padlock the chapel had placed on the museum's door.[50] By the fall, the court had issued an injunction restraining the chapel from restricting the historical society's activities. Historical society directors were able to reopen the gift shop, and the chapel was ordered to refill the society's tanks with heating oil.[51]

An unlikely battle began, and reporters commented on the "unpleasantries." One writer noted, "It is a term used by both the Rev. Sheldon Smith, the chapel's soft-spoken rector, and Meade Jones, the genteel Virginia-born woman who heads the historical society."[52] All participants appealed for support. Jones explained the situation to her sisters in the DAR,[53] and Frank Law, the chapel's carillonneur wrote to "Friends of the Washington Memorial Chapel" protesting that chapel officials were being cast as villains even though they had offered land and $75,000 toward a new building.[54] Smith avoided the subject, but invited the chapel's legal counsel to speak to parishioners on the continuing litigation.[55]

The key legal issue boiled down to determining exactly what Dr. Burk's vision and intent had been. Had he created a single, indivisible entity called the Washington Memorial, making the historical society not a tenant that could be evicted but rather the beneficiary of a trust? As Meade Jones expressed the concept to the Episcopal bishop in Philadelphia, "Valley Forge is a symbol of unity nationally and internationally, and the wholeness of Dr. Burk's concept for the Washington Memorial at Valley Forge, the interpretation of religious and secular life, is the epitome of the lesson lived and remembered at Valley Forge."[56] Her own painstaking research in the society's records showed her that money had been raised all over the nation for building the Washington Memorial, with contributions coming from many people, such as members of the DAR, who would not have made donations to a simple parish church.[57] As evidence for this position, the society's lawyers observed that Burk had used the same stationery for both chapel and historical society business, and that on behalf of the society he had solicited funds for some of the bays of the chapel's cloister.[58] Burk's ambitious plans had been cut off only by his death.

Litigation dragged on for years. Three times the chapel petitioned the court to dissolve the injunction restraining the chapel from evicting the historical society. Enormous expenses were incurred on both sides before the historical society's position was finally upheld by a 1983 ruling that made the injunction permanent, recognizing that the trust Burk formed had given the society a right to stay at the Washington Memorial in perpetuity.

Peace negotiations began around the end of 1984 after a federal court dismissed the chapel's final appeal. Then tentative discussions began between representatives of the chapel and the historical society on how the two organizations could work effectively together to realize the vision of the founder.[59] The period of bitterness had taken its toll and is now looked on with regret by almost all who are active in these organizations. According to Smith, the most lamentable result was that the litigation clouded many friendships between people who had formerly shared interests and worked well together.[60]

Once Meade Jones was relatively certain that the historical society would not be evicted, she stepped up a campaign to professionalize the organization. She sought federal grant money and initiated a corporate membership program and a major fundraising effort. In 1985, the society formally adopted a collections policy, defining the collection as primarily Washingtoniana, encampment-related objects, objects revealing American attitudes toward the Valley Forge experience, and objects attesting to eighteenth-century military life and colonial material culture.[61] Objects that did not conform to the new collections policy could be traded or sold. The society also changed the name of its journal from *Picket Post* to the *Valley Forge Journal*, gave it a more professional look, and began seeking material from academic scholars. It was around this time that a bequest of John Dobson brought the society ten more Washington camp cups, giving them an even dozen of these superb artifacts, which remain among the highlights of the collection.[62]

One of Meade Jones's key accomplishments as president was presiding over the installation of a new permanent exhibit at the society's museum called "Valley Forge, the Reality and the Symbol." Funding from the National Endowment for the Humanities and the J. Howard Pew Freedom Trust made the exhibit's installation possible.[63] The theme came from recommendations of a colloquium panel of historians and museum experts, and the project was directed by Michael Kammen of Cornell University and William T. Alderson of the University of Delaware.[64] By that time, Valley Forge National Historical Park itself was effectively interpreting the story of the encampment, so the display at the museum was intended to complement rather than compete with the park's interpretation. Objects on display not only suggested life in the camp but also showed how the Valley Forge story had developed as a symbol for nineteenth- and twentieth-century Americans, emerging together with a national adulation of George Washington. The exhibit, Kammen explained, showed that Valley Forge had a dual significance: the winter of 1777–1778 had not only shaped the Colonial army but also had served ever since as a lesson about sacrifice and commitment.[65] The exhibit engaged the eye and also the mind, causing visitors to reevaluate some cherished perceptions that many had held since childhood, such as whether Washington had really been observed at Valley Forge kneeling in prayer in the snow.

One of Dr. Burk's key treasures was removed from display at the Washington Memorial when the historical society loaned Washington's marquee to the park, where it could be displayed in a more controlled environment. Before the tent was installed at the park's new Visitor Center, professional textile conservators cleaned and examined it—and made new discoveries, such as the long hidden guild or maker's stamp. Before the tent was reassembled, its weathered fabric was backed with stronger material.[66] The tent remains the centerpiece of exhibits at the park's Visitor Center, where people can view it as it probably looked when Washington used it, furnished with a reproduction camp bed, tables, chest, stools, and other military paraphernalia.

Enough has changed at the Washington Memorial to make one wonder whether Burk would recognize the place if he came back today. But the entity he created to interpret the Valley Forge story has survived. The Washington Memorial is not just a parish church strangely surrounded by a national park; the complex remains a key place to go for interpretation during a Valley Forge visit. On another level, it has itself become an artifact and evidence of the spirit of the early twentieth century and of the way in which the Valley Forge story was being celebrated at that time.

11

New Interpretations at Valley Forge

The biggest change at Valley Forge within the last twenty-five years has not been the administrative transfer of Valley Forge State Park to the National Park Service, but rather the change in how Valley Forge was being interpreted by all those associated with it. Despite some events that were merely glitzy crowd-pleasers, the general trend has been toward the use of new techniques and sources to uncover new information that tends to enrich the traditional Valley Forge story and broaden its appeal.

It was evident that things were changing in 1971, when a reader queried the question-and-answer column of the Valley Forge Historical Society's journal: "Were all the troops at Valley Forge of the Caucasian race?" No, the editor replied, African Americans had served in several regiments, and so had some native Americans.[1] By the end of the 1970s, the contribution of other ethnic groups was being actively chronicled.

In the same decade, it was also acknowledged that significant numbers of women had spent the winter of 1777–1778 at Valley Forge. In years gone by, visitors might have gotten the impression that the only women in the camp were the wives of important men, such as Martha Washington, to whom many secondary sources had assigned roles really more typical of upper-middle-class women in the late nineteenth and early twentieth centuries. In his 1905 drama, Dr. Burk created a scene at Washington's Headquarters in which Martha organizes other ladies in sewing and knitting for the troops. She advises a local woman, "Give your daughters such honest accomplishments as will make them capable housekeepers."[2] A 1950 newspaper article portrayed Martha and the wives of other officers as genteel, Victorian angels of mercy, describing how they patched uniforms, knit scarves, darned stockings, and prepared baskets of food and medicine for the soldiers.[3] Pinkowsky's collection of Valley Forge traditions reinforced this homey image.[4] In 1976, the historical society's journal again broke ground with some new interpretive material on female "camp followers"— ordinary wives and paramours who accompanied soldiers, hauling along the necessary pots, pans, and bedding. Camp followers, it explained, washed and cooked, nursed the sick, spied on the enemy, sometimes stole essential food and supplies, and occasionally followed their men into battle.[5]

As the bicentennial drew closer, major changes were made to the park's key historic houses to ensure that they were proper settings for interpretation and reflected the most current knowledge of the past. The Pennsylvania Historical and Museum Commission drove these projects; park commission minutes suggest that the commissioners were not really involved in the details and were primarily concerned that work be done in time for the bicentennial summer of 1976. The changes were based on research by the National Heritage Corporation, but the sketchy report produced, plus the lack of a completion report, makes it difficult to determine today exactly why certain changes were made.

At Varnum's Quarters, several window openings were changed, floors were replaced, and a stairway was completely reconstructed, some of this work reversing changes that had been made in the 1930s. The project made Varnum's Quarters look the way scholars then believed that an eighteenth-century house in the area might have looked, but over the years so much work had been done on this structure that there was no way to tell whether Varnum's Quarters looked like *this* particular house had looked in the eighteenth century. When this project was later evaluated for the National Park Service, the authors of its historical structure report, John Bruce and Cherry Dodd, wrote: "The result is that, although Varnum's today may exhibit all the characteristics of a small house of the early eighteenth century, virtually all clues indicative of its own unique design have vanished."[6] Tom

McGimsey, formerly the historic architect at the park, seconds this opinion, adding that in his mind Varnum's Quarters had been made somehow "sterile" in that it now lacks the quirky details that would make it seem like real people built the place and lived there.[7]

After the National Park Service approved a grant, changes were also made at Washington's Headquarters. Here too work done in the 1930s was reversed: the kitchen wing roof was once again lowered, and the dogtrot between the kitchen and the main building was rebuilt. Hardware was replaced with pieces that were more in keeping with the period, and the entrance to the root cellar was closed—an unfortunate move in that it kept visitors from understanding the origin of the secret-tunnel legend.[8] The Dodds proclaimed this latest restoration of Washington's Headquarters "the most sophisticated to date"[9] and deemed the updated kitchen wing "historically justifiable."[10] Tom McGimsey agrees—his only significant complaint being that the grade around the building was made too low.[11]

In conjunction with the architectural changes, a sophisticated new furnishing plan encouraging the interpretation of the activities of the occupants of Washington's Headquarters during the winter encampment was developed. It stipulated that furniture be arranged to make the building seem cramped and crowded. Country-style and high-style furniture from various periods would be scattered about to suggest that Washington's belongings were interspersed with those of the house's previous occupant. Visitors were to get the impression that they had arrived at the Headquarters at the busiest time of the day—while Washington was receiving his generals, and his secretaries were hurriedly copying his correspondence. Little details would add to the overall impression, such as a nail in the wall near a shadow line, suggesting that a picture had been taken down when Washington moved in.[12] The plan was used for only a short time, but once the National Park Service was manning Washington's Headquarters they also stressed the various activities and hectic pace of a military command center in their interpretation of this building to visitors.[13]

Some thought was also given to the accuracy of the landscaping around the park's historic houses. After the nineteenth-century dam had been removed from Valley Creek in 1920, none of those responsible for the park had shown any concern that the park itself did not really evoke the winter encampment. Boy scouts had been allowed to plant rose gardens, and various groups and individuals had introduced nonnative memorial trees. When one visitor raised the issue in 1963, park commissioners replied: "Beauty has not ruined Valley Forge. It has given a background against which the story can be told."[14] In 1975, inconclusive research among primary-source materials was done in an attempt to understand how Washington's Headquarters would have been landscaped in the eighteenth century. No immediate changes were executed, however, and when the Dodds evaluated the area in their study of Washington's Headquarters published in 1981, they remarked that the landscaping then "resemble[d] a city park with walks designed for young women with baby carriages and Sunday strollers rather than the rural setting that would have been produced by the orchard, barnyard and gardens of two houses in a small forge community."[15]

In the 1970s, Valley Forge was following the lead of many other institutions by adopting the "Williamsburg Formula," which utilized costumed guides stationed in historic structures to act as interpreters and to demonstrate arts and crafts and other activities. In the summer of 1970, a high school teacher dressed as a Continental soldier stationed himself outside the park's auditorium, where he interpreted the role of a soldier in the Continental line.[16] Many women volunteers costumed as colonial ladies later participated in a program called "Host 76." Between 1974 and 1976, they worked at the park's information desk and in the park's historic houses. Annamaria Malloy supported the project, but the volunteers themselves sometimes felt that the paid park staff resented their efforts. One remarked on the number of visitors who had commented that the volunteers "were distinguishable from the Staff by their degree of enthusiasm and courtesy to visitors."[17]

Despite the new interpretations being made at Valley Forge, the celebration of the bicentennial reflected not scholarship but a desire for spectacle and pageantry. The dissension and demonstrations of the late 1960s and early 1970s had upset many traditionalist Americans, who reacted with nostalgia and expressions of national pride. The summer of 1976 was a kind of holiday at Valley Forge.

The earliest bicentennial plans called for something big, impressive, and costly. In 1971 a suburban coalition suggested that Valley Forge become the focal point for bicentennial celebrations in the entire Delaware Valley. They envisioned the development of a regional recreation center and a performing arts center. A monorail would be built in the park, and a grand pageant would be staged there on July 4.[18] Charles Mather, then chairman of the park commission, publicly replied, "The commission will be open to any and all suggestions for its Bicentennial celebration, but it will insist on an orderly, dignified program in keeping with the hallowed grounds of the park."[19]

More expensive suggestions foundered, and Valley Forge ended up with a modest pageant. Pageants were not new to historic sites, and as early as

1949, park administrators had considered some sort of annual Valley Forge play that would combine history and entertainment.[20] This never materialized, although the Boy Scouts had been permitted to stage pageants during their jamborees. Valley Forge finally got its own official pageant in May 1976, when "The Ballad of Valley Forge" was performed in a temporary amphitheater near the Wayne statue by the Pottstown Symphony Orchestra and a chorus of local residents and high school students. Astronaut Neil Armstrong dramatically read the narrative portions of this combination of music and history based on the letters of George Washington.[21]

A second bicentennial event reenacted a foraging expedition originally conducted by Anthony Wayne. During the winter encampment, Wayne had gone to New Jersey by way of Wilmington to procure provisions for the army. He had driven cattle back to Valley Forge through New Jersey's Mercer County and Bucks, Montgomery, and Chester counties in Pennsylvania. The Salem County Historical Society of New Jersey organized a project in which modern cows retraced the footsteps of their eighteenth-century ancestors. Cattle for the reenactment was provided by Cowtown, New Jersey, a place known for its rodeos. The cows arrived at Valley Forge in June 1976, and the event was locally known as "the Great Cow Chase."[22]

The cows were soundly upstaged by Valley Forge's real bicentennial spectacle, still fondly remembered by some as the Wagon Train Pilgrimage, a nationwide bicentennial event lasting more than a year in which authentically reproduced covered wagons were driven east instead of west over old wagon trails. Each of the fifty states was provided with a wagon, which could be sent on a state tour until it joined one of the other wagon trains coming through. Each major wagon train had a traveling musical show that was performed for local communities at every place the wagon train stopped. Citizens and schoolchildren could sign scrolls rededicating themselves to the principles on which the nation was founded, and these were collected by the wagoneers. The project was also inclusive in that anyone who had a wagon and horses could ride along. Some people took their children out of school for a year to ride with the covered wagons. The project had many corporate sponsors, including Aero-Mayflower Transit Company, Gulf Oil, and Holiday Inns. A division of a prominent Philadelphia advertising firm handled details and public relations.[23]

Annamaria Malloy suggested to the park commissioners that Valley Forge be considered as the eastern termination point for the Wagon Train Pilgrimage, and in 1975 she introduced the wagon train's national coordinator, C. Robert Gruver, to the commissioners, who unanimously approved the plans.[24] The wagon train was scheduled to arrive on July 4, 1976, and remain at Valley Forge for two months, during which participants would host activities for park visitors.

The general public did not seem to question whether this activity was compatible with the cause of historic preservation at Valley Forge, or even appropriate for this site. Unlike the Great Cow Chase, the Wagon Train Pilgrimage did not reenact a historic event connected with the winter encampment. It was, however, a highly entertaining and involving project and a chance for people to reaffirm their loyalty to America. The nationwide program was warmly received, and local criticism was limited to problems with food delivery in Valley Forge and the unauthorized activities of some rogue wagoneers.[25] An editorial in the historical society's journal mentioned damaged grass and remaining litter, but also noted that the participants had left "the feeling that some people in America besides the members of the [Valley Forge Historical] Society remember that Valley Forge is important, and that this Park marks a very decisive time in the nation's history. If the wagons can accomplish that, they're welcome here . . . anytime."[26]

Just one month after Valley Forge became a national park, the National Park Service's Mid-Atlantic regional director (whose name, coincidentally, was Chester Brooks) stated that within three years the National Park Service would prepare a new master plan, a document required by the National Park Service to outline the reserved land's long-term development and use and to act as an operations handbook.[27] This process began in the fall of 1977, but the plan was not published until 1982. The general management team leader recalls that the committee did read the state park's recently published plan but went through the entire National Park Service planning process anyway, gathering input from the public and circulating a draft document for public review to incorporate all the best ideas and create a consensus for future direction.[28]

The final General Management Plan acknowledged Valley Forge's widespread use as a regional recreation area but stated that new emphasis would be placed on preserving and maintaining the historical setting. Attempts were made to achieve a compromise that would accommodate the most popular kinds of recreation while protecting sensitive areas. The final result was the most recent expansion of the park in 1984 on ground north of the Schuylkill, where it was hoped more intensive forms of recreation could be transferred. This plus the 1978 acquisition of the holdings of the Keene Corporation (formerly the Ehret Magnesia Company), which had become

Fig. 29.   General Von Steuben takes a ride. This statue, originally located on Outer Line Drive, was moved in 1979 to the Grand Parade so the general could look down on the place where Washington's army once drilled. This is one of many changes made in the park after it became a national park. (Courtesy, Valley Forge National Historical Park)

completely surrounded by land acquired by the park, brought the park roughly to its current dimensions.

Although the authors of the General Management Plan had solicited input from park users, it took a while for the plan's implications to sink in. Early in 1985, the park superintendent denied a request to allow thousands of Boy Scouts to celebrate the seventy-fifth anniversary of scouting by camping at Valley Forge and holding an elaborate jubilee, originally planned to include concession stands, fireworks, hot-air balloons, helicopter rides, and sky-diving demonstrations in a part of the park that had just been reserved for light recreation only.[29] When the organizers of this event used political influence to overturn the denial, the park superintendent was faced with the challenge of getting them to use the land north of the Schuylkill, in which cause he had the support of a number of conservationist and preservationist groups.[30]

Even after the jubilee organizers agreed to move north, the problem was not resolved. Some of the property acquired in 1984, known as Walnut Hill, was believed to have been somehow associated with the encampment, but its value as a resource was unknown because no professional surveys had yet been made. The National Park Service's regional archaeologist and its regional historian protested that the Valley Forge administrators planned to locate certain jubilee activities on precisely this unsurveyed area.[31]

Although the jubilee was held in October 1985 and park administrators reported that little damage had been done,[32] many of those whose priority was preservation continued to be concerned. The following year, voices were raised in protest when the Boy Scouts were permitted to use the same unsurveyed area a second time for a winter pilgrimage.[33] The protesters questioned the value of having a General Management Plan if its provisions could not be enforced in the face of political pressure exerted by well-connected groups and individuals who continued to look on Valley Forge as primarily recreational greenspace, a dispute that would not be completely resolved even after another decade had passed.

The trend toward a more professionalized interpretation of the Valley Forge encampment after the park's transfer to the National Park Service was more the result of the administration's new emphasis on research than the result of the General Management Plan. In the late 1970s and early 1980s, several major research projects would be carried out, including an architectural analysis of structures in the park, a major historical research project, and a major archaeological survey.

In 1978 and 1979, a broad-scale survey of Valley Forge was conducted by the Museum Applied Science Center for Archaeology (MASCA) at the University of Pennsylvania Museum. This was a comprehensive multidisciplinary project designed to gather information about structures and topographical features at the park. Various new archaeological prospecting techniques were used, including aerial photography and geophysical surveying.[34]

Archaeology was not new at Valley Forge, but previous park administrators had made no attempts to coordinate the programs of outside experts or to produce a long-term plan for future archaeological research. As late as 1960, a park commission report told how a John J. Smith, identified as an "authorized relic hunter," had been permitted to search unsupervised for buttons, buckles, and musket balls.[35] Only in the 1960s were all such ad hoc individual authorizations revoked by the park commission.[36]

The park commission had slowly adopted the better policy of allowing recognized archaeological scholars to create their own agendas. Duncan

Campbell, who had worked with Brumbaugh in excavating the "lost redoubt," returned with small groups in 1962, 1966, and 1975.[37] In 1966, Dr. John L. Cotter, a professor at the University of Pennsylvania and a regional archaeologist for the National Park Service, conducted summer classes there for Penn students.[38] This group excavated hut depressions in a wooded area near the Wayne statue; they identified several hut sites, unearthed the remains of fireplaces, and collected various artifacts.[39] Cotter again conducted summer classes at Valley Forge in the summer of 1972, then digging along the outer line, where troops from Virginia had encamped. His project brought new insight into how hut designs had varied among and even within brigades.[40] Cotter's work overlapped work done in 1965, 1972, and 1973 by Vance Packard Jr., staff archaeologist for the William Penn Museum, who excavated several areas, including some near Washington's Headquarters, Varnum's Quarters, the schoolhouse, and the building known as the site of Huntington's Quarters.[41]

After the transition to the National Park Service, objects recovered in archaeological digs were increasingly prized for their interpretive value. Back in 1973, one park commissioner had questioned their worth, writing: "$10,000 has been spent and we have seven rusty nails, 200 bags of broken arrowheads from a prior era, one cannonball and some fish bones, reported to our local papers on this tremendous 'find.' "[42] As material culture became a more common basis for interpreting the lives of people who left few or no records, encampment remains were studied for the insight they could provide into the life of the ordinary soldier, while other finds provided information on the occupations of persons living and working at Valley Forge both before and after the Revolution.[43] In 1978, the park acquired the Neumann Collection of Revolutionary War artifacts, now on display in the Visitor Center, where visitors can form their own conclusions about camp life from material objects.

One thing the archaeologists never found was evidence of human graves at Valley Forge. Duncan Campbell had sought graves near the Waterman Monument but found only offal pits instead.[44] Subsequent research among primary source materials revealed very few references to soldiers being buried at Valley Forge, but many references to the need to dispose of the remains of butchered cattle and dead horses. A 1983 survey listed eleven to fifteen areas previously marked as grave sites, but how these had become identified as such was not known.[45] A decision was made to preserve the presumed grave sites, but the park is certainly not being interpreted as a mass burial ground today. Says park historian Joseph Lee Boyle, "No substantiated human graves have *ever* been found in the park," which is a significant shift in interpretation from what was being written at the turn of the century.[46]

Material for a new interpretation of the Valley Forge story also came from an ambitious, multidisciplinary project initiated in 1977 that produced a highly controversial document called the *Valley Forge Report*. Park Service historians quickly realized that the Valley Forge story as most people knew it was a romantic blend of history and tradition, a considerable percentage of it untraceable to primary source material. Many accounts of the winter encampment had been based on published primary sources that had been quoted over and over again; others incorporated material that could be traced only as far back as the nineteenth century. It seemed that one of the most celebrated incidents in American history was really one of the least well researched. Therefore, several research historians were hired to collect and collate primary data. They spent a year visiting more than 100 repositories of documents throughout the United States, and even some in Europe. They accumulated more than 10,000 copies of documents and 265 rolls of microfilm, creating a respectable collection of Revolutionary War information. A new interpretation of this material was developed primarily by two historians, Wayne Bodle and Jacqueline Thibaut, who based no assertions on hearsay and very little on published primary sources unless the original documents also had been found. The result was a three-volume work made available between 1980 and 1982 that tended to de-romanticize the Valley Forge experience.

In the first volume, Bodle dealt with the December 1777 march to Valley Forge and the condition of the Continental Army at that time. Many other authors had described ragged, defeated, and disorganized soldiers stumbling along Gulph Road. Bodle remarked, "It is impossible to take seriously both the image and the demonstrable facts of the 1777 campaign,"[47] and maintained that the army had been worse for wear but not in its death throes as an organized force. While the soldiers had been living from hand to mouth, their situation was less desperate than "desperate as usual."[48] As for the traditional image that had emerged primarily from Washington's correspondence, Washington may have exaggerated somewhat. Bodle wrote: "Washington was about to channel the frustration stemming from his current military impotence into a political offensive aimed at the governing bodies which sonorously deliberated at York and Lancaster."[49] Previous historians had interpreted Washington's famous warning to Congress that the army was about to "starve, dissolve, or disperse" literally, but Bodle concluded that the letter had been purposely worded in a way that was calculated to galvanize Congress into action.[50]

Bodle also dispelled the romantic notion that a rabble of farmers and tinkers had been magically transformed into a professional army by Von Steuben at Valley Forge. Bodle suggested that even Von Steuben would not have been able to train a genuine rabble in so short a time, writing: "The pre-Steuben army was already at an organizational crystallization point, needing only a knowledgeable, patient and pragmatic individual with the authority and credibility to translate its latent discipline into increased functional effectiveness."[51]

In the second volume, Jacqueline Thibaut dealt with the cherished image of starving soldiers at Valley Forge by thoroughly examining how support services were operating during this period of the American Revolution. She identified the soldiers' staple foodstuffs as beef, flour, and liquor and examined the source of these supplies and how they were expected to reach the men at Valley Forge. She wrote about the famous "February crisis," a period in mid-February 1778 when Washington's troops at Valley Forge suffered a dearth of meat, describing it as a time of "unmitigated misery for Washington's troops"[52] caused by "a confluence of political dissension and organizational ineptitude."[53] However, Thibaut concluded, "There is no record that anyone starved, although the reduced diet combined with poor quarters was certainly conducive to disease."[54]

If the soldiers were not really starving, were they as naked as previous historians had depicted them? Thibaut wrote: "The troops were a multi-hued lot, clothed in a disparate array of uniforms, civilian clothing, and hunting shirts, and some were every bit as ragged as tradition has depicted them."[55] She noted that lack of footgear was a particularly galling problem, but that during the coldest months soldiers deemed unfit for duty because they were inadequately clothed were confined to their huts and not expected to expose bare limbs to harsh weather.[56]

"Historians have found it almost impossible to resist fashioning the Valley Forge winter into a 'crucial turning point' of the Revolutionary odyssey," Thibaut concluded. In the *Valley Forge Report*, she defines it instead as "an unparalleled convergence of hazards besetting the army, as one support mechanism after another faltered, then failed, threatening the survival of the army as a concerted force."[57] There had been no miraculous delivery from misery, since the Continental Army had not experienced the last of cold, hunger, and ragged clothing. According to Thibaut, Valley Forge was a more mundane turning point in which American government officials grappled for the first time with the difficult and uncharted logistics of supplying an army—the war effort ultimately benefiting from the experience they gained. [58]

Just how revisionist was the new interpretation offered by the *Valley Forge Report?* Historian John Reed, long the editor of the historical society's journal and associated with several Valley Forge organizations, had recently presented the more traditional view in his 1969 book *Crucible of Victory*. Reed had drawn on primary source materials in the available body of knowledge before the research done by the park service historians. The language he chose tended to emphasize suffering and sacrifice: weary soldiers trudging toward Valley Forge in 1777, "leaning for protection against the hard north wind." [59] That December, he claimed, "hunger was everywhere," and by the end of February "not a scrap of meat was available to the troops." [60] In Reed's version, Valley Forge was indeed a turning point, although "the ultimate triumph lay years in advance." At Valley Forge a door had been opened "to freedom and independence," and the spirit and training that Washington's men had gained "would carry that cause to triumph." [61]

In 1976, John B. B. Trussell wrote an interpretation of the Valley Forge experience titled *Birthplace of an Army*, also based on primary sources available before the *Valley Forge Report* was researched. While this work still incorporated many traditional beliefs stated as facts, Trussell's interpretation moved away from the more romanticized version and suggested some of the points that would be made more confidently in the *Valley Forge Report*. Yes, he stated in the preface, Washington's army had suffered at Valley Forge, but the shortages they experienced would not be the worst of their careers. [62] Trussell gave the pre–Valley Forge Continental Army credit for already having some training and structure and for having given a good account of themselves at Brandywine, the Paoli Massacre, and Germantown. [63] While still depicting the Valley Forge experience as a monument to endurance and dedication, its real significance, he contended, was that doctrinal differences had been ironed out, standards had been set, and men had been schooled in their duties, which was enough to make it a turning point of the Revolutionary period equal in importance to the signing of the Declaration of Independence or the confrontations at Saratoga and Yorktown. [64]

Because the *Valley Forge Report* was never made generally available through publication, it was not formally reviewed, and there is no consensus on how America's academic scholars feel about its ultimate value. John Shy, professor of history at the University of Michigan, to whom a draft of the report was sent, praised it, remarking, "Careful rereading has confirmed my preliminary judgement, that they [the three volumes] are excellent work." He continued, "Both the narrative section and the section on the supply crisis are of high quality. Their [the authors'] research is extensive, and it is also accurate. Nowhere else can be found such detailed accounts of their respective subjects, and for the purposes of Valley Forge National Park this detail is not excessive."[65]

Within the park service, the report was reviewed by Charles W. Snell and John Luzader, both experts in the military phases of the Revolution. Both raised serious criticisms, which may have stemmed in part from the fact that the draft submitted to them was already bound, making it seem that changes would not really be considered. Snell wrote: "Much effort has gone into the production of this volume [volume 1] in the form of an extensive search and collection of unpublished letters and documents. These yield information that is of considerable interest but this is not of great use to the park."[66] He contended that the report overall lacked the kind of data that would enable planners to plan for future interpretation and protection of resources.[67] Luzader criticized the report as being merely a "write up" of what the researchers had discovered that suffered from the authors' "collegiality, inexperience in site-oriented military history and the absence in daily professional support and supervision by a historian with a strong background in Revolutionary period military history."[68] Both reviewers suggested that volumes 1 and 3 be rejected and that volume 2 be revised. In 1984, all three volumes were finally approved, with the provision that the report would later be supplemented by additional studies.[69]

The *Valley Forge Report* is now fairly widely used by those studying and interpreting the Valley Forge experience. One bibliography published in 1984 described it as "unsurpassed in information about the encampment." The reviewer also wrote: "This work renders outdated every other written work about Valley Forge. It is highly recommended."[70] The *Valley Forge Report* is also the ultimate basis for what visitors learn on a trip to Valley Forge today. An interpretive prospectus completed in 1982 admitted that telling visitors about military supply problems did not fire the patriotic imagination as much as tales of shivering, starving soldiers, but suggested that Valley Forge be presented as a place where organizational problems were overcome and a support system that could supply a national force was worked out.[71] The same year, information from the *Valley Forge Report* was blended into the movie shown at the Visitor Center. This film, sponsored by the Pennsylvania Society, Sons of the Revolution, and originally made in the 1970s, had previously been a mood piece with little dialogue but lots of moving visual images of deep snow and suffering soldiers. The new version incorporated a soundtrack that diverted the viewer's attention from some of the film's bleak imagery. It was recently acknowledged that it is not realistic to expect seasonal interpreters to read the entire *Valley Forge Report*, but information extracted from this material is used for their training, together with lectures from outside experts.[72]

Members of the public who did get a look at the *Valley Forge Report* did so at a time when a new conservative mood was sweeping America in the 1980s. By then, what iconoclasm had been engendered by Watergate had dissipated, and Americans who were tired of being told what was wrong with their nation welcomed historical accounts that reaffirmed their system. The same feelings of loyalty and patriotism that had led so many to sign the scrolls of the Wagon Train Pilgrimage would lead some to look on the *Valley Forge Report* as an attempt to devalue the Valley Forge experience and rob Americans of traditional heroes. The report engendered enough resentment to linger through the decade. In a two-part article written for a local newspaper in 1989, David Lockwood began:

> Recently, some academicians have attacked the traditional history of the encampment of George Washington's Army at Valley Forge in the winter of 1777–78. Broadly basing their arguments on purported new sources, they question the textbook history's description of weariness, despair, suffering, and heroism of the Army at Valley Forge.[73]

For his own interpretation, Lockwood quoted primary source material tending to emphasize the suffering at Valley Forge and concluded:

> Although the mundane factors of inadequate supplies and a poorly organized supply system largely caused the hardships endured by the soldiers at Valley Forge, they in no way should detract from the Valley Forge experience in the winter of 1777–78 as a symbol of the perseverance and courage of American Continental soldiers in the face of extreme hardships and adversity.[74]

That same year, the board of directors of the Valley Forge Historical Society discussed installing a new interpretive exhibit with the theme "Patriotism," and their minutes revealed the concerns of one director about the impact of the "Bodle Report" on the exhibit that they already had.[75] Did the present exhibit subject Washington to needless criticism, this board member wondered?[76] He later expressed a desire to have the new display reflect John Reed's more traditional interpretation, so that the lesson of "determination, fortitude and love of human freedom" would not die.[77]

Today, an even more revisionist trend of thinking is alive among many scholars, preservationists, and museum professionals and is beginning to be felt at Valley Forge. What if history is a continuum in which all eras and events are equally important? Although land and structures were originally preserved at Valley Forge because it was the site of the winter encampment, that really was just a single short incident in the history of the place. Perhaps the resources preserved here can tell other stories of equal or greater interest.

Tucked away in Valley Forge National Historical Park on the west side of Valley Creek is a structure officially known as the Philander Knox Estate but still popularly called Maxwell's Quarters, even though it is unknown when the first dwelling on the site was built and it is likely that no building existed here during the winter encampment. In the course of its long history, the structure has been vastly remodeled a number of times, most recently around 1913 by the Philadelphia-area architect R. Brognard Okie. In times past, attempts might have been made to restore the house to its supposed eighteenth-century look, but in historical structure studies done in the early 1980s the Dodds recommended that it be preserved and interpreted as an example of a country estate of the early twentieth century. They write that the house as it stands "is invaluable as a physical documentation of a way of life which has almost been rendered extinct at Valley Forge."[78]

Tom McGimsey, a former historic architect at Valley Forge, agrees with this view and even regrets that the Washington Inn was restored to match the colonial look of the Washington Headquarters area. In his mind, the most important period of that particular structure's history was the time it spent serving visitors to Valley Forge as a hotel and restaurant. While the conjectural restoration of a Federal-style building says little about the encampment period, a well-preserved Victorian hotel would have given today's visitors a perspective on another era at Valley Forge. "I can just see Brumbaugh ripping off the wrought iron trim," McGimsey says. "Where did he throw it?"[79]

This new ethic is probably responsible for saving another recent park acquisition called the Kennedy-Supplee House, which is presently a restaurant. This structure was built in 1852 and might once have been declared "unhistorical" and demolished because it had nothing to do with the encampment. Instead, it was placed on the National Register in 1983 and leased for adaptive reuse. A 1986 report stated that the structure was a "highly significant early Victorian residence in the Italian villa style."[80] In his own evaluation, John Dodd praised the Egyptian Revival interior details: "The Kennedy Mansion reaches far beyond the Encampment at Valley Forge in its significance as part of the architectural history of the nation and particularly to the Park Service, as its owner, in its potential as an educational and cultural asset."[81]

It is almost a shame that the same thinking was not applied to the old observation tower demolished in 1988. Engineers had proclaimed the tower a safety hazard, and it had long come to be regarded as historically useless because tall trees had surrounded it and visitors could no longer view the layout of the winter encampment. Yet the tower was an artifact of its own time, and its presence at Valley Forge recalled the atmosphere of the park around the turn of the century.

The central theme of the most recent major study drafted at Valley Forge is that there is more to Valley Forge than the six months Washington spent there with his army. In his 1990 multidisciplinary archaeological study of the area around Washington's Headquarters, James Kurtz states: "The inclusion of the entire historical record helps to ensure that significant resources will be preserved for future generations."[82] He strongly advocates that a broader view be taken of the history and importance of Valley Forge, focusing on periods that have been ignored since the park was created:

> The story of the town of Valley Forge extends well beyond the Revolutionary War encampment. It involves industrial growth and failures, economic bust and booms, ethnic and social strife, and the grass roots formation of a park that today is linked with the suffering of the Continental Army during the winter of 1777 and 1778. It is a story worth telling to the public.[83]

Valley Forge can become a more interesting place than it has ever been. The stories of the Valley Forge encampment, the Valley Forge community, and Valley Forge the historic place—with its legacy of artifacts and interpretations reflecting our changing values and our attitude toward American history—are all interwoven. The study of any single aspect becomes more rewarding when consideration is given to the other two. The full story of Valley Forge is not only worth telling to the public; it is impossible to ignore.

Epilogue:
Valley Forge—Past, Present, Future

No battles were fought at Valley Forge—until after the soldiers marched out. It was after the Revolution that Valley Forge became the scene of intermittent quarrel and strife. Each new trend in historiography and historic preservation brought up new issues for those who held its story dear. Each new trend left documentary remains and contributed to a second history of Valley Forge, equally worthy of attention.

It took the Romantic Era of the nineteenth century to create a Valley Forge worth fighting over. Before professional historians had a chance to dwell much on the winter encampment, antiquarians promoted and glorified the Valley Forge experience. The Colonial Revival Movement intensified America's love affair with its own past, and in its wake organizations were formed to celebrate the Valley Forge experience and preserve its Washington's Headquarters.

The early record of the Centennial and Memorial Association of Valley Forge is one of cooperation with other patriotic groups, such as the Patriotic Order Sons of America and the Daughters of the American Revolution

(DAR). They made Valley Forge a tourist attraction that drew pilgrims to the sacred soil where, it was believed, so many had suffered and died, and this new role for the town, following its decline as an industrial area, actually gave it a renaissance.

The long battle of Valley Forge can be said to have begun when a second lasting entity—the Valley Forge Park Commission, with its mission to establish a park and its power to condemn property—was organized. Private-property owners disputed the amounts they were offered for their dwellings, and business owners complained even more bitterly about actions that inhibited their operations and expansion. Yet the prevailing spirit of nationalism in America put public opinion on the side of the park commission, even when it condemned the property of its rival organization, the Centennial and Memorial Association of Valley Forge.

At the end of the nineteenth and beginning of the twentieth century, the park commission transformed Valley Forge into a memorial park. Monuments sprang up, and the grounds were beautified with flowering dogwoods and attractive vistas. Additional relics of the Colonial and Revolutionary periods were preserved. There were conflicts over where monuments should be located and what they should look like, but consensus that such tributes were appropriate for Valley Forge.

The Rev. Dr. W. Herbert Burk was initially able to coexist peacefully with the park commission. His establishment of the Washington Memorial emphasized the sacred and holy nature of Valley Forge in a period when history and religion both were employed to foster morality. His modest first attempts to interpret the Valley Forge experience, as in his museum collection and his publication of interpretive guides, were not resented.

As the 1920s and 1930s brought a new emphasis on historical accuracy, leaders of the park commission increasingly came into conflict with Burk. Burk objected to expanding the park and to destroying the living communities that expansion entailed. The park commissioners objected to Burk's plans to overwhelm Valley Forge with a cathedral, since there had been no cathedral at Valley Forge in the winter of 1777–1778. The concurrent predilection for tasteful historic sites ensured conflict also over perceived attempts to commercialize Valley Forge. Battles were waged over the specter of hot dog stands, and the mere name of a brewery on a guidebook raised alarm.

As the re-creation of Williamsburg changed tastes in historic preservation, Valley Forge followed suit with its "complete restoration" project, originally planned to give the visitor the feeling of visiting the actual winter encampment. At first, only a few people questioned whether attempts to re-create the past were preferable to merely preserving what was really left of it. As time passed and tastes and styles changed once more, the major projects of the complete restoration drew more and more criticism.

The Cold War brought intensified twentieth-century attempts to use the Valley Forge experience to inspire visitors to greater patriotism and loyalty. Entities then active at Valley Forge seemed almost to enter into competition over which one could achieve this objective best. The new Freedoms Foundation emerged as the clear winner. The most recent conflicts have come about from new professional research done at Valley Forge largely after the park's transfer to the National Park Service. Was the *Valley Forge Report* unnecessarily iconoclastic? Did it in turn overly influence the new interpretive exhibit at the Valley Forge Historical Society's museum?

As times change and trends continue to develop, the surviving major institutions at Valley Forge must keep pace by adjusting their agendas to serve new constituencies. At the moment, they are at peace with one another and going about their business in a spirit of unprecedented cooperation and respect.

On May 3, 1992, there was a special celebration of Evensong at the Washington Memorial to commemorate the alliance between France and the United States that had contributed so materially to America's victory in the Revolution. Because news of the French alliance had come while Washington was at Valley Forge, the Valley Forge Historical Society generally hosts an annual celebration, but this one was special because it was jointly sponsored by the historical society and the chapel. At the end of the service in the Washington Memorial Chapel, Dr. Richard Stinson, the new rector, took Meade Jones, president of the historical society, on his arm, and together they officially unlocked the door that had been closed since 1969. They intended their action to symbolize the dawn of a new age for their two organizations. Each of them shook hands with all guests as they passed from the chapel to the museum for a reception hosted by the historical society.

On June 5, 1993, the Valley Forge Historical Society held its annual meeting in the library at the Washington Memorial, an elegant complex tucked away behind the chapel, but a location so unfamiliar that someone was posted outside to direct the members to its door. In his remarks Dr. Stinson emphasized, "This is your room as well as the chapel's room." Pointing out that on the shelves lining the walls books on history and religion are "co-mingled," he continued: "Our organizations are co-mingled, too." Meade Jones continued the theme, commenting on how Dr. Burk had envisioned a "comprehensive memorial." The cooperation and goodwill established one year earlier was definitely the goal for the future.

In a 1992 interview, Stinson discussed his mission as one of developing the Washington Memorial Chapel as a national shrine. He said he admired the significant achievement of Sheldon M. Smith in making the parish live and function, and like his predecessor wanted to increase attendance through a new "Committee on Growth, Evangelism and Communication." He had been in touch with the park service about joint archaeological investigations, and as a dedicated naturalist he said he would like visitors to appreciate the beauties of nature along with the lessons of history when they visit the Washington Memorial. Stinson was formerly rector at Saint James' Church at Mount Vernon and served a tour as a chaplain in Vietnam. In his mind, the Washington Memorial was no anomaly. "If you've read *Ivanhoe*," he said, "if you believe in the ideals of Christian knighthood, then the Washington Memorial makes perfect sense."[1]

Over the last few years, the Valley Forge Historical Society has been reaching out to new audiences with new programs. The most successful of these is an active Elderhostel program—in fact, the largest such program in the state—administered by C. Robert Gruver, who coordinated the wagon-train event back in 1976. The society also sponsors an annual art exhibit and participated in the popular annual Philadelphia Open House program. In 1993, architectural improvements to the museum portion of the complex made certain areas brighter, more inviting, and more up-to-date in terms of visitor expectations.

West of the park, the Freedoms Foundation underwent a transition during the 1970s when Ken Wells retired and Robert W. Miller was installed as president in 1975. In a 1983 article for the *Philadelphia Inquirer Magazine*, Chuck Bauerlein wrote: "The foundation is, indeed, drifting into a new emphasis on education and spending less of its time and energy 'promoting America.' "[2] In 1992 Miller defined the Freedoms Foundation as "basically an educational institution."[3] The premise that the nation's youth had failed to realize that freedom entails certain responsibilities inspired the foundation's Annual Youth and Leadership Workshops, in which students were instructed in traditional American values and principles. A recent foundation publication comments:

> Although initially the long range value of these programs was open to question, their significance now has become indisputable. Not only do elementary programs provide an important learning activity

supplemental to the school curriculum, but there is an even more important result, namely, the acculturation of children who are immigrants or whose parents are immigrants. Freedoms Foundation programs have helped to mainstream ethnic populations in American history and familiarize children with the nature of American institutions.[4]

Recently the foundation offered some courses for which several universities granted graduate credit. Some of them focused on the history of the American Revolution and the Civil War, and in some the word "freedom" figured prominently in the course titles—such as "Rights, Responsibilities, and Freedom" and "Freedom and the American Presidency."

In October 1994, as this book goes to press, President Robert W. Miller of the Freedoms Foundation has announced his retirement. A search is being conducted for a new president. One of Robert Miller's key accomplishments was the development of a companion to the Bill of Rights called the "Bill of Responsibilities," based on nearly two years of work by American scholars directed by a steering committee. Miller was also proud of the organization's program of Leavey Awards for Excellence in Private Enterprise Education. Endowed by the Thomas and Dorothy Leavey Foundation in 1982, these awards honored those who developed innovative ways to teach about the free enterprise system.

The focus of the organization changed a great deal since Cold War days. In fact, a recent Freedoms Foundation newsletter carried a photograph of Professor Valentin Petrovich Fyodorov, who had been promoting free enterprise in the former Soviet Union. Fyodorov's likeness was captured as he posed next to a copy of the Bill of Responsibilities, which he learned about at a Leavey Awards symposium in 1989. Once the old enemy was gone, foundation administrators appeared to want to put their Cold War heritage behind them. In a 1992 report, a foundation vice president wrote:

> The central purpose of the organization is not—and never was—fighting Communism and socialist theory. Rather, Freedoms Foundation illuminates the advantages of a free society with the purpose of reminding Americans of the blessings and responsibilities of freedom. In the course of fulfilling this mission, it naturally compares the workings of the society dedicated to the idea of freedom with those of societies dedicated to other purposes.[5]

Warren D. (Denny) Beach has been superintendent at Valley Forge National Historical Park since the spring of 1990. Very much a "people person," he enjoys meeting visitors and the members of various organizations active at Valley Forge. "But this is no popularity contest," he states. "We are here to serve the resource. Not everybody understands that."[6] To Beach has fallen the unenviable job of enforcing the provisions of the General Management Plan and balancing the interests of the resource with the demands of the local community. In the summer of 1992, paratroopers from the Eighty-second Airborne Division requested permission for a mass jump into the park as a part of their annual reunion. A similar jump had been permitted in 1989, but Beach denied the request—which, he maintained, did not serve the resource and may have posed a threat to the safety of visitors. Beach stood firm against a host of complaints, like one letter to the editor of the *Philadelphia Inquirer* in which the writer denounced Beach's decision as "just one more step in successive attempts to keep the public from using this historical park."[7] Beach also had to deal with the angry owners of homes adjacent to the park who complained about deer destroying their shrubbery and, most recently, with structural problems in the arch. Probably the biggest park controversy in recent years was the discovery that gay men were using one area of the park for open sexual activity, something that led to a sting operation resulting in more than sixty arrests.

Will the park expand again? Beach says probably not. Instead of buying land, the National Park Service now secures scenic easements to protect the park's remaining buffer areas from any drastic developments. It is hoped that scenic easements will protect much of the privately held land in what used to be Valley Forge village, so that the area retains what remains of its old village flavor.[8]

Recent research in historic preservation at Valley Forge has been done by historic architect Tom McGimsey at a ruined dwelling on the former Walnut Hill Estate on the north side of the Schuylkill River, which had been protected by a hastily erected fence during the Boy Scout activities of 1985 and 1986. McGimsey produced a lengthy multidisciplinary study revealing that this structure, much of it destroyed by fire in 1967, had a wing built in the mid-eighteenth century, and might well have played a part in the winter encampment. According to McGimsey, the house also has "significant building fabric from each of its periods and can help interpret building construction."[9] According to Denny Beach, "We used to have a house and a barn, now we have an historic house and barn. We have to treat them a little differently."[10]

In 1993, Valley Forge National Historical Park hosted a centennial celebration that had been in the works for approximately two years to commemorate the 100th anniversary of the existence of a public park at Valley Forge. Authorized by Denny Beach but coordinated by Joan Marshall-Dutcher, this celebration, like all anniversaries, acknowledged the past but really revealed the attitudes of the present and hinted at plans for the future.

Marshall-Dutcher started by organizing a steering committee and a number of subcommittees. For months, trial balloons were floated and reviewed. At one point, an appearance and speech by the President of the United States was contemplated. Eventually the celebration was limited by the amount of funds that could be raised from corporations and the local community, because the decision had been made to use no federal (taxpayer) dollars. The original plan for a single, elaborate celebration evolved into a year of special events beginning on December 19, 1992 ("March-In Day") and culminating on the weekend of June 19, 1993 ("Evacuation Day").

Marshall-Dutcher's goals included raising the profile of Valley Forge and involving new people in its events. The steering committee had many new faces including local corporate executives and known movers and shakers from other organizations, such as the Junior League and the Friends of Independence Park. One centennial event was an entry in the popular Philadelphia Flower Show, which entailed the organization of a garden group—another first for Valley Forge. The black sorority Delta Sigma Theta participated by funding and dedicating a monument honoring patriots of African descent. The 1993 National Council on Public History was hosted by Valley Forge National Historical Park, and the extremely popular Chester County artist Richard Bollinger created a painting, *Forging a Nation*, set in Valley Forge in December 1777.

Another goal was to make it clear that history did not begin and end at Valley Forge with the winter encampment, so the big weekend celebration held June 19 and 20, 1993, had two focal points. At one location, hundreds of people participated in hourly reenactment programs on eighteenth-century military and camp life, making this the largest reenactment organized at Valley Forge in recent years. In the area around Washington's Headquarters, the focus was different. There, interpreters in Victorian dress explained the layout and life of the now-vanished 1890s Valley Forge village. A special exhibit on the park's nineteenth- and twentieth-century history was mounted in the 1913 train station, and bands playing turn-of-the-century American music performed.

Visitation in the park that weekend alone was estimated at more than

15,000 people. An aggressive publicity campaign resulted in Valley Forge press releases being picked up by the wire services, and the appearance of Valley Forge information in publications as distant as the *Kansas City Star* and the *Chicago Tribune* and as national as *Family Circle* magazine and the *Washington Post*.

Comments overheard at the centennial celebration indicated that this blending of the story of the encampment with other aspects of Valley Forge history was refreshing to some but incomprehensible to others. An emphasis on Valley Forge's "second" history may well spark new controversy, start another battle, and add yet another chapter to that same tale.

Notes

Preface

1. David Lowenthal, *The Past Is a Foreign Country* (Cambridge: Cambridge University Press, 1985), p. 26.

2. Ibid., p. 328.

3. Michael Kammen, *A Season of Youth: The American Revolution and the Historical Imagination* (New York: Alfred A. Knopf, 1978), p. 7.

4. Lowenthal, *The Past Is a Foreign Country*, p. 353.

5. Ada Louise Huxtable, "Inventing American Reality," *New York Review of Books*, December 3, 1992, p. 24.

6. Michael Wallace, "Visiting the Past: History Museums in the United States," *Radical History Review* 25 (1981), 80.

7. Patricia Mooney-Melvin, "Harnessing the Romance of the Past: Preservation, Tourism, and History," *The Public Historian* 13 (Spring 1991), 46.

Chapter 1: The First Hundred Years at Valley Forge

1. John Fanning Watson, "Trip to Valley Forge and the Camp Hills," July 1828, Historical Society of Pennsylvania, Philadelphia, Pa.

2. Ibid.

3. Ibid.

4. Ibid.

5. Michael Kammen, *Mystic Chords of Memory: The Transformation of Tradition in American Culture* (New York: Alfred A. Knopf, 1991), pp. 42, 49, 51, 53.

6. Watson, "Trip to Valley Forge."

7. Ibid.

8. Ibid.

9. Anne F. Rhoads, Douglas Ryan, and Ella W. Aderman, *Land Use Study of Valley Forge National Historical Park* (Valley Forge, Pa.: Valley Forge National Historical Park, 1989 [internally distributed]), pp. i, 185–186.

10. James Kurtz, *Archaeological Inventory and Assessment: The Western Portion* (Washington, D.C.: U.S. Department of the Interior, National Park Service, Mid-Atlantic Regional Office, 1990), pp. 17–23. In describing the industrial village of Valley Forge in the late nineteenth century, I paraphrase the 1987–1988 draft that drew on historical records, interviews, surface reconnaissance, and subsurface testing.

11. Henry Woodman, *The History of Valley Forge* (reprint ed., Oaks, Pa.: John Francis Sr., 1921), pp. 87–88, 96.

12. Jacqueline Thibaut, *In the True Rustic Order: Historic Resource Study and Historical Base Maps of the Valley Forge Encampment, 1777–1778*, vol. 3 of *Valley Forge Report*, ed. Wayne K. Bodle and Jacqueline Thibaut (Valley Forge, Pa.: Valley Forge National Historical Park, 1980–82), p. 67.

13. Theodore W. Bean, *The History of Montgomery County* (Philadelphia: Everts & Peck, 1884), pp. 1123–1124.

14. Rhoads, Ryan, and Aderman, *Land Use Study*, pp. 187–188.

15. Enos Reeves, "Extracts from the Letter-Books of Lieutenant Enos Reeves," *Pennsylvania Magazine of History and Biography* 21 (1897), 235.

16. Kurtz, *Archaeological Inventory*, pp. 26–29, 168, 172.

17. Ibid., pp. 30–31, 49, 232.

18. Harlan D. Unrau, *Administrative History of Valley Forge National Historical Park* (Denver, Colo.: Denver Service Center, U.S. Department of the Interior, National Park Service, 1984 [internally distributed]), p. 20.

19. Kurtz, *Archaeological Inventory*, p. 31.

20. Caleb Jones to Hannah Ogden, March 2, 1837, John Reed Collection, Record Group 10, Valley Forge National Historical Park (hereafter referred to as VFNHP), Valley Forge, Pa.

21. John F. Reed, "Vision at Valley Forge," *Bulletin of the Montgomery County Historical Society* 15 (Fall 1966), 28.

22. "Preamble and Constitution of the Friendly Association for Mutual Interests," Philadelphia, 1826, Reed Collection, VFNHP.

23. William Maclure to Mary D. Fretogeot, July 31, 1826, Reed Collection, VFNHP.

24. Arthur Eugene Bestor Jr., *Backwoods Utopias: The Sectarian and Owenite Phases of Communitarian Socialism in America, 1663–1829* (Philadelphia: University of Pennsylvania Press, 1950), p. 203.

25. Watson, "Trip to Valley Forge."

26. "Harvest Home Meeting of Chester and Montgomery Counties at the Valley Forge Encampment Ground," July 26, 1828, Valley Forge Miscellaneous File, Chester County Historical Society, West Chester, Pa.

27. Ibid.

28. Daniel Webster, *The Works of Daniel Webster*, vol. 2 (Boston: Charles C. Little and James Brown, 1851), p. 277.

29. "Harvest Home Meeting."

30. Webster, *Works*, pp. 278–279.

31. Isaac A. Pennypacker to John Fanning Watson, April 2, 1844, Supplement to Watson's Annals, AM3011, Historical Society of Pennsylvania.

32. Woodman, *History of Valley Forge*, pp. 49–51, 67, 163–165. Woodman gives George Weedon's name as Joseph Wheedon.

33. Ibid., pp. 126–127.

34. George Washington, *The Diaries of George Washington*, ed. Donald Jackson and Dorothy Twohig, vol. 5 (Charlottesville: University Press of Virginia, 1979), p. 179.

35. Woodman, *History of Valley Forge*, pp. 54–56, 63, 100–101, 145.

36. Ibid., p. 91.

37. Ibid., pp. 27–28, 103–104.

38. Ibid., p. 104.

39. Ibid., p. 153.

40. Benson J. Lossing, *Washington: A Biography* (New York: Virtue Emmens & Co., 1860), p. 571.

41. *Daily Local News* (West Chester, Pa., here and hereafter), April 3, 1873.

42. *Daily Local News*, June 4, 1873.

43. *Daily Local News*, August 6, 1873.

44. Karal Ann Marling, *George Washington Slept Here: Colonial Revivals and American Culture, 1876–1986* (Cambridge, Mass.: Harvard University Press, 1988), p. 25.

45. Kammen, *Mystic Chords of Memory*, pp. 217–225; Wallace, "Visiting the Past," pp. 66–67.

46. *Daily Local News*, July 26, 1873.

47. Theodore W. Bean, *Washington at Valley Forge One Hundred Years Ago; or, The Foot-Prints of the Revolution* (Norristown, Pa., 1876), p. 1.

48. Ibid., pp. 54–61.

49. *Daily Local News*, November 13, 1873.

50. George Washington to John Banister, April 21, 1778, in *The Writings of George Washington from the Original Manuscript Sources, 1745–1799*, vol. 11, ed. John C. Fitzpatrick (Washington, D.C.: Government Printing Office, 1934), pp. 284–293.

51. George Washington Parke Custis, *Recollections and Private Memoirs of George Washington by His Adopted Son* (New York: Derby & Jackson, 1860), pp. 208–209.

52. Daniel Webster, *Works*, p. 279.

53. Watson, "Trip to Valley Forge."

54. Woodman, *History of Valley Forge*, p. 62.

55. Watson, "Trip to Valley Forge."

56. *The Casket*, April 1830.

57. William Perrine, "Washington's Christmas at Valley Forge," *Ladies' Home Journal*, December 1898, p. 7.

58. Marling, *George Washington Slept Here*, pp. 4–8.

59. Woodman, *History of Valley Forge*, p. 65.

60. Parke Custis, *Memoirs of Washington*, p. 275n; Lossing, *Washington*, p. 602n.

61. Bean, *Washington at Valley Forge*, p. 3.

62. Mrs. (Isabella) Thomas Potts James, *Memorial of Thomas Potts* (Cambridge, Mass., 1874), pp. 222–223.

63. William Cox Ewing, "Valley Forge Revisited" (1904), in *George Ewing: Gentleman and Soldier of Valley Forge*, ed. Thomas Ewing (Yonkers, N.Y., 1928), p. 58; W. H. Richardson, "Valley Forge," *New England Magazine* 23 (February 1901), 607.

64. *Daily Local News*, July 26, 1875.

65. Woodman, *History of Valley Forge*, p. 101.

66. Unrau, *Administrative History*, pp. 60–61.

67. "Inexpensive Trips Within Easy Reach," *Philadelphia Bulletin*, June 13, 1904.

68. Nathan Jones to "Dear Nephew," August 8, 1890, Reed Collection, VFNHP.

69. Howard DeHaven Ross, *History of the DeHaven Family* (New York: Pandick Press, 1929), pp. 9–13. This is the fourth edition of this work; the publication date of the first edition is unknown, but the second edition was published in 1895.

70. *New York Times*, May 27, 1990.

71. *Daily Local News*, June 27, 1878.

Chapter 2: The Centennial and Memorial Association of Valley Forge

1. *Daily Local News*, December 22, 1877.

2. *Daily Local News*, January 9, 1878.

3. *Daily Local News*, February 9, 1878.

4. H. J. Stager, *History of the Centennial and Memorial Association of Valley Forge* (n.p., 1911), p. 98.

5. Marling, *George Washington Slept Here*, p. 73.

6. Wallace, "Visiting the Past," pp. 64–65.

7. Marling, *George Washington Slept Here*, p. 74.

8. Judith Mitchell, "Ann Pamela Cunningham and Mount Vernon: A Southern Matron's Legacy" (Paper presented at the Fifteenth Annual Conference of the National Council of Public History, Valley Forge, Pa., April 29–May 2, 1993).

9. John Bruce Dodd and Cherry Dodd, *Historic Structure Report: Washington's Headquarters* (Valley Forge, Pa.: Valley Forge National Historical Park, 1981), pp. 1, 5, 17–20. (Hereafter cited as *Washington's Headquarters*.)

10. Stager, *History of the . . . Association*, p. 82.

11. Mitchell, "Ann Pamela Cunningham and Mount Vernon."

12. Marling, *George Washington Slept Here*, p. 44.

13. Stager, *History of the . . . Association*, pp. 18–20.

14. Marling, *George Washington Slept Here*, pp. 78–79.

15. Barbara McDonald Powell, "The Most Celebrated Encampment: Valley Forge in American Culture, 1777–1983" (Ph.D. dissertation, Cornell University, 1983), p. 61.

16. *Daily Local News*, March 18, 1878.

17. Stager, *History of the . . . Association*, p. 82.

18. *Daily Local News*, May 24, 1878.

19. *Daily Local News*, June 5, 1878.

20. *Daily Local News*, May 31, 1878.

21. *Daily Local News*, June 8, 1878.

22. *Daily Local News*, June 4, 1878.

23. "Final Arrangements for the Valley Forge Centennial," *Philadelphia Times*, June 18, 1878.

24. "Program for the First Centenary," in file marked "Valley Forge Centennial and Memorial Association Proceedings, 1879" at Chester County Historical Society.

25. *Proceedings on the Occasion of the Centennial Celebration of the Occupation of Valley Forge by the Continental Army Under George Washington, June 1878* (Philadelphia: J. B. Lippincott & Co., 1879), pp. 3–4, in ibid.

26. Ibid., pp. 7–8.

27. Ibid.

28. Ibid., pp. 38–39.

29. Ibid., pp. 57–61.

30. *Valley Forge Oration of Henry Armitt Brown* (Philadelphia: Loughead & Co., 1895), in Valley Forge Miscellaneous File, Chester County Historical Society.

31. Ibid.

32. Anna Morris Holstein to Francis M. Brooke, June 26, 1878, Francis M. Brooke Collection, Record Group 12, VFNHP.

33. "Woman's Work at Valley Forge," *Daily Local News*, June 24, 1878.

34. Stager, *History of the . . . Association*, p. 11.

35. Ibid., p. 84.

36. *Daily Local News*, January 12, 1882.

37. Stager, *History of the . . . Association*, pp. 16, 218.

38. *Daily Local News*, May 22, 1879.

39. *Daily Local News*, June 4, 1879.

40. *Daily Local News*, June 19, 1879.

41. *Daily Local News*, June 20, 1879.

42. Ibid.

43. *Daily Local News*, June 21, 1879.

44. *Daily Local News*, June 25, 1879.

45. *Daily Local News*, December 9, 1878.

46. *Daily Local News*, October 30, 1885.

47. *Village Record*, July 11, 1882.

48. Stager, *History of the . . . Association*, pp. 99–100.

49. Pamphlet printed by Patriotic Order Sons of America, Reed Collection, VFNHP.

50. Stager, *History of the . . . Association*, p. 227.

51. Ibid.

52. *Daily Local News*, May 22, 1886, and May 31, 1886.

53. Stager, *History of the . . . Association*, pp. 107–108.

54. Ibid., p. 227.

55. Ibid., p. 228.

56. *Daily Local News*, April 8, 1887.

57. Stager, *History of the . . . Association*, p. 219.

58. *Daily Local News*, August 27, 1887.

59. Dodd and Dodd, *Washington's Headquarters*, pp. 32–33, 64, 79.

60. *Daily Local News*, May 29, 1888.

61. "Washington's Headquarters," June 1891, in Valley Forge Miscellaneous File, Chester County Historical Society.

62. Dodd and Dodd, *Washington's Headquarters*, p. 100.

63. Stager, *History of the . . . Association*, pp. 136, 146.

64. *Daily Local News*, June 24, 1907. The Washington Elm was identified by a marker now in the collections of Valley Forge National Historical Park.

65. Anna Morris Holstein to Mrs. James, July 12, 1887, Society Collection, Historical Society of Pennsylvania.

66. Stager, *History of the . . . Association*, p. 147.

67. "The Valley Forge Reservation," in *Historical Sketches: A Collection of Papers Prepared for the Historical Society of Montgomery County, Pennsylvania*, vol. 5 (Norristown, Pa., 1925), p. 378; Unrau, *Administrative History*, p. 59.

68. Stager, *History of the . . . Association*, pp. 113–114, 218.

69. Anna Morris Holstein to Mrs. James, July 12, 1887.

70. *Daily Local News*, April 24, 1888.

71. Anna Morris Holstein to F. D. Stone, June 18, 1892, Society Collection, Historical Society of Pennsylvania.

72. Mary T. McInnes, *History of the Valley Forge Chapter, National Society, Daughters of the American Revolution* (1944).

73. Ibid.

74. Minutes of the Valley Forge Chapter of the Daughters of the American Revolution, October 1, 1900, Valley Forge Chapter, DAR, Norristown, Pa.

75. Ibid., April 5, 1901.

76. Ibid., October 1, 1901.

77. Ibid., April 2, 1900, and October 1, 1900.

78. Stager, *History of the . . . Association*, p. 154.

79. *Daily Local News*, June 19, 1908.

80. Stager, *History of the . . . Association*, p. 155.

81. "Catalog of Historic Articles and Relics in the Room Furnished by the Merion Chapter, DAR," p. 7, in Valley Forge Miscellaneous File, Chester County Historical Society.

82. William Cox Ewing, "Valley Forge Revisited," p. 64.

83. Kurtz, *Archaeological Inventory*, pp. 46, 274.

84. William H. Sayen, "Valley Forge Park," *Bulletin of the Montgomery County Historical Society* 21 (Fall 1978), 222–223.

85. "A Deserted Village," *Philadelphia Press*, September 8, 1895.

86. Clifton Johnson, "Midwinter at Valley Forge," *Women's Home Companion*, January 1902, p. 9.

87. Ibid.

88. *Daily Local News*, June 20, 1887.

89. *Daily Local News*, June 20, 1890.

90. *American Republican*, January 2, 1903.

91. *Daily Local News*, September 29, 1881.

92. *Daily Local News*, October 18, 1890.

93. *Daily Local News*, June 22, 1900.

94. William M. Stephens, "Burial Places of the Soldiers at Valley Forge," *Bulletin of the Montgomery County Historical Society* 3 (April 1942), 155.

95. *Norristown Times Herald*, June 1, 1896. No modern evidence substantiates the presence of a vast number of graves in this area.

96. *Daily Local News*, April 30, 1902.

97. *Norristown Times Herald*, May 25, 1896.

98. Ado. Latch to Francis M. Brooke, January 14, 1898, Brooke Collection, VFNHP. No modern evidence substantiates the presence of a vast number of graves in this area either.

99. "A Deserted Village," *Philadelphia Press*, September 8, 1895.

100. Stager, *History of the . . . Association*, p. 16.

101. Anna Morris Holstein to F. D. Stone, December 29, 1891, Society Collection, Historical Society of Pennsylvania.

102. Anna Morris Holstein to F. D. Stone, June 12, 1892, Society Collection, Historical Society of Pennsylvania.

103. Stager, *History of the . . . Association*, p. 16.

104. *Daily Local News*, March 21, 1890.

105. "To Form a National Park," *Daily Local News*, December 5, 1889.

106. J. F. Seiders, *Thirty Ancestors of Richard Henry Koch* (Pottsville, Pa., 1939), p. 297.

107. Stager, *History of the . . . Association*, pp. 135, 143–144.

108. Ibid., p. 135.

109. Anna Morris Holstein to F. D. Stone, June 21, 1892, Society Collection, Historical Society of Pennsylvania.

110. Stager, *History of the . . . Association*, p. 139.

111. Ibid., p. 160.

Chapter 3: A Rocky Beginning for the Valley Forge Park Commission

1. *Phoenixville Messenger*, July 15, 1882.

2. *Phoenixville Messenger*, July 22, 1882.

3. Kammen, *Mystic Chords of Memory*, pp. 33, 66, 115–166.

4. *Phoenixville Messenger*, December 23, 1882.

5. *Daily Local News*, June 22, 1883. Other newspapers sometimes refer to the "Valley Forge Monument Association."

6. W. Herbert Burk, *Historical and Topographical Guide to Valley Forge* (Norristown, Pa., 1906), p. 84.

7. Stager, *History of the . . . Association*, p. 123.

8. *Daily Local News*, August 12, 1891.

9. Records of the Valley Forge Park Commission, October 1, 1899, Record Group 46 (microfilm), VFNHP.

10. Ibid., June 17, 1893.

11. Sayen, "Valley Forge Park," p. 216.

12. Francis M. Brooke to Frederick D. Stone, October 26, 1893, Record Group 46, Carton #1, General Correspondence, Pennsylvania State Archives, Harrisburg, Pa.

13. Sayen, "Valley Forge Park," p. 206.

14. Editor, "Notes and Queries," *Pennsylvania Magazine of History and Biography* 18 (1894), 384.

15. "Address of Samuel W. Pennypacker to the Patriotic Order Sons of America, 18 June 1898," Valley Forge Miscellaneous File, Chester County Historical Society.

16. Thibaut, *In the True Rustic Order*, vol. 3 of *Valley Forge Report*, pp. 14–17.

17. Records of the Valley Forge Park Commission, July 6, 1893, Record Group 46, VFNHP.

18. *Daily Local News*, August 12, 1891.

19. Records of the Valley Forge Park Commission, September 7, 1893, Record Group 46, VFNHP.

20. "Valley Forge Land Values," *Daily Local News*, January 30, 1894.

21. "President's Report of the Valley Forge Park Commission, 1 February 1894," Record Group 2, VFNHP.

22. *Daily Local News*, April 21, 1894.

23. *Daily Local News*, May 5, 1894.

24. *Daily Local News*, May 23, 1894.

25. Records of the Valley Forge Park Commission, October 18, 1894, Record Group 46, VFNHP.

26. "Valley Forge Land Values," *Daily Local News*, October 23, 1894.

27. "President's Report of the Valley Forge Park Commission, 1 November 1894," Record Group 2, VFNHP.

28. "President's Report of the Valley Forge Park Commission, 22 March 1895," Record Group 2, VFNHP.

29. "Valley Forge Park," *Daily Local News*, June 6, 1895.

30. Valley Forge Park Commission, *Report . . . December 17, 1896*, p. 16.

31. Francis M. Brooke, *To the Senators and Representatives of the Commonwealth of Pennsylvania, February 22, 1897* (Valley Forge, Pa., 1897), p. 8, Brooke Collection, VFNHP.

32. Secretary of the Park Commission to "Dear Senator," March 6, 1899, Record Group 46, Carton #1, General Correspondence, Pennsylvania State Archives.

33. Valley Forge Park Commission, *Report . . . December 27, 1900*, pp. 21–22

34. *Daily Local News*, October 18, 1901.

35. Woodman, *History of Valley Forge*, p. 72.

36. Thibaut, *In the True Rustic Order*, p. 118.

37. "Sullivan's Bridge Monument," in *Historical Sketches*, 4:31, 41–42.

38. *Daily Local News*, April 21, 1894.

39. "For Valley Forge," *Daily Local News*, May 25, 1895.

40. Daniel Hastings to Francis M. Brooke, November 18, 1895, Brooke Collection, VFNHP.

41. "Report on the Waterman Monument," Record Group 2, VFNHP.

42. Brooke, *To the Senators and Representatives*, pp. 7–8.

43. John Faber Miller, counsel for W. M. Stephens, to Francis M. Brooke, December 29, 1897, Brooke Collection, VFNHP.

44. William F. Solly to Francis M. Brooke, April 2, 1898, and April 5, 1898, Record Group 2, VFNHP.

45. Records of the Valley Forge Park Commission, June 2, 1902, Record Group 46, VFNHP.

46. Valley Forge Park Commission, *Report . . . December 16, 1902*, p. 4.

47. Records of the Valley Forge Park Commission, December 20, 1904, Record Group 46, VFNHP.

48. Ibid., April 16, 1908, and December 14, 1910.

49. Valley Forge Park Commission, *Report . . . 1912*, p. 11.

50. W. H. Richardson, "Valley Forge," *New England Magazine* 23 (February 1901), 605.

51. *Norristown Times Herald*, June 1, 1896.

52. Edward W. Hocker, "Valley Forge as a National Park," *Outlook*, April 6, 1901, p. 788.

53. *Daily Local News*, October 3, 1901. Todd got his wish; the daughters held title to this land until 1983, when it was transferred to the national park at Valley Forge. The state of Pennsylvania never did hold title.

54. Valley Forge Park Commission, *Report . . . December 16, 1902*, p. 5.

55. Records of the Valley Forge Park Commission, May 24, 1939, and September 27, 1939, Record Group 46, VFNHP. The Waterman headstone is not normally on view to visitors, and since its removal there has been confusion over the exact location of Waterman's grave. A 1901 newspaper account reported that the shaft had been constructed "right alongside" the grave, but its exact location today is unknown.

56. Records of the Valley Forge Park Commission, October 2, 1901, Record Group 46, VFNHP.

57. Ellis Hampton to Francis M. Brooke, December 6, 1897, Brooke Collection, VFNHP.

58. Records of the Valley Forge Park Commission, July 6, 1904, Record Group 46, VFNHP.

59. Owen Wister, *Lady Baltimore* (New York: Macmillan, 1906), pp. 67–73.

Chapter 4: *The Park Commission Triumphs*

1. Hampton L. Carson, "The Life and Services of Samuel W. Pennypacker," *Pennsylvania Magazine of History and Biography* 41 (1917), 41–42.

2. "State Commission Visits Valley Forge," *Philadelphia Public Ledger*, October 30, 1904.

3. *Daily Local News*, August 10, 1906.

4. *Daily Local News*, January 9, 1908.

5. *Daily Local News*, October 12, 1883.

6. "Save Valley Forge for a National Park," *Philadelphia Press*, December 20, 1900.

7. Unrau, *Administrative History of Valley Forge*, p. 91.

8. "Save Valley Forge for a National Park."

9. Ibid.

10. Ibid.

11. Julius Moritzen, "Valley Forge and the Nation," *Harper's Weekly*, June 22, 1901, p. 628.

12. Letter of the Valley Forge National Park Association, in Valley Forge Miscellaneous File, Chester County Historical Society.

13. *Daily Local News*, December 2, 1901.

14. *Daily Local News*, January 30, 1902.

15. *Daily Local News*, January 31, 1902.

16. "Must Pennsylvania Lose Valley Forge?" *North American*, January 27, 1902.

17. Carson, "The Life and Services of Pennypacker," pp. 41–42.

18. *Daily Republican*, November 28, 1916.

19. Stager, *History of the . . . Association*, p. 86.

20. Records of the Valley Forge Park Commission, June 24, 1893, Record Group 46, VFNHP.

21. "Valley Forge Campground," *Norristown Times Herald*, June 1, 1896.

22. Moritzen, "Valley Forge and the Nation," p. 629.

23. Stager, *History of the . . . Association*, pp. 136–138.

24. Unrau, *Administrative History*, p. 48.

25. Stager, *History of the . . . Association*, p. 150.

26. Valley Forge Park Commission, *Report . . . 1904*, p. 4.

27. Burk, *Historical and Topographical Guide to Valley Forge*, p. 71.

28. Stager, *History of the . . . Association*, pp. 160–161.

29. Ibid., p. 161.

30. Records of the Valley Forge Park Commission, November 8, 1905, Record Group 46, VFNHP.

31. "Historic Real Estate," *Philadelphia Public Ledger*, July 17, 1905.

32. Stager, *History of the . . . Association*, pp. 162–163.

33. Ibid., pp. 164–165.

34. Ibid., pp. 168–170.
35. *Daily Local News*, June 20, 1907.
36. Stager, *History of the . . . Association*, pp. 231–232.
37. Ibid., p. 239.
38. Ibid., pp. 171, 174, 185, 190–191.
39. Records of the Valley Forge Park Commission, November 24, 1905, Record Group 46, VFNHP.
40. Stager, *History of the . . . Association*, pp. 175, 181.
41. Ibid., p. 183.
42. A. H. Bowen to William Sayen, March 3, 1909, Record Group 46, Carton #1, General Correspondence, Pennsylvania State Archives. Not normally on view, this plaque is among the holdings of Valley Forge National Historical Park.
43. Records of the Valley Forge Park Commission, September 18, 1906, Record Group 46, VFNHP.
44. Valley Forge Park Commission, *Report . . . December 30, 1916*, p. 14.
45. Unrau, *Administrative History*, pp. 141; "Museum Committee Reports, 1 November 1916 and 5 June 1916," Record Group 2, VFNHP.
46. Records of the Valley Forge Park Commission, February 4, 1914, Record Group 46, VFNHP.
47. Ibid., September 5, 1917.
48. F. A. Collins, "Valley Forge Memorial Park," *Outlook*, April 11, 1917, p. 657.
49. Unrau, *Administrative History*, pp. 101–103, 110–111.
50. *Daily Local News*, May 5, 1906, and January 9, 1908.
51. John Bruce Dodd, *Classified Structure Field Inventory Report: School House* (Valley Forge, Pa.: Valley Forge National Historical Park, 1979).
52. Valley Forge Park Commission, *Report . . . 1906*, p. 4.
53. Priscilla Walker Sheels to A. H. Bowen, January 27, 1908, Record Group 46, Carton #1, General Correspondence, Pennsylvania State Archives.
54. *Daily Local News*, January 9, 1908.
55. *Daily Local News*, November 11, 1907.
56. Valley Forge Park Commission, *Report . . . 1908*, p. 4.
57. See Chapter 7.
58. Collins, "Valley Forge Memorial Park," p. 657.
59. Records of the Valley Forge Park Commission, July 2, 1913, Record Group 46, VFNHP.
60. Dodd, *Classified Structure Field Inventory Report: School House.*
61. Valley Forge Park Commission, *Report . . . December 17, 1896*, p. 17.
62. Valley Forge Park Commission, *Report . . . 1904*, p. 3.
63. "Inexpensive Trips Within Easy Reach," *Philadelphia Bulletin*, June 13, 1904.
64. Unidentified writer to "Editor," August 10, 1906, Record Group 46, Carton #1, General Correspondence, Pennsylvania State Archives.
65. A. H. Bowen to W. B. Fletcher, September 14, 1908, Record Group 46, Carton #1, General Correspondence, Pennsylvania State Archives.
66. *Daily Local News*, December 2, 1909.
67. "Report of the Special Electric Railway Committee, 6 October 1921 and 1 December 1921," Record Group 2, VFNHP.
68. Valley Forge Park Commission, *Report . . . 1904*, p. 6.
69. John Bruce Dodd, *Classified Structure Field Inventory Report: Observation Tower* (Valley Forge, Pa.: Valley Forge National Historical Park, 1978).
70. "Sullivan's Bridge Monument," pp. 31–32.
71. Portland (Maine) Society of the Sons of the American Revolution, *Maine at Valley Forge* (n.p., 1908), p. 1.

72. Records of the Valley Forge Park Commission, December 18, 1906, Record Group 46, VFNHP.

73. Sons of the American Revolution, *Maine at Valley Forge*, pp. 4–5.

74. *Ceremonies at the Dedication of the Equestrian Statue of Major-General Anthony Wayne Erected by the Commonwealth of Pennsylvania on the Revolutionary Campground at Valley Forge, June 20, 1908* (Harrisburg, Pa.: Harrisburg Publishing Co., 1909), p. 5, in Valley Forge Miscellaneous File, Chester County Historical Society.

75. Ibid., p. 6.

76. "Statue of General Anthony Wayne Dedicated at Valley Forge," *Philadelphia Press,* June 21, 1908.

77. Samuel W. Pennypacker to Francis Rawle, July 6, 1909, Society Collection, Historical Society of Pennsylvania.

78. A. H. Bowen to John Nicholson, July 6, 1909, Record Group 46, Carton #1, General Correspondence, Pennsylvania State Archives.

79. Valley Forge Park Commission, *Report . . . 1910,* p. 11.

80. Superintendent Hartranft to "Valley Forge Park Committee," January 3, 1911, Nicholson Scrapbooks, Historical Society of Pennsylvania.

81. Superintendent Hartranft to "Whom It May Concern," February 10, 1912, Nicholson Scrapbooks.

82. Scrapbook A-7.2, p. 228, Montgomery County Historical Society, Norristown, Pa.

83. *Daily Local News,* June 11, 1913.

84. Ibid.

85. Records of the Valley Forge Park Commission, November 13, 1906, Record Group 46, VFNHP.

86. Burk, *Historical and Topographical Guide,* pp. 69–70, 82.

87. Records of the Valley Forge Park Commission, February 3, 1917, Record Group 46, VFNHP.

88. Unrau, *Administrative History,* p. 156.

89. Superintendent to H. C. Hill, September 27, 1919, Record Group 46, Carton #1, General Correspondence, Pennsylvania State Archives.

90. Ad placed c. 1919, Record Group 46, Carton #1, General Correspondence, Pennsylvania State Archives.

91. "Report of the Committee for the Restoration of Forts, 6 November 1912," Record Group 2, VFNHP.

92. Ibid., November 3, 1915.

93. Ibid., June 5, 1916.

94. Ibid., October 4, 1916.

95. Ibid., June 1, 1917.

96. *Spring City Reporter,* October 14, 1915.

97. "President's Report of the Valley Forge Park Commission, 1 November 1894," Record Group 2, VFNHP.

98. Unnumbered pages from *Congressional Record,* Nicholson Scrapbooks, Historical Society of Pennsylvania.

99. "The Proper Memorial at Valley Forge," *Philadelphia Record,* January 26, 1911.

100. *Norristown Times Herald,* April 12, 1911.

101. Irving Wanger to A. H. Bowen, April 1, 1911, quoted in Park Commission Records for April 5, 1911, Record Group 46, VFNHP.

102. Ibid., April 5, 1911.

103. War Department to W. H. Sayen, December 17, 1913, Record Group 46, Carton #1, General Correspondence, Pennsylvania State Archives.

104. Valley Forge Park Commission to Lindley Garrison, January 12, 1914, Record Group 46, Carton #1, General Correspondence, Pennsylvania State Archives.

105. "America's Memorial Arch to Valley Forge Heroes," *Philadelphia Public Ledger,* June 21, 1914.

106. Valley Forge Park Commission, *Twelfth Biennial Report . . . March 1, 1919.*

107. "National Arch Presentation at Valley Forge, June 19, 1917," Valley Forge Miscellaneous File, Chester County Historical Society.

108. W. H. Sayen to Governor Brumbaugh, May 8, 1917, Record Group 46, Carton #1, General Correspondence, Pennsylvania State Archives.

109. Valley Forge Park Commission, *Report . . . December 30, 1916,* p. 6.

110. Unrau, *Administrative History,* p. 152.

111. Sayen, "Valley Forge," pp. 224–230.

112. Ibid., p. 221.

113. Ebenezer Lund to Richmond L. Jones, October 31, 1917, Reed Collection, VFNHP.

114. Ebenezer Lund to Richmond L. Jones, July 1, 1919, Reed Collection, VFNHP.

115. Undated Memo of Ebenezer Lund, Reed Collection, VFNHP.

116. Superintendent to Samuel G. Dixon, September 6, 1917, Record Group 46, Carton #1, General Correspondence, Pennsylvania State Archives.

117. Superintendent to Dr. Edward Martin, Pennsylvania Commission of Health, August 23, 1919, Record Group 46, Carton #1, General Correspondence, Pennsylvania State Archives.

118. E. B. Cassatt to William A. Patton, September 29, 1915, Record Group 46, Carton #1, General Correspondence, Pennsylvania State Archives.

119. E. B. Cassatt to William A. Patton, May 29, 1919, Record Group 46, Carton #1, General Correspondence, Pennsylvania State Archives.

120. *Daily Local News,* May 5, 1906.

121. F. W. Echfeldt to Edward W. Beale, May 28, 1917, Record Group 46, Carton #1, General Correspondence, Pennsylvania State Archives.

Chapter 5: The Churches at Valley Forge

1. W. Herbert Burk, ed., *The Valley Forge Address of Theodore Roosevelt* (Norristown, Pa., 1909), pp. 30–32, 42–44. Burk's Washington's Birthday sermon appears in this volume.

2. Ibid., p. 32.

3. Ibid., p. 37.

4. W. Herbert Burk, "The Modern Foes of George Washington" (Paper delivered at Morristown, N.J., February 23, 1931), pp. 10–12, in Reed Collection, VFNHP.

5. Burk, *Historical and Topographical Guide* (1906), p. 31.

6. Eleanor H. S. Burk, *In the Beginning at Valley Forge and the Washington Memorial Chapel* (North Wales, Pa.: Norman B. Nuss, 1938), pp. 8–9.

7. *Washington Chapel Chronicle,* April 15, 1915. Copies of this parish newsletter can be found at the Horace Willcox Memorial Library at Valley Forge National Historical Park.

8. *Washington Chapel Chronicle,* November 15, 1912.

9. "At Valley Forge," *Norristown Times Herald,* August 12, 1911.

10. W. Herbert Burk, "Valley Forge: Its Past, Present, and Future," in *Historical Sketches,* 4:242–243.

11. W. Herbert Burk, "The American Westminster," *DAR Magazine* 42 (December 1923), 704–707.

12. Kammen, *Mystic Chords of Memory,* p. 33.

13. Ibid., pp. 198, 205.

14. A. Edward Newton, "Change Cars in Paoli," in *The Greatest Book in the World and Other Papers* (New York: Little, Brown & Co., 1925), p. 147.

15. *Daily Local News,* February 14, 1886.

16. "Valley Forge Memorial Church," *Village Record,* July 20, 1886.

17. *Daily Local News*, August 23, 1888.

18. *Daily Local News*, November 19, 1890.

19. "Reverend James Guthrie Restrained," *Daily Local News*, October 10, 1890.

20. Edward W. Hocker, "Valley Forge as a National Park," *Outlook*, April 6, 1901, p. 789.

21. *Washington Chapel Chronicle*, June 15, 1908.

22. *Daily Republican*, January 13, 1936.

23. "Valley Forge: Successful Celebration of the 125th Anniversary," *Norristown Herald*, June 20, 1903.

24. *Washington Chapel Chronicle*, November 15, 1912.

25. Burk, "American Westminster," p. 703.

26. Ibid., p. 708.

27. Ibid., p. 704.

28. Eleanor Burk, *In the Beginning at Valley Forge*, pp. 12–14.

29. Ibid., pp. 10–11.

30. "The President at Valley Forge," *Norristown Times Herald*, June 20, 1904.

31. Ibid.

32. Ibid.

33. Ibid.

34. "Valley Forge Memorial," *Daily Local News*, February 23, 1909.

35. The Honorable Wilfred Powell, "Address of His Majesty's British Consul, the Honorable Wilfred Powell at the Dedication of the Lectern" (Washington Memorial Chapel, June 15, 1909), in Reed Collection, VFNHP.

36. Burk, *In the Beginning at Valley Forge*, p. 13.

37. W. Herbert Burk, *Making a Museum: The Confessions of a Curator* (n.p., 1926), pp. 5–6, 12–20.

38. Ibid., pp. 30–34.

39. "The Halls of History" (pamphlet), Reed Collection, VFNHP.

40. Burk, *Making a Museum*, pp. 57–69.

41. *Washington Chapel Chronicle*, August 15, 1909.

42. Miss Lee to W. Herbert Burk, July 25, 1909, Curator's Archives at Valley Forge Historical Society, Valley Forge, Pa.

43. *Washington Chapel Chronicle*, August 15, 1909.

44. *Village Record*, September 12, 1909.

45. Burk, *Making a Museum*, p. 42.

46. *Washington Chapel Chronicle*, May 15, 1911.

47. Miss Lee to W. Herbert Burk, April 6, 1916, Curator's Archives at Valley Forge Historical Society.

48. W. Herbert Burk to Burke & Herbert, Bankers, October 13, 1923, and W. Herbert Burk to Mrs. Robert E. Lee, December 13, 1923, Curator's Archives at Valley Forge Historical Society.

49. *Washington Chapel Chronicle*, July 15, 1910.

50. Burk, *Making a Museum*, pp. 48–49.

51. W. Herbert Burk to Mrs. C. M. Crosby, November 1, 1924, March 3, 1925, and n.d., Curator's Archives at Valley Forge Historical Society.

52. Burk, *Making a Museum*, p. 49.

53. Burk, *Historical and Topographical Guide*, preface.

54. Samuel W. Pennypacker to W. Herbert Burk, September 9, 1906, Reed Collection, VFNHP.

55. *Washington Chapel Chronicle*, April 15, 1908.

56. *Washington Chapel Chronicle*, October 15, 1908.

57. *Washington Chapel Chronicle*, February 15, 1911.

58. *Washington Chapel Chronicle*, May 15, 1911.

59. Ibid.

60. W. Herbert Burk to the Wardens and Vestrymen of All Saints' Parish, as reprinted in *Washington Chapel Chronicle*, December 15, 1910.

61. *Washington Chapel Chronicle*, September 15, 1910.

62. *Washington Chapel Chronicle*, October 15, 1910.

63. *Washington Chapel Chronicle*, April 15, 1908.

64. *Washington Chapel Chronicle*, April 15, 1910.

65. Ibid.

66. W. Herbert Burk to "Dear Friend," November 11, 1905, in Reed Collection, VFNHP.

67. W. Herbert Burk to Stock Certificate Holders of Centennial and Memorial Association of Valley Forge, September 29, 1905, in Reed Collection, VFNHP.

68. Stager, *History of the Centennial and Memorial Association,* pp. 225, 235.

69. *Washington Chapel Chronicle*, June 15, 1911.

70. *Washington Chapel Chronicle*, July 15, 1912.

71. *Washington Chapel Chronicle*, July 15, 1913.

72. *Washington Chapel Chronicle*, March 15, 1913.

73. *Washington Chapel Chronicle*, September 15, 1913.

74. Charles Custis Harrison, "Memoirs" (c. 1925–27), pp. 105–106, University of Pennsylvania Archives, Philadelphia, Pa.

75. Samuel W. Pennypacker to Charles Custis Harrison, December 22, 1905, Charles Custis Harrison Papers, University of Pennsylvania Archives.

76. Harrison, "Memoirs," p. 104.

77. Ibid., p. 108.

78. Ibid., pp. 106–107.

79. Ibid., p. 107. The elms have since died of Dutch elm disease.

80. Ibid., pp. 107–108.

81. Ibid., pp. 108–110.

82. "Honor for Creating Memorial," *Philadelphia Public Ledger*, February 9, 1928.

83. W. Herbert Burk, "Valley Forge Miracles: A Sermon Preached in the Washington Memorial Chapel by Rev. W. Herbert Burk, 13 October 1929," in Reed Collection, VFNHP.

84. Burk, "American Westminster," p. 709.

85. Harrison, "Memoirs," p. 107.

86. Burk, "American Westminster," p. 709.

87. Stephen Elmer Slocum, "The American Westminster," *The Mentor* 13 (October 1925), 46.

88. Burk, "American Westminster," p. 713.

89. Eleanor Burk, *In the Beginning at Valley Forge*, p. 31.

90. *Washington Chapel Chronicle*, May 15, 1915.

91. Burk, "American Westminster," pp. 701–703.

92. Eleanor Burk, *In the Beginning at Valley Forge*, p. 33.

93. Burk, "Valley Forge Miracles."

94. Handbill for Victory Hall, in Reed Collection, VFNHP.

95. W. Herbert Burk to Lt. Pat O'Brien, March 13, 1918, in Curator's Archives at Valley Forge Historical Society.

96. Lois B. Cassatt to "Dear ———," January 15, 1919, Reed Collection, VFNHP.

97. Burk, *Making a Museum*, pp. 70–71.

98. *Washington Chapel Chronicle*, March 20, 1909.

99. W. Herbert Burk, "Good News for the Home Lovers of Valley Forge: A Sermon Preached in the Washington Memorial Chapel by Rev. W. Herbert Burk, 22 December 1918," in Reed Collection, VFNHP.

100. Ibid.

Chapter 6: *Historical Accuracy vs. Good Taste: Valley Forge in the 1920s and 1930s*

1. Burk, *Historical and Topographical Guide*, p. 202.
2. "Valley Forge Campground," *Norristown Times Herald*, June 8, 1896.
3. "Land Committee Report," November 4, 1920, Records of the Valley Forge Park Commission, Record Group 46, VFNHP.
4. Charles E. Hires to Governor Gifford Pinchot, January 28, 1924, Record Group 46, Carton #2, General Correspondence, Pennsylvania State Archives.
5. Richmond L. Jones to Sen. T. L. Eyre, March 13, 1920, Record Group 46, Carton #2, General Correspondence, Pennsylvania State Archives.
6. Richmond L. Jones to T. L. Eyre, March 13, 1920, Record Group 46, Carton #2, General Correspondence, Pennsylvania State Archives.
7. "Land Committee Report," January 2, 1919, in Records of the Valley Forge Park Commission, Record Group 46, VFNHP.
8. "Land Committee Report," December 2, 1920, Records of the Valley Forge Park Commission, Record Group 46, VFNHP.
9. Ibid.
10. George Wheeler Stone, "The Mount Joy Forge on Valley Creek," in *The Scope of Historical Archaeology: Essays in Honor of John L. Cotter*, ed. David G. Orr and Daniel G. Crozier (Philadelphia: Temple University Department of Anthropology, 1984), pp. 87–100.
11. Ibid., pp. 94–110.
12. Ibid., pp. 110–119.
13. Jacob Orie Clark to Valley Forge Park Commission, October 5, 1921, Record Group 46, Carton #2, General Correspondence, Pennsylvania State Archives.
14. John S. Kennedy to John P. Nicholson, November 15, 1921, Record Group 46, Carton #2, General Correspondence, Pennsylvania State Archives. "Loups" are masses of iron that have gone partway through the refining process, also spelled "loop" or "loupe" and also called "blooms."
15. Richmond L. Jones to J. S. Kennedy, November 17, 1921, Record Group 46, Carton #2, General Correspondence, Pennsylvania State Archives.
16. Richmond L. Jones to J. S. Kennedy, December 5, 1921, Record Group 46, Carton #2, General Correspondence, Pennsylvania State Archives.
17. "Digging Begins in Two Parts of Park for Foundations of Shop Burned by British," *Philadelphia Inquirer*, December 2, 1928.
18. Helen Schenck, "The Upper Forge at Valley Forge" (Report for the Museum of Applied Science Center for Archaeology [MASCA], November 1984), pp. 27–31.
19. Jerome Sheas, "The Forges at Valley Forge," *Picket Post*, July 1944, p. 6.
20. Schenck, "The Upper Forge," p. 74.
21. Ibid., p. 77.
22. "1776 Smithy Found," *Philadelphia Public Ledger*, March 6, 1932. This story appeared at the time actual preparations were being made to dismantle the building.
23. Records of the Valley Forge Park Commission, July 10, 1929, Record Group 46, VFNHP.
24. Albert C. Myers, "Statement Regarding Hay Creek Forge," Records of the Valley Forge Park Commission, inserted after the minutes of March 28, 1934, VFNHP.
25. Israel R. Pennypacker, *The Valley Forge Burned by the British Troops, September 1777, and an Analysis of the Myers Report* (June 1929), p. 11, in Valley Forge Miscellaneous File, Chester County Historical Society.
26. Ibid., pp. 6–7.
27. Israel R. Pennypacker, *The Burned Valley Forge: Judge Koch's Report and the Evidence Contrary to Its Conclusions* (November 1929), p. 13, in Reed Collection, VFNHP.
28. Jacob Orie Clarke to Israel R. Pennypacker, July 25, 1930, Record Group 2, VFNHP.

29. Jacob Orie Clark to Israel R. Pennypacker, August 11, 1930, Record Group 2, VFNHP.

30. George Schultz to Israel R. Pennypacker, May 14, 1930, Record Group 2, VFNHP.

31. Records of the Valley Forge Park Commission, April 23, 1930, Record Group 46, VFNHP.

32. Albert C. Myers, "Statement Regarding the Hay Creek Forge," Records of the Valley Forge Park Commission, inserted after minutes of March 28, 1934, Record Group 46, VFNHP.

33. George Schultz to Gilbert Jones, February 12, 1945, Record Group 2, VFNHP.

34. Records of the Valley Forge Park Commission, November 12, 1925, VFNHP.

35. Dodd and Dodd, *Washington's Headquarters*, pp. 37–38.

36. Richard A. Koch to Members of the Park Commission, May 19, 1931, Records of the Valley Forge Park Commission, 7 May 1931 [*sic*], Record Group 46, VFNHP.

37. George Edward Brumbaugh and Albert Ruthruaff, "Report Regarding Architectural Services at Valley Forge National Historical Park Prior to Its Administration by the U.S. Department of the Interior," March 31, 1980, Record Group 2, VFNHP.

38. Horace Wells Sellers to Albert C. Myers, April 7, 1932, in Dodd and Dodd, *Washington's Headquarters*, pp. F9–F10.

39. Dodd and Dodd, *Washington's Headquarters*, p. 41.

40. Records of the Valley Forge Park Commission, March 22, 1933, Record Group 46, VFNHP.

41. Ibid., April 26, 1933, and May 24, 1933.

42. Laura Lee, "George Washington's Headquarters at Valley Forge Gets Old Period Furniture," *Philadelphia Bulletin*, February 19, 1934.

43. Horace Wells Sellers to Ellis Paxson Oberholtzer, January 11, 1927, Records of the Valley Forge Park Commission, January 13, 1927, Record Group 46, VFNHP.

44. Records of the Valley Forge Park Commission, June 28, 1933, Record Group 46, VFNHP.

45. John Bruce Dodd and Cherry Dodd, *Historic Structure Report: Varnum's Quarters* (Valley Forge, Pa.: Valley Forge National Historical Park, 1981), pp. 11, 12. (Hereafter referred to as *Varnum's Quarters*.)

46. Ibid., p. 36.

47. "Varnum's Encampment Quarters Is a Fine Work of Restoration," *Picket Post*, October 1945, p. 25.

48. Records of the Valley Forge Park Commission, January 24, 1961, and December 20, 1960, Record Group 46, VFNHP. Staff at Valley Forge National Historical Park believe that the objects furnishing Varnum's Quarters today are not the DAR objects. Exactly what happened to those is unknown. They may have been removed from the park by the Pennsylvania Historical and Museum Commission when Valley Forge became a national park in 1976.

49. "Israel Pennypacker Reviews the Work of the Valley Forge Park Commission," *Norristown Times Herald*, December 7, 1932.

50. Ibid.

51. Emily D. Stephens, *The Story of the Eviction of the Stephens Family; or, Tyrannic Rule at Valley Forge* (Norristown, Pa.: Author, 1937), Valley Forge Miscellaneous File, Chester County Historical Society.

52. Records of the Valley Forge Park Commission, April 24, 1935, Record Group 46, VFNHP.

53. Ellis Paxson Oberholtzer to E. C. Smith, May 16, 1934, Record Group 46, Carton #6, General Correspondence, Pennsylvania State Archives.

54. *Daily Republican*, October 3, 1935.

55. *Daily Republican*, November 19, 1935.

56. Letter from Governor to Edward C. Shannon, January 18, 1936, text reprinted in *Daily Republican*, February 7, 1936.

57. Records of the Valley Forge Park Commission, 28 July 1937, Record Group 46, VFNHP.

58. Ibid., November 12, 1935.

59. Ibid., special session held July 3, 1942.

60. *Daily Republican,* July 7, 1942.

61. Gilbert Jones to Karl F. Scheidt, January 29, 1943, Record Group 46, Carton #3, Commission Correspondence, Pennsylvania State Archives.

62. Records of the Valley Forge Park Commission, April 29, 1923, VFNHP.

63. Executive Meeting Minutes, January 12, 1923, in Minutes of the Valley Forge Historical Society.

64. Ibid., June 25, 1923.

65. W. Herbert Burk to "The Student Body," February 1, 1921, General Files of the Valley Forge Historical Society.

66. W. Herbert Burk to "My Dear Compatriot," January 26, 1923, Valley Forge Miscellaneous File, Chester County Historical Society.

67. Sixth Annual Report of the Valley Forge Historical Society, June 19, 1924, in Minutes of the Valley Forge Historical Society.

68. W. Herbert Burk to James B. Bailey, August 31, 1926, Washington Memorial Chapel Files, Defenders' Gate, Valley Forge, Pa.

69. W. Herbert Burk to G. H. Morgan, Chair of Valley Forge Park Commission, October 12, 1926, General Files of the Valley Forge Historical Society.

70. Burk, *Historical and Topographical Guide,* p. 38.

71. W. Herbert Burk to the Rt. Rev. Thomas Garland, July 12, 1926, Washington Memorial Chapel Files.

72. "The National Washington Memorial Church," Valley Forge Miscellaneous File, Chester County Historical Society.

73. "New Valley Forge Church Is Started," *Philadelphia Public Ledger,* February 23, 1928.

74. Valley Forge Park Commission, *Report . . . 30 August 1927 to 1 June 1929,* p. 8.

75. Israel R. Pennypacker, "Valley Forge," *American Mercury,* March 7, 1926, p. 344.

76. "Valley Forge a National Problem," Society Collection, Historical Society of Pennsylvania.

77. Records of the Valley Forge Park Commission, December 12, 1928, Record Group 46, VFNHP.

78. Ibid., October 10, 1928.

79. "Dr. Burk Charges Animus to Chapel," *Philadelphia Bulletin,* December 18, 1928.

80. "Dr. Burk in Row over Auto Ban at Valley Forge," *Philadelphia Inquirer,* December 18, 1928.

81. Records of the Valley Forge Park Commission, May 8, 1929, Record Group 46, VFNHP.

82. "Valley Forge Manor at Historical Valley Forge" (c. 1927 advertisement), Valley Forge Miscellaneous File, Chester County Historical Society.

83. Valley Forge Park Commission, *Report . . . 30 August 1927 to 1 June 1929,* p. 6.

84. Israel R. Pennypacker, *Address of Israel R. Pennypacker Made Before Pennsylvania Society and New York Color Guard Sons of the Revolution at Valley Forge, June 7, 1930* (Philadelphia: John T. Palmer Co., 1930), p. 7, in Valley Forge Miscellaneous Files, Chester County Historical Society.

85. Records of the Valley Forge Park Commission, September 12, 1928, Record Group 46, VFNHP.

86. W. Herbert Burk, "What Shall We Do with Valley Forge?" Reed Collection, VFNHP.

87. W. Herbert Burk, "Valley Forge Miracles: A Sermon Preached in the Washington Memorial Chapel by W. Herbert Burk, 13 October 1929," Reed Collection, VFNHP.

88. Records of the Valley Forge Park Commission, March 25, 1931, Record Group 46, VFNHP.

89. Ibid., October 28, 1931.

90. Minutes of the Valley Forge Historical Society, June 19, 1929, Valley Forge Historical Society.

91. Records of the Valley Forge Park Commission, March 25, 1931, Record Group 46, VFNHP.

92. Lawrence Ritchey to Israel R. Pennypacker, April 16, 1931, Records of the Valley Forge Park Commission, April 22, 1931, Record Group 46, VFNHP.

93. Records of the Valley Forge Park Commission, May 27, 1931, Record Group 46, VFNHP.

94. W. Herbert Burk to Mrs. C. H. Hinchman, May 18, 1931, General Files of the Valley Forge Historical Society.

95. Ellis Paxson Oberholtzer to W. Herbert Burk, May 25, 1931, Oberholtzer Papers, Historical Society of Pennsylvania.

96. "President Hoover's Visit on Memorial Day, 30 May 1931," pp. 13–17, Reed Collection, VFNHP.

97. "President Hoover at Valley Forge," *Norristown Times Herald*, May 30, 1931.

98. William R. Gardner to Officers of the Valley Forge Historical Society, July 12, 1933, in Minutes of the Valley Forge Historical Society, inserted after the 1933 annual report.

99. *Coatesville Record*, April 13, 1931.

100. Records of the Valley Forge Park Commission, April 5, 1941, Record Group 46, VFNHP.

101. Valley Forge Park Commission, *Report . . . 26 July 1939 to 1 January 1943*, p. 18.

102. Minutes of the Valley Forge Historical Society, June 19, 1930, Valley Forge Historical Society.

103. Valley Forge Historical Society Treasurer to ———, November 17, 1933, General Files of the Valley Forge Historical Society.

104. "Museum Report," in Minutes of the Valley Forge Historical Society, June 19, 1938, Valley Forge Historical Society.

105. *Daily Republican*, August 2, 1929.

106. Records of the Valley Forge Park Commission, July 22, 1931, Record Group 46, VFNHP.

107. Ibid., July 27, 1932.

108. Ibid., September 28, 1932.

109. "Israel Pennypacker Reviews Work of the Valley Forge Park Commission," *Norristown Times Herald*, December 7, 1932.

110. Cornelius Weygandt, *The Blue Hills* (New York: Henry Holt & Co., 1936), p. 113.

Chapter 7: The "Complete Restoration" of Valley Forge

1. *Daily Republican*, June 21, 1935.

2. Ibid.

3. Gilbert Jones, "Future May Learn from the Past," *Picket Post*, October 1944, p. 2.

4. Gilbert Jones, "People's Mandate to Restore the Valley Forge Encampment Urged by Park Commissioners," *Picket Post*, April 1946, p. 6.

5. Ibid., p. 7.

6. Ibid., p. 16.

7. Michael Wallace, "Visiting the Past: History Museums in the United States," *Radical History Review* 25 (1981), 76–77; Kammen, *Mystic Chords of Memory*, pp. 359–362.

8. Charles B. Hosmer Jr., *Preservation Comes of Age: From Williamsburg to the National Trust, 1926–1949*, 2 vols. (Charlottesville, Va.: Preservation Press, 1981), 1:65–67.

9. Wallace, "Visiting the Past," p. 77.

10. Ada Louise Huxtable, "Inventing American Reality," *New York Review of Books*, December 3, 1992, p. 24.

11. Wallace, "Visiting the Past," p. 73.

12. Kammen, *Mystic Chords of Memory*, pp. 504–505.

13. Valley Forge Park Commission, *Report . . . 24 October 1935 to 1 January 1939*.

14. *Daily Local News*, January 28, 1936.

15. Ibid.

16. *Daily Republican*, December 3, 1936.

17. *Daily Republican*, December 8, 1936.

18. *Coatesville Record*, November 30, 1936.

19. "Valley Forge Restoration Attacked and Defended," *Philadelphia Bulletin*, December 2, 1936.

20. Ibid.

21. Gilbert Jones, quoted in an interview in the *Daily Republican*, August 15, 1938.

22. *Daily Republican*, December 28, 1938.

23. *Daily Republican*, June 6, 1939.

24. Harry Emerson Wildes, *Valley Forge* (New York: Macmillan, 1938), p. 311.

25. Gilbert Jones, "Commissioners Urge Restoration of Valley Forge Encampment," *Picket Post*, July 1944, p. 12. Fort Mordecai Moore is identified in current park literature as the unnumbered redoubt just south of Redoubt #2. Stirling Redoubt is now identified as an unnumbered redan east of Inner Line Drive just north of Conway's Brigade. Fort George Washington is called Redoubt #3. The rifle pit is now identified as a redan on Mount Joy below the inner line earthworks and above Redoubt #3; it is not identified on park literature. According to Classified Structure Field Inventory reports done on these structures by John Bruce Dodd in 1979, Fort Mordecai Moore was incorrect in many details, Stirling Redoubt was located where a redoubt had perhaps never existed, and the rifle pit might not have been a rifle pit at all but another field work.

26. Records of the Valley Forge Park Commission, November 25, 1942, Record Group 46, VFNHP.

27. Jones, "People's Mandate," p. 11.

28. Records of the Valley Forge Park Commission, July 26, 1944, Record Group 46, VFNHP.

29. Ibid., July 24, 1946.

30. Ibid., November 27, 1946.

31. Valley Forge Park Commission, *Report . . . January 1947 to January 1951*, p. 4.

32. George Edwin Brumbaugh to Norris D. Wright, October 5, 1946, George Edwin Brumbaugh Papers, Box 66, Winterthur Museum and Gardens, Wilmington, Delaware.

33. "Report Covering Certain Buildings and Areas in Valley Forge National Park," Brumbaugh Papers, Box 8.

34. George Washington, *The Writings of George Washington from the Original Manuscript Sources, 1745–1799*, ed. John C. Fitzpatrick, vol. 10 (Washington, D.C.: Government Printing Office, 1933), p. 171.

35. Typed copy of the poem "Valley Forge" by Dr. Albigence Waldo from *The Historical Magazine*, vol. 7, 1863, in Brumbaugh Papers, Box 66.

36. Frank E. Schermerhorn, "Roof-Log from a Hut at Valley Forge," *Picket Post*, April 1948, p. 23. The same poem also appeared in the April 1947 issue of *Picket Post* with the title "Ode to the Last Log of a Soldiers' Hut." In this version the last line read: "To Chance of God and faith in Washington."

37. *Coatesville Record*, July 6, 1905.

38. *Philadelphia Record*, September 26, 1909.

39. Edgar Williams, "That Log Cabin in Valley Forge," *Philadelphia Inquirer Magazine*, June 14, 1959.

40. All these log structures are still visible at Valley Forge except for the guard huts, which were no longer needed once the park guards were furnished with motor vehicles and radio communication. Because they were also confusing to visitors, who thought they were replica huts, they were all taken down except for one near the arch, which houses equipment for the arch lights.

41. *Philadelphia Record*, September 26, 1909.

42. Records of the Valley Forge Park Commission, January 21, 1948, Record Group 46, VFNHP.

43. "Camp Huts Again Rising on Historic Winter Encampment as Restoration Work Goes On," *Picket Post*, July 1947, pp. 28–29.

44. "Specifications for Log 'Hutts,'" Brumbaugh Papers, Box 70.

45. "Rigors of Washington's Winter at Valley Forge Recalled by Restoration Project," *New York Herald Tribune*, August 24, 1947.

46. Milton G. Baker to Norris D. Wright, August 5, 1947, Brumbaugh Papers, Box 66.

47. Records of the Valley Forge Park Commission, July 23, 1947, Record Group 46, Valley Forge National Park.

48. Ibid., November 26, 1947.

49. Plans for the first Levittown were announced on May 7, 1947, and by 1949 some 4,000 units were sold. Within a few more years, Levittown communities contained literally thousands of nearly identical houses on regularly spaced parallel streets. It is interesting to note that William Levitt employed mass production techniques he himself had learned while erecting military housing during World War II.

50. Norman Randolph to Thomas W. Sears, July 16, 1948, Brumbaugh Papers, Box 66.

51. Records of the Valley Forge Park Commission, January 25, 1948, Record Group 46, VFNHP.

52. Ibid., February 25, 1948, and May 26, 1948.

53. "Report Concerning Certain Buildings and Areas in Valley Forge National Historic Park," Brumbaugh Papers, Box 8.

54. Ibid.

55. Norman Randolph to Members of the Military Works Committee, August 31, 1948, Brumbaugh Papers, Box 66.

56. "Press Release: Knox Artillery Shop Restoration at Valley Forge Park," Brumbaugh Papers, Box 66.

57. Norman Randolph to Norris D. Wright, September 23, 1948, Brumbaugh Papers, Box 66.

58. George Edwin Brumbaugh, "Report to the Valley Forge Park Commission on the Colonel William Dewees Mansion, Valley Forge," *Picket Post*, January 1950, p. 16.

59. Unpublished book manuscript by George Edwin Brumbaugh, Brumbaugh Papers, Box 108.

60. Brumbaugh, "Report . . . on Dewees Mansion," pp. 13–16.

61. John Bruce Dodd and Cherry Dodd, *Historic Structure Report: The David Potts House* (Valley Forge, Pa.: Valley Forge National Historical Park, 1981), p. 41. (Hereafter referred to as *David Potts House.*)

62. George Edwin Brumbaugh to Norman Randolph, January 17, 1948, Brumbaugh Papers, Box 66.

63. George Edwin Brumbaugh to Norris Wright, December 18, 1948, Brumbaugh Papers, Box 66.

64. Dodd and Dodd, *David Potts House*, p. 69.

65. Brumbaugh, "Report . . . on Dewees Mansion," p. 17.

66. Dodd and Dodd, *David Potts House*, pp. 20, 36–43.

67. *Report . . . January 1947–January 1951*, p. 19.

68. George Edwin Brumbaugh to Norman Randolph, April 22, 1952, Brumbaugh Papers, Box 66.

69. Records of the Valley Forge Park Commission, December 19, 1955, Record Group 46, VFNHP.

70. Ibid., May 22, 1956.

71. Ibid., April 22, 1958.

72. George Edwin Brumbaugh to Milton G. Baker, August 22, 1966. Brumbaugh Papers, Box 66.

73. Report titled "Reconstruction of Soldiers' Huts, Valley Forge State Park Research Documentation," n.d., Record Group 2, VFNHP.

74. Records of the Valley Forge Park Commission, December 19, 1958, Record Group 46, VFNHP.

75. Ibid., February 23, 1960.

76. Ibid., April 26, 1960.

77. Ibid., May 22, 1962.

78. Edward Pinkowsky, *Washington's Officers Slept Here* (Philadelphia: Sunshine Press, 1953), p. 19.

79. Records of the Valley Forge Park Commission, May 28, 1963, Record Group 46, VFNHP.

80. Ibid., April 26, 1965. It is now called the Steuben Memorial.

81. Ibid., September 27, 1965.

82. Ibid., December 20, 1965.

83. Interview with Tom McGimsey, historic architect at Valley Forge National Historical Park, August 5, 1992.

84. G. U. Dryanski, "What Happened to the Forge at Valley Forge?" *Philadelphia Inquirer Magazine*, July 22, 1962, p. 4.

85. Helen Schenck, "The Upper Forge at Valley Forge," *Journal of the Museum of Applied Science Center for Archaeology*, November 1984, pp. 40–41.

86. Records of the Valley Forge Park Commission, June 23, 1968, Record Group 46, VFNHP.

Chapter 8: New Uses for an Old Story

1. W. Herbert Burk to E. B. Cassatt, December 4, 1920, General Files of the Valley Forge Historical Society.

2. W. Herbert Burk to Jessie Tuttle, October 18, 1921, General Files of the Valley Forge Historical Society.

3. W. Herbert Burk to Mrs. William Pierce, October 4, 1923, General Files of the Valley Forge Historical Society.

4. Israel R. Pennypacker, "Valley Forge," *American Mercury*, March 7, 1926, p. 343.

5. Records of the Valley Forge Park Commission, June 13, 1928, Record Group 46, VFNHP.

6. Records of the Valley Forge Park Commission, August 20, 1928, Record Group 46, VFNHP.

7. Ibid., June 28, 1933.

8. Ibid., October 24, 1934.

9. Theresa L. Wilson to W. Herbert Burk, October 25, 1926, General Files of the Valley Forge Historical Society.

10. Minutes of the Valley Forge Historical Society, September 25, 1939.

11. Address given by John Robbins Hart at the Washington Memorial Chapel, April 27, 1941, Valley Forge Miscellaneous File, Chester County Historical Society.

12. John Robbins Hart, *Valley Forge During World War II* (New York: American Historical Co., 1944), pp. 21, 22, 29.

13. Walker Haeuster to Valley Forge Park Commission, June 22, 1939, Record Group 46, Carton #2, Commission Correspondence, Pennsylvania State Archives.

14. Edward C. Shannon to Governor Arthur James, June 30, 1939, Record Group 46, Carton #2, Commission Correspondence, Pennsylvania State Archives.

15. Records of the Valley Forge Park Commission, September 27, 1939, Record Group 46, VFNHP.

16. Ibid., January 27, 1943.

17. Valley Forge Park Commission, *Report . . . January 1943–January 1947*, pp. 12–13.

18. Records of the Valley Forge Park Commission, June 23, 1943, Record Group 46, VFNHP.

19. R. J. Gillis to L. Ralph Phillips, February 2, 1942, Record Group 46, Pennsylvania State Archives.

20. Gilbert Jones to the Hon. Michael Francis Doyle, September 1, 1942, and Hon. Michael Francis Doyle to L. Ralph Phillips, August 31, 1942, both in Record Group 46, Pennsylvania State Archives.

21. Records of the Valley Forge Park Commission, April 25, 1945, Record Group 46, VFNHP.

22. Script for Evacuation Day radio program, June 18, 1944, Record Group 2, VFNHP.

23. Records of the Valley Forge Park Commission, September 26, 1945, Record Group 46, VFNHP.

24. "U.S. Carrier Valley Forge Goes into Commission with Mementos of the Historic Winter Encampment," *Picket Post*, January 1947, pp. 47–49.

25. *Daily Republican*, November 30, 1945.

26. Kammen, *Mystic Chords of Memory*, pp. 586–587, 657.

27. Wallace, "Visiting the Past," p. 82.

28. Valley Forge Park Commission, *Report . . . January 1947–January 1951*, pp. 18–19.

29. Records of the Valley Forge Park Commission, October 26, 1949, Record Group 46, VFNHP.

30. "National Jamboree of the Boy Scouts of America, 1950" (pamphlet), Reed Collection, VFNHP.

31. McCullough's articles were reprinted in a souvenir booklet printed in 1950 and titled "Jamboree 1950 as reported in the Philadelphia Inquirer." The material quoted here comes from the article originally printed on June 25, 1950. A copy of the booklet is in the Reed Collection, VFNHP.

32. Ibid., article of July 8, 1950.

33. Ibid., article of July 1, 1950.

34. Ibid., article of July 3, 1950.

35. Ibid., article of July 1, 1950.

36. Ibid., article of July 5, 1950.

37. "Official Map of Boy Scout Jamboree 1957," Reed Collection, VFNHP.

38. Collier Rhoads, "Slip of Tongue Elevates Nixon as Crowds Cheer," *Norristown Times Herald*, July 13, 1952.

39. "Spectacular Show, Fireworks Give Jamboree Brilliant Start," *Norristown Times Herald*, July 18, 1964.

40. "Question Box," *Picket Post*, January 1965, pp. 29–30.

41. Records of the Valley Forge Park Commission, February 24, 1965, Record Group 46, VFNHP.

42. Report titled "Patterns of the Past: Geophysical and Aerial Reconnaissance at Valley Forge," ed. Elizabeth Ralph and Michael Parrington, Valley Forge National Historical Park Archives.

43. Records of the Valley Forge Park Commission, November 28, 1971, Record Group 46, VFNHP.

44. Ibid., September 27, 1971.

45. Address of Dwight D. Eisenhower, reported in *Four Years of Work for Freedom, 1949–1953* (Valley Forge, Pa.: Freedoms Foundation, August 31, 1953), Freedoms Foundation Archives, Valley Forge, Pa.

46. Newsletter of Freedoms Foundation, January 1965, Freedoms Foundation Archives. Over the years, the title of this publication has been changed several times; it will consistently be referred to here as Newsletter of Freedoms Foundation.

47. Chuck Bauerlein, "Teaching America About Freedom," *Philadelphia Inquirer Magazine*, December 18, 1983, p. 27.

48. *The Archive*, June 23, 1949.

49. Typed transcript, "E. F. Hutton's Remarks on 22 October 1949," Freedoms Foundation Archives.

50. President's Report, in *Four Years of Work for Freedom, 1949–1953*.

51. E. F. Hutton to K. D. Wells, May 31, 1949, Wells Correspondence, Freedoms Foundation Archives.

52. Undated, untitled typed account of the history of the Freedoms Foundation based on staff recollections, Freedoms Foundation Archives.

53. Address of E. F. Hutton to Rotary Club in Miami, February 9, 1949, Wells Correspondence, Freedoms Foundation Archives.

54. Report of Don Belding, in *Four Years of Work for Freedom, 1949–1953*.

55. Freedoms Foundation, *Report from Valley Forge, 40th Anniversary Edition* (Valley Forge, Pa., 1989), p. 2.

56. From the Credo of the Freedoms Foundation as it appeared on the cover of *Atlantic Magazine*, April 1949. In full, the articles were: "Right to worship God in one's own way; Right to Free speech and press; Right to assemble; Right to petition for grievances; Right to privacy in our homes; Right to habeas corpus—no excessive bail; Right to trial by jury—innocent till proved guilty; Right to move about freely at home and abroad; Right to own private property; Right to work in callings and localities of our choice; Right to bargain with our employers; Right to go into business, compete, make a profit; Right to bargain for goods and services in a free market; Right to contract about our affairs; Right to the service of government as a protector and referee; Right to freedom from 'arbitrary' government regulation and control." A current copy of the Credo shows that some wording has been changed since this appeared in 1949. The Credo now includes "Right to *peaceably* assemble; Right to petition for *redress of* grievances; Right to trial by jury—innocent *until* proved guilty; Right to bargain with our employers *and employees*." The "Right to free elections and personal secret ballot" appears in the current version but not in this 1949 version.

57. "On the Cover," *Atlantic Magazine*, April 1949, inside cover.

58. *Daily Republican*, April 18, 1949.

59. *Daily Republican*, November 19, 1949.

60. *Daily Republican*, February 22, 1958.

61. "VP Nixon Presents Awards at Freedoms Foundation Ceremonies," *Norristown Times Herald*, February 22, 1953.

62. Report of the address of Cecil B. DeMille at Freedoms Foundation, in Reed Collection, VFNHP.

63. "Two Area Winners of Freedom Awards," *Norristown Times Herald*, November 21, 1949.

64. Descriptions of school awards program in *Four Years of Work for Freedom, 1949–1953*.

65. Greg Walter, "Snow Job at Valley Forge," *Philadelphia Magazine*, February 1968, p. 71.

66. Ibid., p. 73. This is not to suggest that McCarthy had any connection with the Freedoms Foundation. Nothing uncovered in the research for this book indicated that this was the case.

67. Letter to Editor from Harry Sayre, President of UPA-CIO, *The Archive*, April 19, 1951.

68. Radio Reports Inc. Script for Freedoms Foundation to Air 12:00 Noon, June 3, 1949, Freedoms Foundation Archives.

69. Taped Radio Spot Commercials, Freedoms Foundation Archives.

70. *Freedoms Handbook*, Freedoms Foundation Archives.

71. Bauerlein, "Teaching America About Freedom," p. 27.

72. E. F. Hutton's remarks on October 22, 1949.

73. Ibid.

74. Freedoms Foundation souvenir, Reed Collection, VFNHP.

75. Quoted in *Daily Republican*, August 18, 1949.

76. Message of Kenneth D. Wells, in Newsletter of Freedoms Foundation, June 1957.

77. E. F. Hutton's remarks on October 22, 1949.

78. Fact Sheet on Freedoms Foundation Library, Freedoms Foundation Archives.

79. "Mementos of Freedom," *Philadelphia Inquirer Magazine*, December 8, 1963, p. 7.

80. *The Medal of Honor Grove: Its Origins and History* (Valley Forge, Pa.: Freedoms Foundation, n.d.).

81. Records of the Valley Forge Park Commission, May 23, 1918, Record Group 46, Pennsylvania State Archives.

82. Interview with Robert Miller, President, Betty Miller (his wife), and Dr. Charles Hepburn, Vice President, at Freedoms Foundation, Valley Forge, Pa., September 10, 1992.

83. John F. Reed, "Dedication at Valley Forge," *Picket Post*, January 1968, p. 27.

84. *Daily Republican*, April 28, 1952.

85. *Daily Republican*, June 23, 1958.

86. Records of the Valley Forge Park Commission, December 20, 1960, Record Group 46, VFNHP.

87. Ibid., May 23, 1961.
88. Ibid., October 26, 1964.

Chapter 9: *The Siege of Valley Forge*

1. Traffic Regulations for Dogwood Display Sundays, 1936, Record Group 46, Pennsylvania State Archives.
2. "A Threat to the Hallowed Acres," *Norristown Times Herald*, August 26, 1949.
3. Records of the Valley Forge Park Commission, April 28, 1948, and May 26, 1948, Record Group 46, VFNHP.
4. Ibid., March 25, 1930.
5. Ibid., June 25, 1963.
6. Ibid., May 28, 1963.
7. Ibid., September 25, 1967.
8. Kenneth D. Wells to Joseph Neff Ewing, January 27, 1958, General Files of the Valley Forge Historical Society.
9. "New Post Office at Valley Forge Dedicated," *Picket Post*, October 1964, pp. 18–19, 29.
10. "Two Hundred Attend Hearing for Commercial Plan in Schuylkill Township," *Daily Republican*, November 20, 1962.
11. John F. Reed to Schuylkill Township Supervisors, November 21, 1962, Reed Collection, VFNHP.
12. "Valley Forge Crisis" (Joseph Perron, 1967), Reed Collection, VFNHP.
13. Records of the Valley Forge Park Commission, January 15, 1968, Record Group 46, VFNHP.
14. Ibid., April 22, 1968.
15. Ibid., February 26, 1968.
16. Ibid., November 25, 1968.
17. Ibid., March 25, 1968.
18. Ibid., June 14, 1968.
19. Ibid., February 23, 1970.
20. Ibid., February 22, 1971.
21. Phyllis and Charles Martin to Charles E. Mather, March 14, 1971, Record Group 46, Pennsylvania State Archives.
22. Records of the Valley Forge Park Commission, March 22, 1971, Record Group 46, VFNHP.
23. Ibid., July 23, 1973.
24. Ibid., June 23, 1969.
25. Ibid., August 31, 1970.
26. Quoted in "Valley Forge Ok's Vets Antiwar Rally," *Norristown Times Herald*, September 1, 1970.
27. Records of the Valley Forge Park Commission, September 28, 1970, Record Group 46, VFNHP.
28. Robert Fowler, "Rabbi, Wife Wounded by Guard," *Philadelphia Inquirer*, October 18, 1970.
29. Robert Fowler, "Guard Suspended in Shooting of Rabbi in Valley Forge Park," *Philadelphia Inquirer*, November 7, 1970.
30. Pat Sheehy, " 'No Peace on Earth' Say Veterans Camped at Park," *Today's Post*, December 27, 1971.
31. "Hoodlum Hangout at Valley Forge," *Philadelphia Inquirer*, May 8, 1969.
32. Press Release from Valley Forge State Park, May 21, 1971, Record Group 46, Pennsylvania State Archives.
33. Robert Bridges, "Hoodlums Desecrate Valley Forge, Commissioner Says," *Philadelphia Bulletin*, July 14, 1971.

34. Jerome Sheas's Report in Records of the Valley Forge Park Commission, inserted after December 28, 1970, Record Group 46, VFNHP.

35. Ibid.

36. Minutes of the Valley Forge Historical Society, October 24, 1968.

37. Maria Goddard to Joane Fulcoly, March 21, 1968, Record Group 2, VFNHP.

38. Records of the Valley Forge Park Commission, March 4, 1974, Record Group 46, VFNHP.

39. S. K. Stevens to M. M. Ammerman, September 14, 1971, Record Group 46, Pennsylvania State Archives.

40. Gertrude Kimble to Valley Forge Park Commission, June 1, 1971, Record Group 46, Pennsylvania State Archives.

41. Interview with Meade Jones, President, Valley Forge Historical Society, August 7, 1992.

42. "Society's Stolen Artifacts Recovered by Police," *Picket Post*, 3rd quarter 1977, pp. 18–20.

43. Robert Fowler, "Valley Forge Guards Pocket Fees from Guided Tours of Shrine," *Philadelphia Inquirer*, January 7, 1971.

44. Robert Fowler, "Valley Forge Park Chief Admits Taking Kickbacks," *Philadelphia Inquirer*, February 9, 1971.

45. Robert Fowler, "Head of Park Is Ousted at Valley Forge," *Philadelphia Inquirer*, March 16, 1971.

46. Records of the Valley Forge Park Commission, May 21, 1973, Record Group 46, VFNHP.

47. Ibid., July 22, 1974.

48. "State of the Union," January 22, 1973, a handwritten report inserted in Records of the Valley Forge Park Commission, Record Group 46, VFNHP.

49. Special Status Committee Report, March 4, 1974, in Records of the Valley Forge Park Commission, Record Group 46, VFNHP.

50. Records of the Valley Forge Park Commission, June 24, 1974, Record Group 46, VFNHP.

51. Ibid., September 23, 1974.

52. Pennsylvania Historical and Museum Commission, and Gilboy, Stauffer & Giombetti, Stibinski & Davies, Architects, Engineers, and Planners, *A Master Plan for Valley Forge State Park* (Harrisburg, Pa., April 20, 1975), p. 2.

53. Ibid., p. 8.

54. Ibid., p. 54.

55. Ibid., pp. 8, 14.

56. Ibid., p. 15.

57. Ibid., p. 52.

58. Records of the Valley Forge Park Commission, September 23, 1974, Record Group 46, VFNHP.

59. Statement of Jack Schwartz, May 5, 1975, in Records of the Valley Forge Park Commission, inserted after June 23, 1975, Record Group 46, VFNHP.

60. Ibid.

61. Records of the Valley Forge Park Commission, April 22, 1974, Record Group 46, VFNHP.

62. "State of the Union," handwritten report in Records of the Valley Forge Park Commission, April 23, 1973, Record Group 46, VFNHP.

63. Records of the Valley Forge Park Commission, February 24, 1975, Record Group 46, VFNHP.

64. "Valley Forge Park Fee Suggestion Is Rapped by Commission," *Norristown Times Herald*, February 24, 1976.

65. Records of the Valley Forge Park Commission, February 28, 1976, Record Group 46, VFNHP.

66. Horace Mather Lippincott, "The Problem of a College in a City," in Brumbaugh Papers, Box 67, Winterthur Museum.

67. "The Valley Forge Ideal and the University of Pennsylvania," Brumbaugh Papers, Box 89.

68. "Report of the Philadelphia Committee on the Establishment of a College of Liberal Arts at Cressbrook Farm, Valley Forge, and Embodying a Plan for Such a College. Submitted at the

Baltimore Conference of the Association of Pennsylvania Alumni, October 24–25, 1935," Brumbaugh Papers, Box 67.

69. Ibid.

70. George Edwin Brumbaugh to E. Wallace Chadwick, June 27, 1935, Brumbaugh Papers, Box 67.

71. "Tredyffrin Board Delays Decision on Chesterbrook," *Today's Post*, December 12, 1971.

72. Unrau, *Administrative History*, p. 533.

73. Records of the Valley Forge Park Commission, December 21, 1971, Record Group 46, VFNHP.

74. *Daily Local News*, February 11, 1972.

75. Margaret Giacalone, "We Need Chesterbrook," *Suburban and Wayne Times*, April 27, 1972.

76. Unrau, *Administrative History*, pp. 534–535.

77. Records of the Valley Forge Park Commission, April 28, 1975, Record Group 46, VFNHP.

78. Coleman McCarthy, "Valley Forge: A New Struggle for the Sacred Ground," *Philadelphia Inquirer* (Washington Post News Service), June 8, 1975.

79. Records of the Valley Forge Park Commission, August 26, 1936, Record Group 46, VFNHP.

80. Ibid., December 18, 1962.

81. Records of the Valley Forge Park Commission, April 26, 1976, Record Group 46, VFNHP.

. 82. Unrau, *Administrative History*, p. 545.

83. Editorial, *Philadelphia Bulletin*, May 14, 1974.

84. Records of the Valley Forge Park Commission, December 24, 1975, Record Group 46, VFNHP.

85. Ibid., February 28, 1976.

86. Unrau, *Administrative History*, pp. 529, 530, 535–536.

87. Ibid., pp. 537, 539, 541.

88. Records of the Valley Forge Park Commission, June 24, 1974, Record Group 46, VFNHP.

89. Ibid., September 22, 1975.

90. House Committee on Interior and Insular Affairs, Subcommittee on National Parks and Recreation, *Hearings on H.R. 2257, H.R. 5621 and H.R. 7989*, 94th Cong., 1st sess., September 29, 1975.

91. Ibid., pp. 15–16.

92. Ibid., p. 65.

93. Ibid., pp. 80–81.

94. Ibid., pp. 82–83.

95. Ibid., p. 125–127.

96. Ibid., pp. 45–51.

97. Unrau, *Administrative History*, pp. 563–564, 566–567, 569.

98. Ibid., pp. 570–571.

99. Ibid., p. 609.

100. "Only Gradual Changes at the Park," *Picket Post*, 4th quarter 1976, p. 21.

101. "Valley Forge Unit to Be 'Watchdogs,' " *Norristown Times Herald*, September 28, 1976.

102. Unrau, *Administrative History*, pp. 613–614.

Chapter 10: A Struggle for Growth and Professionalism at the Washington Memorial

1. This point is made in much correspondence and literature originating at the Washington Memorial during Burk's day. In fact, the parish newsletter, the *Washington Chapel Chronicle*, is subtitled "A Record of Religion and Patriotism."

2. Obituary for Dr. John Robbins Hart, *Daily Republican*, September 19, 1967.

3. *Daily Local News*, January 1, 1936.

4. *Daily Republican*, August 20, 1937.

5. John Robbins Hart to Walter L. Wright, July 3, 1941, Washington Memorial Chapel Files, Defenders' Gate.

6. John Neff Ewing to John Robbins Hart, July 10, 1941, Washington Memorial Chapel Files.

7. "Daughters of American Revolution Go Forward in Plans to Build Bell Tower for Valley Forge," *Picket Post*, July 1946, p. 26.

8. *Daily Republican*, September 24, 1941.

9. *Daily Local News*, February 24, 1942.

10. "Memorial Tower Fund of DAR over $60,000," *Picket Post*, January 1947, p. 41.

11. "Daughters of the American Revolution Campaign for Thanksgiving Bell Tower Is Nearing the Goal Fixed at $100,000," *Picket Post*, April 1947, p. 31.

12. "National Carillon Soon to Be Housed in Tower Provided by Funds Obtained by Daughters of American Revolution," *Picket Post*, July 1947, p. 31.

13. Gertrude S. Carraway, "Valley Forge Bell Tower Cornerstone Relaid," *DAR Magazine* 84 (August 1950), 652–653.

14. "Demolition of Original Chapel and Teddy Roosevelt Letters Link Memories of Great Memorial," *Picket Post*, January 1948, p. 47.

15. *Daily Republican*, September 21, 1939.

16. Minutes of the Valley Forge Historical Society, July 28, 1941.

17. Executive Meeting Minutes of the Valley Forge Historical Society, October 12, 1942.

18. Ibid., May 10, 1943.

19. Directors' Meeting Minutes of the Valley Forge Historical Society, November 13, 1944.

20. Annual Meeting of the Valley Forge Historical Society, January 13, 1947.

21. *Daily Local News*, February 9, 1957.

22. "Tom Thumb's Family Sees Midget's Piano," *Picket Post*, October 1947, p. 22. The piano is still among the holdings of the historical society but not on view to visitors.

23. Gilbert Jones to Mr. Joseph B. Ganser, March 2, 1945, General Files of the Valley Forge Historical Society. The fate of this object is unknown today.

24. "Letters by George Washington Found in a Museum's Dust," *Kansas City Star*, April 8, 1951. The signet ring has since been stolen from the museum.

25. John Robbins Hart to Dear Director, in Minutes of the Valley Forge Historical Society, filed after March 10, 1952.

26. Minutes of the Valley Forge Historical Society, December 8, 1958.

27. "Society Museum Must Present Drama, Not Cabinet of Curios or Castoffs," *Picket Post*, January 1945, p. 9.

28. Lloyd Eastwood-Siebold, "A New Day Is Dawning," *Picket Post*, October 1950, p. 4.

29. "The Valley Forge Library," *Picket Post*, February 1962, p. 40.

30. Henry C. Biddle to Parishioners and Friends of the Chapel, August 4, 1965, in Reed Collection, VFNHP.

31. Interview with Dr. Sheldon M. Smith, retired rector of Washington Memorial Chapel, June 24, 1992.

32. Ibid.

33. Frank Law to Mr. Moll, January 30, 1968, Record Group 46, Pennsylvania State Archives.

34. Records of the Valley Forge Park Commission, February 28, 1976, Record Group 46, VFNHP.

35. Minutes of the Valley Forge Historical Society, December 9, 1967.

36. W. L. Cremers of the vestry to Francis Forbes, 3rd vice president of Valley Forge Historical Society, in Minutes of the Valley Forge Historical Society, filed after February 13, 1968.

37. Records of the Valley Forge Park Commission, March 24, 1969, Record Group 46, VFNHP.

38. Interview with Dr. Sheldon M. Smith, June 24, 1992.

39. Minutes of the Valley Forge Historical Society, December 15, 1969.

40. Howard Gross to the vestry, May 25, 1972, in Minutes of the Valley Forge Historical Society, filed after June 26, 1972.

41. Secretary of the Vestry William Gesner to Howard Gross, June 19, 1972, General Files of the Valley Forge Historical Society.

42. Building Inspector, Notes on Inspection, July 11, 1972, General Files of the Valley Forge Historical Society.

43. Margaret Roshong to Park Commissioners, March 2, 1970, Records of the Valley Forge Park Commission, March 23, 1970, Record Group 46, VFNHP.

44. Margaret Roshong to Charles E. Mather, March 21, 1970, Records of the Valley Forge Park Commission, March 23, 1970, Record Group 46, VFNHP.

45. Records of the Valley Forge Park Commission, September 24, 1973, Record Group 46, VFNHP.

46. Proposed Agreement between Valley Forge Historical Society and Pennsylvania Historical and Museum Commission, May 14, 1975, Records of the Valley Forge Park Commission, May 14, 1975, Record Group 46, VFNHP.

47. Minutes of the Valley Forge Historical Society, December 11, 1976.

48. Ibid., April 1, 1978.

49. Minutes of the Valley Forge Historical Society, May 23, 1979.

50. Ibid.

51. Minutes of the Valley Forge Historical Society, November 10, 1979.

52. Julia Cass, "Valley Forge Pits a Church Against History," *Philadelphia Inquirer*, January 6, 1980.

53. Meade Jones to Dear DAR Member, October 1, 1979, in Litigation Papers of the Valley Forge Historical Society, Valley Forge, Pa.

54. Frank Law to Friends of the Washington Memorial Chapel, January 1980, General Files of the Valley Forge Historical Society.

55. Sheldon Smith to Dear Friends, May 19, 1980, reprinted in *Chapel Dateline*, filed in Litigation Papers of the Valley Forge Historical Society.

56. Meade Jones to the Rt. Rev. Lyman C. Ogilby, July 6, 1979, General Files of the Valley Forge Historical Society.

57. Interview with Meade Jones, President of the Valley Forge Historical Society, August 7, 1992.

58. William Scott Margaree III to Meade Jones, March 29, 1978, in Litigation Papers of the Valley Forge Historical Society.

59. Minutes of the Valley Forge Historical Society, December 15, 1984.

60. Interview with Dr. Sheldon M. Smith, June 24, 1992.

61. Collections Policy adopted in 1985, in Minutes of the Valley Forge Historical Society, January 26, 1985.

62. Press release by the Valley Forge Historical Society, February 22, 1982, in Litigation Papers of the Valley Forge Historical Society.

63. "Valley Forge Historical Society Permanent Exhibit Opened July 4, 1984," *Valley Forge Journal*, December 1984, p. 146.

64. "Message from the President," *Valley Forge Journal*, June 1982, p. 5.

65. Michael Kammen to Meade Jones, November 24, 1981, in Minutes of the Valley Forge Historical Society, January 30, 1982.

66. Toby Raphael, "An American Treasure Preserved," *Picket Post*, 2nd quarter 1979, pp. 15–17.

Chapter 11: New Interpretations at Valley Forge

1. "Question Box," *Picket Post*, July 1971, p. 40.

2. W. Herbert Burk, *Washington at Valley Forge: A Drama*, act 1, scene 4.

3. "General's Wife Played Dominant Role in Camp," *Daily Republican*, June 30, 1950.

4. Edward Pinkowsky, *Washington's Officers Slept Here* (Philadelphia: Sunshine Press, 1953), p. 6.

5. Virginia L. Atkinson, "Campfollowers of the American Revolution," *Picket Post*, Summer 1976, pp. 13–17. To this day, little is known about women at Valley Forge, mainly because there is no primary source material. We do know that certain officers' wives were present and did gather together to socialize, but whether they made any contribution to the welfare of the common soldiers is unknown. It is also known that campfollowers were present, and their roles as nurses and laundresses are mentioned. Exactly how these women lived and where they were housed is unknown.

6. Dodd and Dodd, *Varnum's Quarters*, p. 14.

7. Interview with Tom McGimsey, August 5, 1992.

8. Dodd and Dodd, *Washington's Headquarters*, pp. 43–45, 54.

9. Ibid., p. 46.

10. Ibid., p. 125.

11. Interview with Tom McGimsey, August 5, 1992.

12. Anne Woodward, *A Furnishing Plan for the Headquarters of General George Washington at Valley Forge, Pa.* (Valley Forge, Pa.: Valley Forge State Park, 1974), pp. 1, 10–11, 19, 37, 43, 65.

13. Valley Forge National Historical Park, *Interpretive Prospectus* (Valley Forge, Pa., February 15, 1982), p. 9.

14. Records of the Valley Forge Park Commission, November 26, 1963, Record Group 46, VFNHP.

15. Dodd and Dodd, *Washington's Headquarters*, p. 53. Since then, many changes have been made in the interests of historical accuracy.

16. Joan Perkolup, " 'Soldier' Puts Life into Revolutionary Tales at Valley Forge," *Philadelphia Bulletin*, August 23, 1970.

17. Betty Sampson, "History of the Valley Forge Living History Volunteers, 1974–1976," in Record Group 2, VFNHP.

18. Records of the Valley Forge Park Commission, April 26, 1971, Record Group 46, VFNHP.

19. "Park Panel Sets Strict 'Bicen' Policy," *Norristown Times Herald*, May 1, 1971.

20. Alfred Stern, "A Preliminary Report on Operation Valley Forge," June 1949, in Record Group 2, VFNHP.

21. Barry Spyker, "Ballad of Valley Forge: Hills Come Alive with Music," *Norristown Times Herald*, May 10, 1976.

22. "The Great Cow Chase" (handbill), Reed Collection, VFNHP.

23. Press Kit for Bicentennial Wagon Train Pilgrimage, in Record Group 2, VFNHP.

24. Records of the Valley Forge Park Commission, March 24, 1975, Record Group 46, VFNHP.

25. George H. Ebner to Creed C. Black, n.d., in Records of the Valley Forge Park Commission, June 28, 1976, Record Group 46, VFNHP.

26. Editorial, *Picket Post*, 4th quarter 1976, p. 4.

27. Unrau, *Administrative History*, p. 608.

28. Interview with Richard Wells, April 22, 1993. At the time the GMP was written, Wells was team captain of the Planning Team, Mid-Atlantic/North Atlantic Team, Denver Service Center.

29. Wallace B. Elms to Regional Director, December 7, 1984; Alfred H. Link to Joseph W. Westner, December 18, 1984; Wallace B. Elms to Regional Director, February 8, 1985. The papers in notes 29 through 33 were privately obtained through public information officer, National Park Service, Mid-Atlantic Regional Office, Philadelphia.

30. Wallace B. Elms to Regional Director, February 8, 1985, Mary C. Carroll to Edwin G. Holl, March 15, 1985.

31. James W. Coleman Jr. to Regional Director, September 23, 1985.

32. Supplementary Case/Incident Report, October 5, 1985, no. 850839, VFNHP.

33. Wayne Bodle to Dr. Larry E. Tise, March 14, 1986, William Penn Mott Jr. to John Fowler, July 29, 1986.

34. Helen Schenck, "Archaeological Prospecting at Valley Forge," *Journal of the Museum of Applied Sciences Center for Archaeology*, December 1978, p. 16.

35. Valley Forge Park Commission, *Report . . . 1 June 1958 to 31 May 1960*, Records of the Valley Forge Park Commission, September 27, 1960, Record Group 46, VFNHP.

36. Records of the Valley Forge Park Commission, February 24, 1964, VFNHP.

37. Michael Parrington, Helen Schenck, and Jacqueline Thibaut, "The Material World of the Revolutionary War Soldier at Valley Forge," in *The Scope of Historical Archaeology: Essays in Honor of John L. Cotter*, ed. David G. Orr and Daniel G. Crozier (Philadelphia: Temple University, Department of Anthropology, 1984), pp. 132–133; Douglas C. George, *Archaeological Collection Management at Valley Forge* (Philadelphia: U.S. Department of the Interior, National Park Service, February 1986), p. 32.

38. Parrington, Schenck, and Thibaut, "Material World of the Revolutionary Soldier," p. 130.

39. John L. Cotter, "Preliminary Report on Archaeological Investigations at the Pennsylvania Encampment at Valley Forge, July–October, 1966," pp. 1–8, Record Group 2, VFNHP.

40. Parrington, Schenck, and Thibault, "Material World of the Revolutionary Soldier," pp. 134–138.

41. George, *Archaeological Collection Management*, pp. 48–51.

42. "State of the Union," handwritten report inserted in Records of the Valley Forge Park Commission, January 22, 1973, Record Group 46, VFNHP.

43. George, *Archaeological Collection Management*, p. 6.

44. "Patterns of the Past: Geophysical and Aerial Reconnaissance at Valley Forge," report edited by Elizabeth Ralph and Michael Parrington, Valley Forge National Historical Park Archives.

45. Louis J. Venuto to Chief of Interpretation, August 31, 1983, Valley Forge National Historical Park Archives.

46. Interview with Joseph Lee Boyle, historian at Valley Forge National Historical Park, April 14, 1993.

47. Wayne K. Bodle, *The Vortex of Small Fortunes: The Continental Army at Valley Forge, 1777–1778*, vol. 1 of *Valley Forge Report* (Valley Forge, Pa.: Valley Forge National Historical Park, 1980–82), p. 76.

48. Ibid., pp. 77, 81.

49. Ibid., p. 97.

50. Ibid., p. 123.

51. Ibid., p. 351.

52. Jacqueline Thibaut, *The Fatal Crisis: Logistics and the Continental Army at Valley Forge, 1777–1778*, vol. 2 of *Valley Forge Report*, ed. Wayne K. Bodle and Jacqueline Thibaut (Valley Forge, Pa.: Valley Forge National Historical Park, 1980–82), pp. 227, 237.

53. Ibid., p. 267.

54. Ibid., p. 339.

55. Ibid., p. 371.

56. Ibid., p. 392.

57. Ibid., pp. 664–665.

58. Ibid., p. 666.

59. John F. Reed, *Valley Forge: Crucible of Victory* (Monmouth Beach, N.J.: Philip Freneau Press, 1969), p. 5.

60. Ibid., p. 41.

61. Ibid., p. 68.

62. John B. B. Trussell Jr., *Birthplace of an Army: A Story of the Valley Forge Encampment* (1976; reprint, Harrisburg: Pennsylvania Historical and Museum Commission, 1983), p. iii.

63. Ibid., pp. 5–10, 111.

64. Ibid., p. 116.

65. John Shy to Gil Lusk, August 20, 1979, Valley Forge National Historical Park Archives.

66. Charles W. Snell to Chief Historian, November 17, 1980, Valley Forge National Historical Park Archives.

67. Charles W. Snell to Chief Historian, November 18, 1980, Valley Forge National Historical Park Archives.

68. John Luzader to Chief Historian, n.d., Valley Forge National Historical Park Archives.

69. Memorandum to Associate Director of Cultural Resources from Regional Director of Mid-Atlantic Region, March 2, 1984, Files of the Mid-Atlantic Regional Office, National Park Service, Philadelphia. The additional studies included a demographic analysis of the Continental Army at Valley Forge; a study on the life of the common soldier at Valley Forge; a study of revisionist interpretations of the Valley Forge encampment; a study of the impact of regional geography economics and demography on the Valley Forge encampment; and a study of the organization and effective strength of the main Continental Army. So far, only the first additional study has been done.

70. Richard L. Blanco, *The War of the American Revolution: A Selected Bibliography of Published Sources* (New York: Garland, 1984), entry no. 737.

71. Valley Forge National Historical Park, *Interpretive Prospectus* (Valley Forge, Pa., February 15, 1982), pp. 2, 3, 6.

72. Interview with Bob Dodson, Chief of Interpretation at Valley Forge National Historical Park, August 3, 1992.

73. David M. Lockwood, "The Symbolism of Valley Forge Restored," *Suburban and Wayne Times*, July 20, 1989.

74. David M. Lockwood, "Suffering of Washington's Army Was Very Real," *Suburban and Wayne Times*, July 27, 1989.

75. Minutes of the Valley Forge Historical Society, November 18, 1989.

76. Ibid., January 18, 1990.

77. Ibid., March 18, 1990.

78. John Bruce Dodd and Cherry Dodd, *Historic Structure Report: The Philander Knox Estate* (Valley Forge, Pa.: Valley Forge National Historical Park, 1981), p. 116.

79. Interview with Tom McGimsey, historic architect at Valley Forge National Historical Park, August 5, 1992.

80. *The Kennedy-Supplee Mansion* (Wayne, Pa.: Middle States Preservation, December 1986), p. 2.

81. John Bruce Dodd, *Classified Structure Field Inventory Report, Kennedy-Supplee Mansion* (Valley Forge, Pa.: Valley Forge National Historical Park, 1979).

82. James Kurtz, *Archaeological Inventory and Assessment: The Western Portion* (Washington, D.C.: U.S. Department of the Interior, National Park Service, Mid-Atlantic Regional Office, 1990), introduction.

83. Ibid., p. 297.

Epilogue: Valley Forge—Past, Present, Future

1. Interview with Dr. Richard Stinson, rector of Washington Memorial Chapel, August 13, 1992.

2. Chuck Bauerlein, "Teaching America About Freedom," *Philadelphia Inquirer Magazine*, December 18, 1983, p. 28.

3. Interview with Robert W. Miller, President, Betty Miller (his wife), and Charles Hepburn, Vice President, Freedoms Foundation, September 11, 1992.

4. *1990: The Year in Review* (Valley Forge, Pa.: Freedoms Foundation, n.d.).

5. Charles Hepburn, "An Examination of Certain Passages from Barbara MacDonald Powell, 'The Most Celebrated Encampment: Valley Forge in American Culture, 1777–1983,'" p. 7, in Vertical Files at Horace Willcox Library, VFNHP.

6. Interview with Denny Beach, August 3, 1992.

7. Al Kerr to Editor, *Philadelphia Inquirer*, March 29, 1992.

8. Interview with Denny Beach, August 3, 1992.

9. Thomas Clinton McGimsey, "Untangling the History of the Pawling Wetherill House at Walnut Hill Estate" (M.S. thesis, University of Pennsylvania, 1992), pp. 70–71, available at Horace Willcox Memorial Library, VFNHP.

10. Interview with Denny Beach, August 3, 1992.

Bibliography

Books, Articles, Published Reports, and Proceedings

Atkinson, Virginia L. "Campfollowers of the American Revolution." *Picket Post,* Summer 1976, pp. 13–17.

Bauerlein, Chuck. "Teaching America About Freedom." *Philadelphia Inquirer Magazine,* December 18, 1983, pp. 26–28.

Bean, Theodore W. *The History of Montgomery County.* Philadelphia: Everts & Peck, 1884.

——. *Washington at Valley Forge One Hundred Years Ago; or, The Foot-Prints of the Revolution.* Norristown, Pa.: Author, 1876.

Bestor, Arthur Eugene, Jr. *Backwoods Utopias: The Sectarian and Owenite Phases of Communitarian Socialism in America, 1663–1829.* Philadelphia: University of Pennsylvania Press, 1950.

Blanco, Richard L. *The War of the American Revolution: A Selected Bibliography of Published Sources.* New York: Garland, 1984.

Bodle, Wayne K., and Jacqueline Thibaut. *Valley Forge Report.* 3 vols. Valley Forge, Pa.: Valley Forge National Historical Park, 1980–82.

> Vol. 1: *The Vortex of Small Fortunes: The Continental Army at Valley Forge, 1777–1778,* by Wayne K. Bodle.
> Vol. 2: *The Fatal Crisis: Logistics and the Continental Army at Valley Forge, 1777–1778,* by Jacqueline Thibaut.
> Vol. 3: *In the True Rustic Order: Historic Resource Study and Historical Base Maps of the Valley Forge Encampment, 1777–1778,* by Jacqueline Thibaut.

Brooke, Francis M. *To the Senators and Representatives of the Commonwealth of Pennsylvania, 22 February 1897.* Valley Forge, Pa., 1897.

Brown, Henry Armitt. *Valley Forge Oration of Henry Armitt Brown.* Philadelphia: Press of Loughhead & Co., 1895.

Brumbaugh, George Edwin. "Report to the Valley Forge Park Commission on the Col. William Dewees Mansion, Valley Forge." *Picket Post,* January 1950, pp. 11–18.

Burk, Eleanor H. S. *In the Beginning at Valley Forge and the Washington Memorial Cathedral.* North Wales, Pa.: Norman B. Nuss, 1938.

Burke, W. Herbert. "The American Westminster." *DAR Magazine* 42 (December 1923), 784–787.

——. *Historical and Topographical Guide to Valley Forge.* Norristown, Pa., 1906. Also published in 1920 and 1928 by Norman B. Nuss (North Wales, Pa.).

——. *Making a Museum: The Confessions of a Curator.* N.p., 1926.

————. *The Valley Forge Address of Theodore Roosevelt.* Norristown, Pa., 1909.

————. "Valley Forge: Its Past, Present, and Future." In *Historical Sketches: A Collection of Papers Prepared for the Historical Society of Montgomery County.* Vol. 4, pp. 235–247.. Norristown, Pa., 1910.

————. *Washington at Valley Forge: A Drama.* N.p., 1905.

"Camp Huts Rising Again on Historic Winter Encampment as Restoration Work Goes On." *Picket Post,* July 1947, pp. 28–29.

Carraway, Gertrude. "Valley Forge Bell Tower Cornerstone Relaid." *DAR Magazine* 84 (August 1950), 652–653.

Carson, Hampton L. "The Life and Services of Samuel W. Pennypacker." *Pennsylvania Magazine of History and Biography* 41 (1917), 1–125.

Ceremonies at the Dedication of the Equestrian Monument of Major-General Anthony Wayne Erected by the Commonwealth of Pennsylvania on the Revolutionary Campground at Valley Forge, 20 June 1908. Harrisburg, Pa.: Harrisburg Publishing Co., State Printer, 1909.

Collins, F. A. "Valley Forge Memorial Park." *Outlook,* April 11, 1917, pp. 655–657.

Custis, George Washington Parke. *Recollections and Private Memoirs of George Washington by His Adopted Son.* New York: Derby & Jackson, 1860.

"Daughters of the American Revolution Campaign for Thanksgiving Tower Is Nearing the Goal Fixed at $100,000." *Picket Post,* April 1947, pp. 31–32.

"Daughters of the American Revolution Go Forward in Plans to Build Bell Tower for Valley Forge." *Picket Post,* July 1946, pp. 24–27.

"Demolition of Original Chapel and Teddy Roosevelt Letters Link Memories of Great Memorial." *Picket Post,* January 1948, pp. 47–49.

Dodd, John Bruce. *Classified Structure Field Inventory Reports* (unless otherwise noted, all published in 1979 by Valley Forge National Historical Park):

Blacksmith Shop	*Observation Tower* (1978)
Fort Mordecai Moore	*Redoubt #2*
Group III Replicas of Soldiers' Huts	*Schoolhouse*
Kennedy-Supplee Mansion	*Stirling Redan*
Mount Joy Redan	

Dodd, John Bruce, and Cherry Dodd. *Historic Structure Reports* (all published in 1981 by Valley Forge National Historical park):

The Philander Knox Estate
Varnum's Quarters
Washington's Headquarters

Dryanski, G. U. "What Happened to the Forge at Valley Forge?" *Philadelphia Inquirer Magazine,* July 22, 1962, pp. 4–5.

Eastwood-Siebold, Lloyd. "A New Day Is Dawning." *Picket Post,* October 1950, p. 4.

Environmental Assessment Draft General Management Plan. Denver, Colo.: Denver Service Center, U.S. Department of the Interior, National Park Service, June 1980.

Ewing, William Cox. "Valley Forge Revisited." In *George Ewing: Gentleman and Soldier of Valley Forge.* Edited by Thomas Ewing. Yonkers, N.Y., 1928.

Four Years of Work for Freedom, 1949–1953. Valley Forge, Pa.: Freedoms Foundation, August 31, 1953.

George, Douglas C. *Archaeological Collection Management at Valley Forge.* Philadelphia: U.S. Department of the Interior, National Park Service, 1984.

Hart, John Robbins. *Valley Forge During World War II.* New York: American Historical Co., 1944.

Hocker, Edward W. "Valley Forge as a National Park." *Outlook*, April 6, 1901, pp. 787–790.

Hosmer, Charles B., Jr. *Preservation Comes of Age: From Williamsburg to the National Trust, 1926–1949*. 2 vols. Charlottesville, Va.: Preservation Press, 1981.

Huxtable, Ada Louise. "Inventing American Reality." *New York Review of Books*, December 3, 1992, pp. 24–29.

Jackson, John W. *Pinnacle of Courage*. Gettysburg, Pa.: Thomas Publications, 1992.

James, Mrs. (Isabella) Thomas Potts. *Memorial of Thomas Potts*. Cambridge, Mass., 1874.

Johnson, Clifton. "Midwinter at Valley Forge." *Women's Home Companion*, January 1902, pp. 9–10, 44.

Jones, Gilbert. "Commissioners Urge Restoration of Valley Forge Encampment." *Picket Post*, July 1944, pp. 11–14.

———. "Future May Learn from the Past." *Picket Post*, October 1944, p. 2.

———. "People's Mandate to Restore the Valley Forge Encampment Urged by Park Commissioners." *Picket Post*, April 1946, pp. 6–16.

Kammen, Michael. *Mystic Chords of Memory: The Transformation of Tradition in American Culture*. New York: Alfred A. Knopf, 1991.

———. *A Season of Youth: The American Revolution and the Historical Imagination*. New York: Alfred A. Knopf, 1978.

The Kennedy-Supplee Mansion. Wayne, Pa.: Middle States Preservation, December 1986.

Kurtz, James. *Archaeological Inventory and Assessment: The Western Portion*. Washington, D.C.: U.S. Department of the Interior, National Park Service, Mid-Atlantic Regional Office, 1990.

Lossing, Benson J. *Washington: A Biography*. New York: Virtue Emmens & Co., 1860.

Lowenthal, David. *The Past Is a Foreign Country*. Cambridge: Cambridge University Press, 1985.

Marling, Karal Ann. *George Washington Slept Here: Colonial Revivals and American Culture, 1876–1986*. Cambridge, Mass.: Harvard University Press, 1988.

McInnes, Mary T. *History of the Valley Forge Chapter, National Society, Daughters of the American Revolution*. N.p., 1944.

"Mementos of Freedom." *Philadelphia Inquirer Magazine*, December 8, 1963, pp. 6–7.

"Memorial Tower Fund of DAR over $60,000." *Picket Post*, January 1947, p. 41.

"Message from the President." *Valley Forge Journal*, June 1982, p. 5.

Mitchell, Judith. "Ann Pamela Cunningham and Mount Vernon: A Southern Matron's Legacy." Paper presented at the Fifteenth Annual Conference of the National Council on Public History, Valley Forge, Pa., April 29–May 2, 1993.

Mooney-Melvin, Patricia. "Harnessing the Romance of the Past: Preservation, Tourism, and History." *The Public Historian* 13 (Spring 1991), 35–48.

Moritzen, Julius. "Valley Forge and the Nation." *Harper's Weekly*, June 22, 1901, pp. 628–629.

"National Carillon to Be Housed in Tower Provided by Funds Obtained by Daughters of American Revolution." *Picket Post*, July 1947, p. 31.

"New Post Office at Valley Forge Dedicated." *Picket Post*, October 1964, pp. 18–19, 29.

Newton, A. Edward. "Change Cars in Paoli." In *The Greatest Book in the World and Other Papers*. New York: Little, Brown & Co., 1925.

1990: The Year in Review. Valley Forge, Pa.: Freedoms Foundation, n.d.

"Notes and Queries." *Pennsylvania Magazine of History and Biography* 18 (1894), 384.

"Only Gradual Changes at the Park." *Picket Post*, 4th quarter 1976, pp. 21–22.

Parrington, Michael, Helen Schenck, and Jacqueline Thibaut. "The Material World of the Revolutionary Soldier at Valley Forge." In *The Scope of Historical Archaeology*:

Essays in Honor of John L. Cotter. Edited by David G. Orr and Daniel G. Crozier. Philadelphia: Temple University Department of Anthropology, 1984.

Pennsylvania Historical and Museum Commission, and Gilboy, Stauffer & Giombetti, Stibinski & Davies, Architects, Planners, and Engineers. *A Master Plan for Valley Forge State Park*. Harrisburg, Pa., April 20, 1975.

Pennypacker, Israel R. *Address of Israel R. Pennypacker Made Before Pennsylvania Society and New York Color Guard Sons of the Revolution at Valley Forge, June 7, 1930*. Philadelphia: John T. Palmer Co., 1930.

———. *The Burned Valley Forge: Judge Koch's Report and the Evidence Contrary to Its Conclusions*. N.p., 1929.

———. "Valley Forge." *American Mercury Magazine*, March 7, 1926, pp. 341–345.

———. *The Valley Forge Burned by the British Troops, September 1777, and an Analysis of the Myers Report*. N.p., 1929.

Perrine, William. "Washington's Christmas at Valley Forge." *Ladies' Home Journal*, December 1898, p. 7.

Pinkowsky, Edward. *Washington's Officers Slept Here*. Philadelphia: Sunshine Press, 1953.

Powell, Barbara McDonald. "The Most Celebrated Encampment: Valley Forge in American Culture, 1777–1983." Ph.D. dissertation, Cornell University, 1983.

Proceedings on the Occasion of the Centennial Celebration of the Occupation of Valley Forge by the Continental Army Under George Washington, June 1878. Philadelphia: J. B. Lippincott & Co., 1879.

"Question Box." *Picket Post*, April 1964, October 1964, January 1965, and July 1971.

Raphael, Toby. "An American Treasure Preserved." *Picket Post*, 2nd quarter 1979, pp. 11–18.

Reed, John F. "Dedication at Valley Forge." *Picket Post*, January 1968, pp. 26–27.

———. *Valley Forge: Crucible of Victory*. Monmouth Beach, N.J.: Philip Freneau Press, 1969.

———. "Vision at Valley Forge." *Bulletin of the Montgomery County Historical Society* 15 (Fall 1966), 28.

Reeves, Enos. "Extracts from the Letter-Books of Lieutenant Enos Reeves." *Pennsylvania Magazine of History and Biography* 21 (1897), 235–265.

Report from Valley Forge, 40th Anniversary Edition. Valley Forge, Pa.: Freedoms Foundation, 1989.

Rhoads, Anne F., Douglas Ryan, and Ella W. Aderman. *Land Use Study of Valley Forge National Historical Park*. Valley Forge, Pa.: Valley Forge National Historical Park, 1989.

Richardson, W. H. "Valley Forge." *New England Magazine* 23 (February 1901), 597–608.

Roshong, Margaret D. "Sheas Family Association with Valley Forge." *Picket Post*, July 1967, pp. 34–36.

Ross, Howard DeHaven. *History of the DeHaven Family*. New York: Pandick Press, 1929.

Sayen, William H. "Valley Forge Park." *Bulletin of the Montgomery County Historical Society* 21 (Fall 1978), 205–237.

Schenck, Helen. "Archaeological Prospecting at Valley Forge." *Journal of the Museum of Applied Science Center for Archaeology*, December 1978, pp. 16–17.

———. "The Upper Forge at Valley Forge." Report done for the Museum of Applied Science Center for Archaeology (MASCA), November 1984.

Schmerhorn, Frank E. "Ode to the Last Log of a Soldier's Hut." *Picket Post*, April 1947, p. 43.

———. "Roof-Log from a Hut at Valley Forge." *Picket Post*, April 1948, p. 23.

Seiders, J. F. *Thirty Ancestors of Richard Henry Koch*. Pottsville, Pa., 1939.

Sheas, Jerome. "The Forges at Valley Forge." *Picket Post*, July 1944, pp. 3–6.

Slocum, Stephen Elmer. "The American Westminster." *The Mentor* 13 (October 1925), 45–48.

"Society Museum Must Present Drama, Not Cabinet of Curios or Castoffs." *Picket Post*, January 1945, p. 9.

"Society's Stolen Artifacts Recovered by Police." *Picket Post*, 3rd quarter 1977, pp. 18–20, 39.

Sons of the American Revolution, Portland, Maine, Society. *Maine at Valley Forge*. N.p., 1908.

Stager, H. J. *History of the Centennial and Memorial Association of Valley Forge*. N.p., 1911.

Stephens, Emily D. *The Story of the Eviction of the Stephens Family; or, Tyrannic Rule at Valley Forge*. Norristown, Pa. N.p., 1937.

Stephens, William M. "Burial Places of the Soldiers at Valley Forge." *Bulletin of the Montgomery County Historical Society* 3 (April 1942), 154–156.

Stone, George Wheeler. "The Mount Joy Forge on Valley Creek." In *The Scope of Historical Archaeology: Essays in Honor of John L. Cotter*. Edited by David G. Orr and Daniel G. Crozier. Philadelphia: Temple University Department of Anthropology, 1984.

"Sullivans Bridge Monument." In *Historical Sketches: A Collection of Papers Prepared for the Historical Society of Montgomery County, Pennsylvania*. Vol. 4, pp. 31–44. Norristown, Pa.: The Organization, 1910.

"Tom Thumb's Family Sees Midget's Piano." *Picket Post*, October 1947, p. 22.

Trussell, John B. B., Jr., *Birthplace of an Army: A Story of the Valley Forge Encampment*. Harrisburg: Pennsylvania Historical and Museum Commission, 1983. Originally published in 1976.

"U.S. Carrier Goes into Commission with Mementos of the Historic Winter Encampment." *Picket Post*, January 1947, pp. 47–49.

U.S. Congress. House of Representatives. Subcommittee on National Parks and Recreation of the Committee on Interior and Insular Affairs. *Hearings on HR 2257, HR 5621, and HR 7989*. 94th Congress, 1st Session, September 29, 1975.

Unrau, Harlan D. *Administrative History of Valley Forge National Historical Park*. Denver, Colo.: Denver Service Center, U.S. Department of the Interior, National Park Service, 1984.

"Valley Forge Historical Society Exhibit Opened July 4 1984." *Valley Forge Journal*, December 1984, pp. 146–148.

"The Valley Forge Library." *Picket Post*, February 1962, pp. 40–41.

Valley Forge National Historical Park. *Interpretive Prospectus*. Valley Forge, Pa.: Valley Forge National Historical Park, February 15, 1982.

Valley Forge Park Commission. Reports for various years:

Report . . . December 17, 1896.
Report . . . December 27, 1900.
Report . . . December 16, 1902.
Report . . . 1904.
Report . . . 1906.
Report . . . 1908.
Report . . . 1910.
Report . . . 1912.
Report . . . December 30, 1916.
Twelfth Biennial Report . . . March 1, 1919.
Report . . . 30 August 1927 to 1 June 1929.
Report . . . 1931–1935.
Report . . . 26 July 1939 to 1 January 1943.
Report . . . January 1943 to January 1947.
Report . . . January 1947 to January 1951.

"The Valley Forge Reservation." In *Historical Sketches: A Collection of Papers Prepared for the Historical Society of Montgomery County, Pennsylvania*. Vol. 5, pp. 369–381. Norristown, Pa., 1915.

"Varnum's Quarters Is a Fine Work of Restoration." *Picket Post*, October 1945, pp. 25–26.

Wallace, Michael. "Visiting the Past: History Museums in the United States." *Radical History Review* 25 (1981), 63–96.

Walter, Greg. "Snow Job at Valley Forge." *Philadelphia Magazine*, February 1968, pp. 71–75, 148–154.

Washington, George. *The Diaries of George Washington.* Edited by Donald Jackson and Dorothy Twohig. Vol. 5. Charlottesville: University Press of Virginia, 1979.

———. *The Writings of George Washington from the Original Manuscript Sources, 1745–1799.* Edited by John C. Fitzpatrick. Washington, D.C.: Government Printing Office, 1931–1944.

Webster, Daniel. *The Works of Daniel Webster.* Vol. 2. Boston: Charles C. Little and James Brown, 1851.

Weygandt, Cornelius. *The Blue Hills.* New York: Henry Holt & Co., 1936.

Wildes, Harry Emerson. *Valley Forge.* New York: Macmillan, 1938.

Williams, Edgar. "That Log Cabin at Valley Forge." *Philadelphia Inquirer Magazine,* June 14, 1959, pp. 6–7.

Wistar, Owen. *Lady Baltimore.* New York: Macmillan, 1906.

Woodman, Henry. *The History of Valley Forge.* Oaks, Pa.: John Francis Sr., 1921. Letters originally published in 1850.

Primary Source Material Collections

Chester County Historical Society, West Chester, Pa.:

Clipping Files. (There is a separate section for Valley Forge. See below.)

Valley Forge Centennial and Memorial Association Proceedings, 1879.

Valley Forge Miscellaneous File (Several unnumbered boxes in the vault; items are in alphabetical order).

Defenders' Gate, Valley Forge, Pa. Washington Memorial Chapel Parish Files. (Items are presently in unmarked boxes in the cellar.)

Freedoms Foundation, Valley Forge, Pa. Freedoms Foundation Archives. (Items consisting of reports, ephemera, and correspondence were pulled for me by the librarian. Materials were not organized in named collections except for Ken Wells's correspondence, which was in boxes marked as such.)

Historical Society of Pennsylvania, Philadelphia, Pa.:

AM3011.

John Fanning Watson, "Trip to Valley Forge and the Camp Hills," July 1828.

Nicholson Scrapbooks.

Oberholtzer Papers.

Society Collection.

Montgomery County Historical Society, Norristown, Pa. Newspaper Clipping Scrapbooks.

National Park Service, Mid-Atlantic Regional Office, Philadelphia, Pa. Files.

Pennsylvania State Archives, Harrisburg, Pa. Records of the Valley Forge Park Commission. Record Group 46. (There are minute books on microfilm, and loose correspondence that is divided into "general correspondence" and "commission correspondence.")

University of Pennsylvania Archives, Philadelphia, Pa. Charles Custis Harrison Papers.

Valley Forge Chapter of the Daughters of the American Revolution, Norristown, Pa. Minutes of the Organization.

Valley Forge Historical Society, Valley Forge, Pa.:

Curator's Archives. (Materials are kept in separate file cabinets relating to items in the museum collections.)

General Files. (A file cabinet in the basement, contents in no particular order.)

Litigation Papers. (Separate boxes holding materials relating to the recent litigation with Washington Memorial Chapel.)

Minutes of the Organization.

Valley Forge National Historical Park (VFNHP), Valley Forge, Pa.:

Horace Willcox Memorial Library, Vertical Files.

Record Group 2.

John Reed Collection, Record Group 10.

Francis M. Brooke Collection, Record Group 12.

Records of the Valley Forge Park Commission, Record Group 46.

(Minutes of the organization are kept on microfilm, duplicating what exists in Harrisburg.)

Archives. (The term "Archive" refers to inactive files kept on the second floor at Administrative Headquarters. At some point, these will be archived.)

Winterthur Museum and Gardens, Wilmington, Del. George Edwin Brumbaugh Papers.

Chester County Historical Society Newspaper Clipping Files

The following Philadelphia-area newspapers have articles about Valley Forge. Clippings were made by the Chester County Historical Society and are retained in their files.

American Republican, 1852–1903.
The Archive, 1949–1951.
The Casket, 1830.
Coatesville Record, 1905–1936.
Daily Local News, 1873–1972.
Daily Republican, 1916–1967.
Kansas City Star, 1951.
North American, 1902.
Philadelphia Bulletin, 1904–1936.

Philadelphia Inquirer, 1928.
Philadelphia Press, 1895–1908.
Philadelphia Public Ledger, 1904–1928.
Philadelphia Record, 1909–1911.
Philadelphia Times, 1878.
Phoenixville Messenger, 1882.
Spring City Reporter, 1915.
Village Record, 1882–1909.

Valley Forge National Historical Park Newspaper Clipping Files

The following newspapers contained information about Valley Forge. Clippings were collected by the staff at Valley Forge Park. Information is available in the park's scrapbooks, filed in Record Group 2.

Philadelphia Bulletin, 1970–1974.
Philadelphia Inquirer, 1969–1980.

Suburban and Wayne Times, 1972.
Today's Post, 1971.

Other Newspapers Consulted

New York Herald Tribune, 1947.   *Philadelphia Inquirer,* 1992.
New York Times, 1990   *Suburban and Wayne Times,* 1989.
Norristown Times Herald, 1896–1976.

Washington Chapel Chronicles. 1908–1920. (Actually the Washington Memorial Chapel parish newsletter. Copies are available at Horace Willcox Memorial Library at Valley Forge National Historical Park.)

Interviews

Beach, Warren D. (Denny). Superintendent at Valley Forge National Historical Park. August 3, 1992.

Boyle, Joseph Lee. Historian at Valley Forge National Historical Park. April 14, 1993, and informal talks from 1990 to 1993.

Dodson, Bob. Chief of Interpretation at Valley Forge National Historical Park. August 3, 1992.

Jones, Meade. President of Valley Forge Historical Society. August 7, 1992.

Kalbach, E. Scott. Chief Ranger at Valley Forge National Historical Park. April 21, 1993.

Marshall-Dutcher, Joan. Historian at Valley Forge National Historical Park. June 5, 1992, and informal talks from 1990 to 1993.

McGimsey, Tom. Historic architect at Valley Forge National Historical Park. August 5, 1992.

Miller, Robert, Betty Miller, and Charles Hepburn. Respectively, president of the Freedoms Foundation, his wife, and the foundation's vice president. September 10, 1992.

Smith, Rev. Dr. Sheldon M. Retired rector at Washington Memorial Chapel. June 24, 1992.

Stinson, Rev. Dr. Richard. Rector at Washington Memorial Chapel. August 13, 1992.

Wells, Richard. Formerly team captain of the Planning Team, Mid-Atlantic / North Atlantic Team, Denver Service Center. April 22, 1993.

Index

Adams, John Quincy, 6
Alderson, William T., 196
American Mercury, 120
Anderson, Isaac, 111
Annals of Philadelphia, 1, 2
Armstrong, General John, monument to, 69
Armstrong, Neil, 203
Atlantic Magazine, 165

Bake House, 149. *See also* Washington Inn
Baker, Milton, 140–41
The Ballad of Valley Forge, 203
Bartholomew, Mrs. S. R., 92
Bauerlein, Chuck, 163, 176, 218
Beach, Warren D. (Denny), 220, 221
Bean, Theodore W., 10–12, 13, 22, 35, 39, 57
Belding, Don, 162, 163, 164, 166
Bethel Colored Church, 9
Bicentennial Celebration, 184, 200, 202–4
bloody footprints, image of, 11–12, 74, 130
Bodle, Wayne, 208–9, 212
Bollinger, Richard, 221
Bowen, A. H., 51, 67
Boyd, D. Knickerbocker, 129–30
Boyle, Joseph Lee, 207–8
Boy Scouts. *See* National Boy Scout Jamborees
Brandywine, Battle of, 3, 210
Brooke, Francis M., 36, 40, 41, 44, 45, 48, 49, 51
Brooks, Chester, 204
Brown, Henry Armitt, 23, 40, 54
Bruker, Wilbur M., 169
Brumbaugh, George Edwin, 137–51, 154, 213

Brumbaugh, Martin, 70, 74, 76, 102, 106, 137
Burk, Eleanor, 82, 88, 91
Burk, Rev. Jesse Y., 82, 91
Burk, Rev. W. Herbert, 80, 81–103, 105, 106, 107, 118–27, 155–57, 170, 186, 187, 188, 189, 190, 191, 197, 200, 216
Bush-Brown, Henry K., 66–67

Campbell, J. Duncan, 144, 206–7
Cassatt, E. B., 80, 155
Centennial Celebration (of 1876), 9–10
Chesterbrook, 181–82, 185–86
Chew, Mary J. B., 92
"chicken thief monument," 51
Civilian Conservation Corps (CCC), 133, 134
Civil Rights Movement, xiii
Clarke, Jacob Orie, 108, 109, 111–12
Clay, Henry, 6
Cleveland, Grover, 35
Cold War, xiii, 159–70, 217, 219
"Colonel Dewees Mansion," 149. *See also* Washington Inn
Colonial Dames. *See* National Society of the Colonial Dames of America
Colonial Revival Movement, 9–11, 33, 86, 145, 168, 215
Colonial Williamsburg, 130–32, 135, 154, 159, 216
communism, 159–60, 163, 166, 169
Cone, Andrew, 22
Cone, Mary E. Thropp, 22–23, 37–39
Cotter, John L., 207
County Line Expressway, 173
Crawford, Robert, 34–35

Cret, Paul Philippe, 73–74
Crosby, Mrs. C. M., 93
Cunningham, Ann Pamela, 18, 20
Custis, George W. Parke, 11, 13
Cutler, Anna, 78
Cutler, Thomas, 78

Daily Local News, 24–26, 28, 32, 39–40, 42,
    44, 46, 54
DAR. *See* Daughters of the American
    Revolution
D'Ascenzo, Nicola, 100
Daughters of the American Revolution
    (DAR), 10, 36, 55, 116, 174, 188–89,
    195, 215
  Chester County Chapter, 30, 62
  Merion Chapter, 30
  Philadelphia Chapter, 78, 114
  Valley Forge Chapter, 30, 68, 91, 100
"David Potts House," 149. *See also*
    Washington Inn
Defenders' Gate, 87, 95, 191
DeHaven, Holstein, 45
DeHaven, Jacob, 14
DeKalb, General Baron Johan, 7
Delaware Marker, 69
Delta Sigma Theta, 221
DeMille, Cecil B., 165
Dewees, William, 4, 89, 108, 153
Dobson, John, 196
Dodd, Cherry, 200, 202, 213
Dodd, John Bruce, 200, 202, 213, 214
Doylestown Intelligencer, 7
Draemel, Milo F., 141
Duff, James H., 137
Duponceau, Peter S., 6, 152
Duportail, Brigadier General Louis, 42, 109
Duportail House, 180
Duportail map, 41–42, 70, 82, 108, 109, 140
Durante, Jimmy, 167

Earle, Alice Morse, 10
Earle, George H., 116, 117, 133
Ehret Magnesia Company, 78, 204
Eisenhower, Dwight D., 161, 162, 164, 165
era of monuments. *See* Valley Forge:
    monuments at
Evacuation Day (June 19) celebrations,
    17–18, 21–23, 24–26, 31–32, 85–86,
    102, 120, 150, 158, 189, 221–22
Evans, Stephen, 108

Fechner, Robert, 133
Fields, Gracie, 157
Fine, John, 150
Ford, Gerald, 186
Ford, Henry, 132
Fort Greene, 144
Fort Huntington (Redoubt #4), 51, 69,
    70–71, 76
Fort John Moore (Redoubt #2), 135, 137,
    142–44, 154
Fort Mordecai Moore, 135, 142, 240 n. 25
Fort Muhlenberg, 144
Fort Washington (Redoubt #3), 51, 70, 76,
    135, 240 n. 25
Fowler, Robert, 177–78
Fox, Richard, 181, 185
Francis, John U., 117
Franklin, Ben, 2
Free and Accepted Masons (Freemasons), 25,
    120, 169, 189
Freedoms Foundation, 162–70, 173–74, 217,
    218–19, 244 n. 56, 244 n. 66
  awards program, 164–66
  Bill of Responsibilities, 219
  Credo, 164–65, 167, 244 n. 56
  Independence Garden, 168
  Medal of Honor Grove, 168
Freemasons. *See* Free and Accepted Masons
Friendly Association for Mutual Interests, 5

Garland, Rt. Rev. Thomas J., 97, 119–20
Germantown, Battle of, 3, 210
Gettysburg, 45, 54, 66, 88, 126
Greenfield Village, 132
Gross, Howard, 193
Gruver, C. Robert, 203–4, 218
Guthrie, James M., 84–85

"Halls of History," 91–92, 101, 118, 119,
    139
Hampton, Ellis, 51
Harding, Warren G., 123
Harper's Weekly, 22, 57
Harrison, Charles Custis, 97–99
Hart, Rev. John, 157, 158, 159, 169, 187–91
Hartranft, S. S., 67–68
Harvest Home Meeting of Chester and
    Montgomery Counties, 5–6
Haupt, L. M., 42
Hayes, Rutherford B., 17
Hensel, W. U., 98

Hewes, Deborah, 113
Heyl, John F., 152
Hickman, Lawrence C., 134
Hires, Charles E., 106
historic preservation, women and, 20
history, American attitudes toward, xi–xiv, 2, 18–19, 38, 52
Hollenbach, Edwin H., 141, 150
Holstein, Anna Morris, 20, 23, 24, 27, 28–30, 34–35, 36, 57, 100
Holstein, William, 24
Hoover, Herbert, 116, 123–24, 165
Hope, Bob, 167
Hosmer, Charles B., 131
"Host 76," 202
"Hot Dog War," 116–17
Houdon, Jean Antoine, statue of George Washington, 124, 125
Howard, Daniel, 48
Howe, Sir William, 3, 108
Huntington's Quarters, 33, 123, 124, 207
Hutton, E. F., 162, 163–64, 166, 167, 168
Huxtable, Ada Louise, xiii, 132, 133

Inner Line Drive, 64

Jackson, Andrew, 6
James, Mrs. (Isabella) Thomas Potts, 13, 147
Jenkins, Mrs. Charles F., 168
John Havard House, 41
Johnson, Clifton, 31
Jones, Gilbert, 117–18, 130, 134
Jones, James, 5, 20
Jones, L. Davis, 194
Jones, Meade, 177, 194–97, 217–18
Jones, Nathan, 14, 34
Jones, Richmond L., 106, 109

Kammen, Michael, xi, 83, 159, 196, 197
Kennedy, Alexander, 4
Kennedy's Hollow, 4. *See also* Port Kennedy
King of Prussia, development of, 173–75, 181–82
Knox, Philander, 88
Koch, Richard M., 111, 113
Kriebel, H. W., 121
Kurtz, James, 214

Lafayette, Marquis de, 91
Laird, Warren P., 86
Lancaster New Era, 44

Lane, Frankie, 167
Law, Frank, 192, 195
Lee, Charles, 100
Lee, Mary Custis, 92
Lee, Robert E., 92
"Letitia Penn Schoolhouse," 62–64, 107, 207
Lincoln, Abraham, 87, 95
Lockwood, David, 212
Lossing, Benson J., 9, 13
"lost redoubt." *See* Fort John Moore
Lovell, Fannie B., 93
Lowenthal, David, xi, xii
Lund, Ebenezer, 78–79, 105
Lusk, H. Gilbert, 186
Luzader, John, 211

McCarthy, Colman, 182
McCormick, Lawrence, 41
McCullough, John M., 160–61, 243 n. 31
McGimsey, Tom, 200–201, 213, 220
McGroury, James, 139
McInnes, Rebecca, 35
McIntire, Carl, 175, 176
McKinley, William, 50, 56
Maclure, William, 5
McMenamin, B. F., 44, 80
McMenamin, George, 44
Maine Marker, 66
Malloy, Annamaria, 180, 181, 182, 185, 186, 202, 203–4
Marling, Karal Ann, 9, 13
Marshall-Dutcher, Joan, 221
Martin, Edward, 135–37
Mason, J. Alden, 144
Massachusetts Monument, 69
Mather, Charles, 202
Medary, Milton B., 86, 100
Media Record, 42
Meier, Judith A., 14
Michener, James, 174
Mifflin, Thomas, 108
Miller, Robert W., 218–19
Mills, Ruth, 165
Montgomery, Charles B., 109
Mooney-Melvin, Patricia, xiii–xiv
Morris, Robert, 99
Mount Joy Forge, 108
Mount Vernon, 18, 106–7
Mount Vernon Ladies' Association, 18, 20, 24
Museum Applied Science Center for Archaeology (MASCA), 206

Myers, Albert Cook, 111–12, 134

National Boy Scout Jamborees, 160–62, 177, 203, 205–6, 220
National Heritage Corporation, 200
National Memorial Arch, 72–76, 79, 102, 123, 137, 182, 186
National Memorial Association. *See* Valley Forge Memorial Association
National Park Association, 56
National Park Service, 133, 134, 171, 186, 200–201, 204–6, 207, 208–12, 213–14, 217, 219–22
    General Management Plan, 204–6, 220
National Peace Chime, 188
National Society of the Colonial Dames of America, 10, 55
National Society, Daughters of the Revolution of 1776, 50, 131, 139
National Sojourners, 189
Nesbit, Michael, 25
New Jersey Monument, 69
New York Times, 182
Nixon, Richard, 161, 165, 184
Norristown Times Herald, 57, 83

Oberholtzer, Ellis Paxson, 134
Ogden, Hannah, 11, 20–21, 24
Ogden, Stanley L., 10–11
Okie, R. Brognard, 213
Outer Line Drive, 64, 71, 175, 205
Owen, Robert, 5

Packard, Vance, Jr., 207
Paoli Massacre, 3, 210
Patriotic Order, Sons of America (POS of A), 26–28, 29, 30, 31–32, 36, 41, 55, 58, 85, 106–7, 116, 118, 156, 169, 215
patriotism, 52, 55, 73, 99, 155, 159, 247 n. 1
Patriot's Hall. *See* "Halls of History"
Pattison, Robert E., 35, 40
Pennsylvania Columns, 67–68
Pennsylvania Department of Forests and Waters, 112, 141, 178
Pennsylvania Historical and Museum Commission, 152, 174, 177, 178–80, 181, 183, 184, 185, 200–201, 237 n. 48
Pennsylvania Magazine of History and Biography, 41
Pennsylvania Society of the Sons of the Revolution, 129–30, 138, 142, 211

Pennsylvania Turnpike, 172
Pennypacker, Isaac A., 7, 41
Pennypacker, Israel R., 111–12, 118, 120–21, 122, 123, 126, 156
Pennypacker, Samuel W., 41, 53, 56–57, 58, 62, 63, 66–67, 69, 76, 83, 85, 94, 98
Penrose, Boies, 55–56
"Perpendicular Gothic" (architectural style), 86, 100. *See also* Washington Memorial Chapel Complex
Perron, Joseph, 174
Peters, Richard, 147
Pezak, John, 152
Philadelphia and Reading Railroad Company, 9
Philadelphia Baptist Association, 85
Philadelphia Bulletin, 121, 176, 184
Philadelphia Inquirer, 163, 176, 182, 218, 220
Philadelphia Magazine, 166
Philadelphia Press, 31
Philadelphia Public Ledger, 59, 74, 187
Philadelphia Record, 139
Phoenixville and Bridgeport Electric Railway Company, 52
Phoenixville Daily Republican, 57
Phoenixville Messenger, 37–38, 44
Phoenixville, Valley Forge & Strafford Electric Railway Company, 64
Picket Post, 196
Pinchot, Gifford, 126
Pinkowsky, Edward, 152–53, 200
Port Kennedy, 4, 31, 33, 64, 78, 82, 85, 102–3, 121, 173, 194
POS of A. *See* Patriotic Order, Sons of America
Potts, David, 4, 108
Potts, Isaac, 4, 12–13
Potts, John, 108
Potts, Ruth Anna, 13
Powell, Wilfred, 89
Pratt, Bela, 100

Quigg, Frank, 122–23

Randolph, Norman, 141, 144, 145, 147, 150
Reader's Digest, 165
Redoubt #1, 49
Redoubt #2, 144, 154
Redoubt #3, 51, 70, 76, 135, 240 n. 25
Redoubt #4, 51, 69, 70–71, 76
Reed, George Edward, 55

Reed, John, 152, 210, 213, 174
Reed, Nathaniel, 185–86
Reeves, Enos, 4
Riddle Mansion, 107
Robarts, John O. K., 38–39
Rockefeller, John D., Jr., 130–31, 134
Rogers Building, 107
Rogers, Charles, 4, 8, 9, 10
Rogers, John, 4
Rogers, John J., 140
Romantic Era, xii, 2, 9, 215
Roosevelt, Franklin D., 133, 158
Roosevelt, Theodore, 56, 86, 88–89
Roshong, Margaret, 193
Ross, Howard DeHaven, 14

Scheidt, Karl F., 117–18
Schenck, Helen, 109
Schermerhorn, Frank E., 138, 240 n. 36
Schmid, Sergeant Al, 158
Schnadelbach-Braun Partnership, 151
Schollenberger collection, 92. *See also*
    Washington Memorial Chapel
    Complex: museum
Schollenberger, Thomas H., 92
Schultz, George W., 109, 112
Schulze, Dick, 185
Schuylkill Expressway, 172–73
Schweizer, J. Otto, 71
Scott, Hugh, 185, 186
Sellers, Horace Wells, 112–14
Shapp, Milton, 181, 184–85, 186
Shaw, Sarah, 10
Shy, John, 210–11
Slab Tavern, 151–52
Smith, Isaac W., 10, 17, 31
Smith, Kate, 166–67
Smith, Rev. Sheldon M., 191–93, 194–96,
    218
Snell, Charles W., 211
Snyder, Garrett, 145–46
Society of the Cincinnati, 10
Sons of the American Revolution, 10, 48,
    116, 134
Sparks, Jared, 41
Speaker, Fred, 176
Stager, Henry J., 18, 27, 57, 60
Stalin, Joseph, 159
Star Redoubt (Redoubt #1), 49, 70, 115
Stephens, Emily D., 115–16
Stephens, Sarah, 7

Stephens, William, 33, 49, 115–16
Steuben. *See* Von Steuben
Steuben Memorial. *See* Von Steuben's
    Quarters
Steuben Society of America, 151–52
Stevens, Rev. C. Ellis, 85
Stevens, S. K., 152, 177, 184
Stinson, Rev. Richard, 217–18
Stirling, Major General William Lord, 164
Stirling Redoubt, 135, 240 n. 25
Stone, Frederick D., 30, 35, 41
Sullivan, Major General John, 46
Sullivan's Bridge, 46, 49, 66
    monuments, 46–48
Sussel, Arthur, 113

Tait, Rt. Rev. Francis M., 124
Taylor, Roy A., 185
Tencate, Fred A., 57
Thibaut, Jacqueline, 208–10
314th Infantry Cabin, 139
Thropp, Isaiah, 4
Todd, I. Heston, 21, 48–49, 50, 85, 229
    n. 53
Trego, W. T., 124
Truman, Harry, 161
Trussel, John B. B., 210

United Nations, 159
United States Department of the Interior, 133
University of Pennsylvania, 180–81

Valley Creek Restoration, 105–6, 108
"Valley Forge" (the aircraft carrier), 158
Valley Forge
    arch, 72–76, 79, 102, 123, 137, 182, 186
    archaeological finds and excavations,
        108–9, 110, 119, 135, 144, 154, 162,
        206–7
    blacksmith shop. *See* Valley Forge: Knox
        Artillery Shop
    brigade markers, 66
    cathedral, 119–20, 121, 216
    "complete restoration" of, 129–54, 216–17
    covered bridge, 173
    crime at, 177–78
    Delaware Marker, 69
    dogwoods, 69, 171, 172, 216
    encampment, 2–3, 147, 208–10
    forge reconstruction at, 109–12, 135,
        153–54

ghost stories, 34

industries, 4–5, 20, 31, 32, 78–79, 107–8

Kennedy-Supplee House, 213–14

Knox Artillery Shop, 135, 137, 145, 154, 179

land acquisitions, 42–44, 62, 76, 78, 102–3, 121–23, 126, 133, 215, 220

landscaping, 29, 69–70, 71, 79, 114, 141, 201–2, 216

Maine Marker, 66

maps, 41–42, 43, 65, 136

Massachusetts Monument, 69

Maxwell's Quarters, 177, 213

monuments at, 38–39, 46–51, 66–69, 71–76, 132, 216, 221

national park, creation of, 54–57, 184–86

New Jersey Monument, 69

observation tower, 66, 135, 137, 158, 214

observatory, 8, 9

possible burials at, 33–34, 50, 68, 83, 121, 141, 169, 182–83, 207–8

post-encampment period, eighteenth century, 3–4

post office at, 173

pre-encampment period, eighteenth century, 2–3, 107–8

preservation of, early calls for, 7, 34–35, 39–40

railroad station, 52, 169

replica huts, 129–30, 134, 135, 137, 138–41, 150–51, 154, 240 n. 40, 241 n. 49

road construction, 64

schoolhouse, 62–64, 107, 207

secret tunnel, 13–14

state park, 36, 40–52, 53–80, 85, 105–24, 129–54, 155–62, 169–70, 171–86, 193–94, 200–204, 216–17

tourist account, earliest, 1, 2

utopian community, 5

veterans' cemetery, proposed, 182–84

visitor center, 124, 125, 197, 207

women at, 199–200, 250 n. 5

Valley Forge Centennial Association, 17–20. *See also* Valley Forge Centennial and Memorial Association

Valley Forge Centennial and Memorial Association, 20–36, 39, 55, 57–61, 79, 88, 96, 107, 113, 215–16, 231 n. 42

Valley Forge DAR Monument, 68, 71

Valley Forge Historical Society, 102, 119, 169, 177, 186, 189–90, 192–97, 212, 217–18

Valley Forge Journal, 196

Valley Forge Mansion House Hotel, 11, 152–53

Valley Forge Memorial Association, 39, 46, 72

Valley Forge Museum of American History (at Washington Memorial), 91–93, 118–19, 189–90, 192–94, 195, 196–97

Valley Forge National Historical Park, 185–86, 196, 211, 221

Valley Forge Park Commission, 40–52, 53–80, 102–3, 105–7, 108–24, 129–30, 132–33, 134–37, 139, 140–45, 147, 148–52, 154, 155–56, 157–62, 169–70, 171–76, 178–80, 181–85, 193–94, 206–7, 216

    creation of, 40–41, 42

    Subcommittee on Sex, Hippies, and Whiskey Swillers, 176

Valley Forge Report, 208–13, 217, 252 n. 69

Valley Forge Worsted Mills, 78–79

Varnum, Brigadier General James, 48, 49

Varnum's Quarters, 33, 76–78, 114–15, 200–201, 207, 237 n. 48

Veterans Administration, 182–83

Victory Hall. *See* "Halls of History"

Vorhees, David, 54

Von Steuben, Major General Friedrich Wilhelm Baron, 6, 209

    statue of, 71–72, 157, 205

Von Steuben's Quarters, 135, 151–52, 154

Vroon, Peter, 184, 185

Wagon Train Pilgrimage, 203–4

Walker, Daniel, 108

Wallace, Michael, xiii, 131

Walnut Hill, 206, 220

Walter, Greg, 166

Wanger, Irving P., 56, 73–74

Warren, Mercy Otis, 28

Washington Association, 19

Washington Chapel Chronicle, 94, 96, 97, 100–101

Washington, George, xii, 2, 3, 7–8, 9, 11, 12, 13, 14, 19, 25, 41, 73, 81–82, 87, 89, 124, 138, 139, 151, 167, 169, 190, 208–9

at prayer at Valley Forge, 12–13, 81–82, 91, 92, 100, 169
Washington Inn, 42, 59, 69, 79, 85, 116, 135, 137, 140, 145–49, 152, 154, 213
Washington, Martha, 28, 190, 200
Washington Memorial Chapel Complex, 81–103, 122, 123, 124, 139, 169, 187–97, 216, 217–18
  bell tower and carillon, 188–89, 192
  library, 190–91
  museum, 91–93, 118–19, 189–90, 192–94, 195, 196–97, 217
  weddings at, 188, 191–92
  windows, 99
Washington Post, 182
Washington Reviewing His Troops at Valley Forge, 124
Washington's Birthday, 20, 27, 81, 85, 89, 96, 119, 120
Washington's Headquarters
  Morristown, N.J., 18–19
  Newburgh, N.Y., 18
  Valley Forge, Pa., 2, 5, 11, 12, 13–14, 18, 19–20, 23, 24, 25, 26, 35, 36, 38, 57–58, 59, 60, 61, 64, 69, 88, 92, 96, 107, 111, 112–14, 124, 138, 145, 153, 158, 175, 179, 200, 202, 207, 213, 214, 221; furnishings at, 29–31, 36, 62, 113–14, 201; restorations of, 28–29, 62, 112–13, 201
Washington's marquee, 92–93, 190, 197
Waterman, John, 48, 49, 50, 165, 230 n. 55
"Waterman Monument," 46, 48–51
Watson, John Fanning, 1, 2, 5, 7, 11, 13, 41

Wayland, Henry L., 14–15
Wayne, General Anthony, 203
  statue of, 66–67, 71, 79, 80, 203
Wayne, John, 167
Wayne's Woods, 34, 207
Webster, Daniel, 6–7, 11
Weedon, General George, 7
Weems, Mason L. (Parson), 12
Wells, Kenneth D., 162, 163, 164, 167–68, 169, 173, 218
Wetherill, William, 48
Weygandt, Cornelius, 126
Whitaker, Rt. Rev. O. W., 85, 95
Wildes, Harry Emerson, 135
Willcox, Horace, 179
William Penn Museum, 207
Williams, Joseph, 108
"Williamsburg Formula," 202
Wilson, Eleanor, 69
Wilson, Woodrow, 69, 101
Wirth, Conrad L., 133
Women's Companion, 31
Wood, Alan, Jr., 89
Wood, Mary H., 89
Wood, R. Francis, 51
Woodman, Henry, 7–9, 11, 13, 46, 117, 142
Woolman, Henry F., 180
World War I, 71, 74–75, 100–101, 139
World War II, xiii, 157–59, 189
Wright, Norris D., 137, 141

Yeager, Waters Dewees, 15

Zinn, Colonel George A., 70